Pulling Myself Together

Denise Welch has had lead roles in hit dramas such as *Soldier Soldier*, *Spender*, *The Vice*, *Down to Earth* and *Coronation Street*. Most recently she starred as Steph Haydock in *Waterloo Road*, for which she won the Best Actress Award two years running at the 2009 and 2010 *TV Quick* and *TV Choice* Awards. She is a regular presenter on *Loose Women*, where she has won the hearts of the British people for her honesty and witty humour. She lives in Cheshire with her husband, actor Tim Healy, and her two sons, Matthew and Louis.

DENISE WELCH

Pulling Myself Together

PAN BOOKS

First published 2010 by Sidgwick & Jackson

First published in paperback in 2011 by Pan Books
an imprint of Pan Macmillan, a division of Macmillan Publishers Ltd
Pan Macmillan, 20 New Wharf Road, London N1 9RR
Basingstoke and Oxford
Associated companies throughout the world
www.panmacmillan.com

ISBN 978-0-330-51301-2

The acknowledgements on page 351 constitute an extension of
this copyright page.

A CIP catalogue record for this book is available from
the British Library.

Typeset by Ellipsis Books Limited, Glasgow
Printed in the UK by CPI Mackays, Chatham ME5 8TD

Visit **www.panmacmillan.com** to read more about all our books
and to buy them. You will also find features, author interviews and
news of any author events, and you can sign up for e-newsletters
so that you're always first to hear about our new releases.

To my beloved sons, Matthew and Louis,

for loving me enough not to read this until I'm six feet under!

Pulling Myself Together

Prologue

6 a.m. I pull up outside the *Coronation Street* studios. I smile at the security guard on the door as I pass him. It's a forced smile, a painted smile that masks the anguish I'm feeling, but hopefully he can't tell the difference.

On my way to my dressing room, I greet various members of the cast and crew, saying hello and pretending to laugh at their jokes. Over the years I've learned how to disguise my depression, so none of them have any idea how desperate I feel. No one knows what's going on inside me.

I knew today would be bad from the moment I woke up. As soon as I opened my eyes, a dark cloud descended, huge and heavy, weighing me down. My limbs felt like lead as I dragged myself out of bed, wretchedly wishing I could just curl up under the duvet and hide from the world.

This depression has the most horrendous effect on me. The blackness is crushing; the day ahead looms like a giant, oppressive mountain that I'm being forced to climb. How on earth am I going to get through it?

There was no warning that I would feel this way. I felt fine yesterday. I was looking forward to today and my big scene with Michael Le Vell, who plays my lover, Kevin Webster. It's a crucial scene, full of tension and drama, the kind of acting challenge I really enjoy. I love this role; I love playing Natalie Horrocks. Getting a part in *Coronation Street* is the best thing that's happened in my career. So why am I feeling so terrible?

I dump my bag in my dressing room and make my way to hair and make-up. The room is glaringly bright and filled with the smell of hairspray, perfume and cosmetics; people are chatting away, despite the early hour. I sit down and someone offers me a cup of tea, which I gratefully accept. But when I take a sip of the hot, milky liquid, I find it almost impossible to swallow, as if something is blocking my throat, something dark that wants to choke me. I look at my hand, clasped around the mug, and see that it's trembling. Has anyone else noticed that I'm shaking? I quickly put the mug down, slopping tea onto the table.

Abigail, the make-up artist, gives me a strange look. 'Are you all right, Denise? You look like you've seen a ghost,' she says. The room goes quiet.

My heart pounds with anxiety. What am I going to say? I force myself to be normal. 'You mean the ghost of Ena Sharples that's staring back at me in the mirror?' I reply, as lightheartedly as I can. 'Take a look at those bags! You'd better get busy with that concealer.'

Everyone laughs, but I barely hear them. I'm staring at my reflection, at my sad face, at the deadness in my eyes, and I'm wondering how I can carry on, feeling the way I do. As Abigail works her magic I begin to look better, but the deadness remains in my eyes, and the blackness is still behind them. Why won't it go away? Make it go away! It's been more than seven years since I started suffering these intense bouts of depression, and today I'm feeling as bad as I've ever felt. I don't know how to cope. I've got this big scene with Michael. What if I mess it up?

'Are you sure you're OK?' Abigail asks, breaking into my thoughts.

I sigh softly. 'I'm fine, really,' I say. 'Just tired.'

A runner comes to get me. 'Are you ready to go?'

'I'll be with you in a moment,' I reply.

I walk back to my dressing room in a haze, pick up my bag and head for the bathroom. In the toilet, I open my wallet and take a tiny envelope out of one of the pockets.

There's a blurry battle going on in my head as I tip a small amount of white powder onto a shelf and shape it into a line with my bank card. My thoughts are a complete jumble: I know I shouldn't be doing this, but I'm convinced that it's the only way I can get through. 'Don't do it! It's not the answer,' I tell myself. But it helps me to cope. How else am I going to survive the day? As I roll up a ten-pound note, I block out my objections. I press a finger against one of my nostrils and inhale the white powder through the other.

Thirty seconds later, I'm feeling better. The dark cloud is beginning to clear. I feel more lucid, more alert. I'm going to be OK. I quickly size up what remains in the tiny envelope and decide that it's enough to keep me going for the day. I check my nose for any telltale signs that I've been taking cocaine. No one must know. It would be terrible if anyone found out. What if someone guesses? No, I mustn't think about that.

When I come out of the bathroom, the runner is waiting for me. 'Ready?' he asks.

I smile warmly at him. 'Ready,' I say firmly.

As I follow him onto the set, where the director and Michael are waiting, I concentrate on going over my lines. They haven't a clue how difficult it has been to arrive at this moment and I'm determined not to let them know. Anyway, now that I'm feeling normal and can focus on my work, there's nothing for them to notice.

By the time the director shouts, 'Action!' I know this is going to be a great scene. But as I gear up for Natalie's confrontation with Kevin, I wonder what the hell I think I'm doing. Using cocaine to get through my working day? There's no way of justifying it and I can hardly bear to think about it. How on earth has my life come to this?

Chapter One

Over the years, I've been to see a few quacky, cranky people who haven't been able to accept that depression isn't necessarily linked to the scars of an unhappy childhood. They've made me doubt myself at times, when I've been at my lowest and most vulnerable, and questioning whether my memories were true or false only increased my anxiety and confusion. But now I'm sure that I was blessed with a very happy childhood. When I look back, I can see that I was a very contented child.

When I go through my baby pictures, I get a really warm feeling. I have a vivid memory of being in my pram, in the sunshine, looking out at a lovely trellised wall covered in roses. Mum tells me that I was a beautiful baby, but she must have been wearing rose-tinted glasses because I think I was a rather odd-looking child!

I was born on 22 May 1958 at Tynemouth Infirmary near Whitley Bay, Tyne and Wear, and was named Jacqueline Denise. My parents thought that Jacqueline was lovely and 'very French' and then proceeded to call me Denise. Coincidentally, both my mother and father were born at Tynemouth Infirmary as well, in the same bed, in the same ward, in the same year, a month to the day apart.

Mum came from a very working-class Irish Catholic family. She worshipped her dad, John George, who was known as Mick or Jack, depending on who he was talking to. Granddad was great friends with Sir Matt Busby. He had gone down the pits early in life, before becoming a professional footballer. He played for Reading, Manchester City and Queens Park Rangers and narrowly missed playing in the 1934 FA Cup final, after being injured in the semi-final while playing for Manchester City. My granny was a staunch Labour supporter and I remember heated debates between her and my dad about politics when I was a child. Dad was very fond of Granny, but he was a small businessman and a Tory voter and he used to love winding her up.

My dad was from a very middle-class English family. His father was a terrible snob and Mum's family didn't remotely live up to his idea of who was suitable for his son, Vincent. Mum and Grandpa never saw eye to eye as a result. They tolerated each other, but there was definitely a personality clash there.

My mum says now, 'Look at your dad, he's just like your grandpa!' It's true that Dad has become more like his father as he's got older, physically and in his gait. He is also very fiery, which is definitely a Welch family trait – I've inherited it too! But Grandpa was a real disciplinarian. He would make you chew your peas thirty times; he was a total control freak. Nevertheless, my sister Debbie and I adored him. We were equally close to our maternal grandparents.

Mum used to say that Dad's mum, Nana, was a proper lady. She was always immaculate and looked like she'd just stepped out of a fashion magazine. I have a strong image of her in a dog's-tooth check pencil skirt with a little jacket, a hat and beautiful shoes. When she began to suffer from dementia in later life, it was really sad because she was this vision of the perfect lady and such a lovely person with it.

Dad's family were 'the Welches of Whitley Bay'. My great-uncle Tom had a big factory at North Shields which produced packaged sweets like Welch's Football Chews and Welch's Lollies. My grandpa, his brother, had a smaller firm in Whitley Bay called John W. Welch. Grandpa's factory was very old-fashioned and produced the type of sweets that were weighed out by the quarter-pound from big jars on local cornershop shelves. He invented Black Bullets, dark rolled mints that any Geordie over the age of thirty would immediately recognise. You don't see them much anymore, but they were really popular back then. Toffee, however, was what Welch's were most famous for. Treacle toffee, plain toffee and rum-and-butter toffee were all well-known Welch's varieties.

My parents were twenty-one when I was born. Mum was a psychiatric nurse at Prudhoe Hospital and Dad was doing an economics degree at Newcastle University when Mum got pregnant. These days, most parents would probably encourage their son to continue his education regardless, especially if they had a bit of money like my dad's family did. But no, Dad was whipped out of higher education by his father and set to work for John W. Welch as a sales rep.

Dad resented being forced to leave university and become a rep because he was totally overqualified for the job. He always intended to resume his education and qualify as an accountant, but he never had the chance. What made it worse was that everybody assumed that he was a major shareholder in Welch's Toffees, as the company was known locally, when in reality the share-holding rights fell to his older brother, David, who was perhaps the favoured one when it came to the business side of things. David was committed to the family firm, whereas it was quite obvious that Dad always wanted to do something different. I sometimes used to think of them as the Whitley Bay version of Bobby and JR – though David's not really like JR!

Not only did Grandpa have a factory, but he also had a couple of small shops as well, so if I ever find myself in one of the few remaining old-fashioned sweet shops, I'm suddenly hit by one of the most evocative smells of my childhood, that sugary, musty smell of sweets stored in big jars. It's the smell of happiness, really, because it was such a happy time. Nana used to take Debbie and me to the shop in Gateshead for a treat and we also went to the sweet factory with Dad every Saturday morning, where the Black Bullets were hand-rolled and chopped and the scent of toffee filled the air. I'll never forget the blackcurrant lollies coming out of the oven, purple, hot and gooey.

They used to call me Truly Scrumptious at school, but funnily enough I never really had a sweet tooth, probably because I was surrounded by confectionery. Debbie and I were on the A-list of every children's party, because we'd turn up with a big jar of toffees. That was our calling card. Perhaps as a result, everybody had this image that we were quite well-to-do because we were associated with the famous family firm. But I think that Dad always struggled financially. It wasn't until we were much older that we realised just how much our parents had sacrificed for us.

Because Mum and Dad didn't have any money when I was born, we lived in the family home to start with. Grandpa and Nana had this fantastic big house on the seafront at Cullercoats, North Shields. It was a massive 1900s corner terrace overlooking the sea, with a summer house and a greenhouse at the end of its long garden. At one point, Grandpa and Nana lived in the middle section of the house; my dad's sister Cynthia and her husband David and their children lived downstairs; and, just after they had me, my mum and dad lived in the flat on the top floor. Thirty years later, when I'd just had my son Matthew, I went upstairs to look at the flat, which was now Auntie Cynthia's kitchen. My God, it was tiny! I just don't know how Mum and Dad managed to exist there.

The upside of having young parents was that we never missed out on their company. I remember being taken to parties all the time and our tiny flat was constantly full of people. My parents have always been very sociable and we did everything together as a family. When we went on holiday to France or Spain, it would often be with a whole crowd of Mum and Dad's friends, the same friends they have today. They love to live life to the full and can't bear to miss anything. Dad's a real entertainer and a complete exhibitionist. He's seventy-three now and he still dresses up as a woman, given half the chance. More of that later!

Like Dad, Mum's self-expression comes out in the way she dresses. She has this amazing ability to transform herself: she'll go upstairs in her dressing gown looking like a complete wreck and come down looking every bit as glamorous as Joan Collins. She was always very out there in terms of fashion, very ahead of her time, and people have commented on her sense of style for as long as I can remember. To this day she has an ability to mix and match a top from Marks with a Matalan skirt and look like the belle of the ball.

It's not like Mum has ever had the money to go out and buy the newest pieces. She's never been a slave to *Vogue* or anything like that. She was always very trendy, though. She would have made a great stylist. Clothes were her way of making a statement, which was sometimes quite embarrassing for her children. I particularly remember the day she picked me up from a party wearing a chainmail dress that exposed her midriff. Everybody else's mum was wearing a neat twin-set and my mother arrived looking like Cleopatra, with her hair in a black bob and her chains on.

Mum gave up working as a nurse when I was born, although she did a little bit of modelling from time to time. When I say modelling, it was actually getting a few quid for appearing in the occasional local fashion show. She had a fantastic figure. She also has fabulous hands and nails, so she did some hand modelling too.

As I've said, I was a happy child, but there were three things that used to bother me when I was very small: for some reason I hated it when Mum put her hair up, wore trousers or sat on Dad's knee. One of my very first memories is of coming out of the toy cupboard under the stairs and being furious at the sight of Mum in Capri pants with her hair up. I don't know what a psychiatrist would say about it because I have no idea why I reacted this way, and neither does Mum! Perhaps it's because Mum was, and still is, very attractive; both my parents are. Certainly, as I became older, I didn't always like the way Mum attracted the attention of men, although why wouldn't she?

Whatever the reason, Mum said it was a nightmare! She was a glamorous young woman in her early twenties who loved to be fashionable, but her three-year-old daughter insisted on dictating her wardrobe. It's bizarre because these days I love the Capri pants look. At least it didn't last beyond early childhood.

When I was three, my sister Debbie was born. One of my earliest memories is of my mum carrying my new baby sister down the path to our house. I can't remember Mum being pregnant with Debbie, but I can remember the day she arrived home. Apparently, I wasn't jealous of the baby, but I had to be involved with her care and Mum practically had to pretend that she was my baby daughter, so that I wouldn't stick pins in her and all that stuff young siblings do.

Just before Debbie was born, we moved to a three-bedroom semi in Woodleigh Road, Monkseaton, just outside Whitley Bay. Being so young, Mum and Dad loved to have parties, and the house was always full of people. I have a strong memory of wailing, 'When is everyone go-ho-ho-ho-ing home?' at around four in the morning (although it was probably only about eleven at night) and of my parents saying, 'Oh, have another glass of cola, you'll be fine.' It was something I later vowed never to do to my children. Fast forward to now and . . . whoops!

A friend of Mum and Dad, 'Auntie' Audrey, ran my nursery school. She remains a friend to this day. Audrey was very elegant and always looked properly dressed. You never saw her without her make-up, hair and nails done. The walls of the school were painted a cross between lavender and cornflower-blue, and to this day it's a colour that I find very comforting. It really calms me down. In fact, when I was very ill with depression, I had carpets of that exact colour put down in the house and they had the effect of a comfort blanket.

When I go to my son Louis's school around Christmas, the smell of glue and glitter instantly brings back memories of my infant school, which I loved. The highlight of my life in those days was when Mum would take me into Newcastle after school. I can still remember the feeling of exhilaration. Children are so spoilt these days that I sometimes wonder if Louis ever experiences the same heady level of pure excitement that used to overcome me when Mum picked me up and took me to Bainbridge's department store, which had an olde worlde tea room called the Chattery. Louis would probably rather stick pins in his eyes than go to the Chattery with me, but I found it thrilling. In my memory, it was always winter when we went. The dark nights made it feel even more exciting. It's funny because I hate the winter now.

Wearing fluorescent sashes on dark winter mornings, Debbie and I walked about a mile and a half to get to our next school, Appletree Gardens junior school. It was there that we had the mickey taken out of us about our sweetie factory connection. We had these brown, shiny coats and some of the kids called them 'toffee anoraks'. However, that was as bad as it ever got and I feel incredibly fortunate that I was never bullied at school. The thought of what kids sometimes do to each other makes me feel physically sick, now that I have children of my own.

Saying that, there was this one boy called Richard who was pretty mean to me for a short time. He kept prodding me – non-stop, if I remember correctly. Unfortunately for us both, I went home and told Mum.

The next day, to my utter dismay, I came out of school to find a crowd had gathered. In the centre, I saw my mum, my granny and poor Richard, whom my mum had by the ear. 'Kick him! Go on, kick him!' Mum ordered. I just stood there, absolutely mortified.

Later, my dad drove me to Richard's house and I waited outside in total horror while Dad told his dad what had been going on. Then I heard Richard's dad go into the house and yell at Richard, 'And you, a cub scout!'

Back then, it wasn't a question of going through 'the correct channels'. My parents were just so protective that they thought they'd sort it out themselves. Looking back, it pleases me that they did something about it, although Richard's dad was obviously horrified and God knows what happened to Richard when we'd left.

Even though my parents didn't have much money, I've always felt I was to the manor born, snatched from a royal cradle somewhere hot and taken to Whitley Bay! Mum said that I was the kind of kid who could never understand why the grown-ups might want me to go to bed. Well, why would they, considering what I was bringing to the table in terms of humour and conversation? I was constantly coming downstairs when they had friends over, scurrying around the room, trying to take sips from people's wine glasses. I was also very dramatic, Mum says. One evening, I appeared on the stairs and said, 'Come on, let's all go to the Rex!' The Rex was the posh hotel where Mum and Dad had had their first date, and it was legendary in my mind.

One of my dad's best friends is Ian La Frenais, and he is also my godfather. Ian went on to become a comedy writer, famous for *The Likely Lads*, *Porridge* and *Auf Wiedersehen, Pet*, but he was just Uncle Ian in the early days, one of Mum and Dad's gang. He lived with his parents, Auntie Gladys and Uncle Cyril, at the end of the road, so we were down at their house a lot. Later, he became a very glamorous figure to me. He was always very trendy, and still is.

When I was eight, I begged Ian to draw up outside my school in his incredible black Silver Cloud Rolls Royce, the likes of which Whitley Bay had never seen. Rolls Royces didn't look like glorified Audis back then. They used to glide along in majestic splendour and it was an event if one arrived in your street. I made Mum organise the trip and she and Ian duly arrived at the school gates one lunchtime with his friends, the actors Tom Courtenay and Rodney Bewes. Thrilled, I stepped grandly into the car, feeling like a movie star, hoping that all my schoolmates were watching.

We drove ten minutes to the coast for fish and chips. When we had finished eating, I was anxious to get back to school in time for the end of the lunch break, so that anyone in the playground who hadn't seen me getting into Ian's Rolls Royce would see me getting out of it when they dropped me back. Apparently, as I got out of the car, I shrugged and said, 'Oh well, back to reality!'

When Ian moved to London and we went down to see him, our visits usually took in a recording of *The Likely Lads* at the BBC, which I totally took for granted. Likewise, it felt completely natural when Ian took us to Alvarez restaurant on the King's Road, with actresses like Sheila Fearn and Joan Sims. I was absolutely in my element.

During the filming of the second series of *The Likely Lads*, Rodney Bewes came to stay with us, which was obviously quite impressive because he was starring in the country's most popular sitcom. At the time, I wasn't remotely thinking about being an actress, but it felt completely normal to me when people came over to ask Rodney for his autograph.

We lived opposite the church where the Brownies held their meetings and inevitably they heard that Rodney was staying with us. One night, I looked out of the front window and there were about thirty Brownies at the door, come to ask if they could have his autograph. So I went upstairs to his room and said, 'There are thirty Brownies outside. Do you mind just coming downstairs?'

'No, I'm not coming down. I'm learning my lines,' he said grumpily.

'You get out of that bed and get downstairs!' my mother called, perhaps forgetting he wasn't one of her children.

'No!' he yelled back.

I'll never forget the look of disappointment on the Brownies' faces; it has stayed with me to this day, which is probably why I would never refuse to give someone my autograph. Rodney and I laugh about it now, but he always insists that he can't remember it.

When we went to London to see Ian, Mum would always take us to a children's clothes shop on the King's Road called And Mother Wouldn't Like It. The shop stocked outrageous gear that the northeast hadn't seen the likes of. 'But I don't want to wear it!' Debbie and I would protest as she togged us out in beaded trousers and big Baker Boy hats, on one of our trips down south. I remember thinking, 'My God, this is just too trendy for Whitley Bay!' But Mum would insist. As a result, we were ahead of the game, but not really comfortable with it. When you're ten, you just want to conform. You don't want to be different.

Mum was always saying, 'Oh, that looks very French!' or 'That looks very Italian!' She loved the chic way French women could wear something very simple, pick a flower, put it in their hair and look amazing. (This French thing is a recurring theme, isn't it? Mum was obsessed with all things French, which may be why I've ended up playing a French teacher in *Waterloo Road*!) But sometimes she didn't quite get it right, as far as Debbie and I were concerned.

There's one occasion that particularly sticks out in my mind, when we went to the circus while on holiday on the Isle of Wight. It was one of those really miserable English holidays when it just pours down all day, every day, and the afternoon we went to the circus was no different. That was the day Mum insisted that it was incredibly chic in France to wear big white knickers with a blazer and socks, and in this case she made us wear our school blazers.

'We don't care if it's chic; we are not going out in just our pants!' we kept saying.

'Just look in any of the magazines if you don't believe me!' she argued. 'It's totally *à la mode.*' In other words, we had no choice.

At the circus, we took our blazers off and sat with them over our knees, so that no one could see we weren't wearing skirts. Then, of course, Coco the Clown pointed at me and said, 'I need someone to help me with this trick. You, little girl, come and help me!'

I felt like I was acting out *The Emperor's New Clothes* as I walked down the steps in my white knickers and blazer. The way I remember it now, it was like a horror film, with the entire audience sniggering and saying, 'She's got no clothes on!'

To this day, when I bring it up, Mum says, 'Don't be silly! People were commenting on how lovely you looked.' Believe me, they weren't. I was only small, yet I can remember people saying, 'Do you think she knows she's only got her underwear on?' It was a nightmare. Now, of course, we love the fact that Mum was so ahead of the times, fashion-wise.

The house I grew up in was the kind of house you draw when you're a child, with a sloping roof, four windows and a door. There was a porch that joined on to the house next door, with a little path leading up to it through the garden and shrubbery. Downstairs, there was a little hall with three rooms off it: a lounge, for posh; a living room; and a kitchen. There was a hatch between the living room and the kitchen and I once saw Mum and Dad having a fight through it. Dad was brandishing a toasting fork and Mum was wielding a knotted tea towel.

I bet that if you asked any of their friends who they thought would have been most likely to split up, out of all the couples, it would have been my mum and dad, Vin and Annie, because they're like chalk and cheese. Yet of all those couples they knew then who are still in our lives today, it's my parents who have stayed together.

They had a very volatile relationship and made no bones about arguing in front of us. It was upsetting because Dad didn't realise how scary he could be. Their arguments were usually about nothing: Mum would be really cross that Dad hadn't rung from the rugby club or something, and Dad would go into this ridiculous rant, as if the world had ended. Then, five minutes later, it would all be fine. It really used to get Deb and me down when we had friends staying over because neither Mum nor Dad would make concessions if other people were there.

I remember putting notes under the door that said, 'Please don't argue!' I often wondered whether they were going to split up. After a particularly big row, Dad took Debbie and me to the Spanish City Amusement Park. While we were queuing for the big wheel, I said to Dad, 'Are you and Mum going to get divorced?'

There was an agonising pause and then Dad said, 'No, don't be so daft! We've just had a row.' He can't remember it now, so I don't know if divorce was ever something they were considering. It's only when you're older that you realise your parents were just two very young people who fell in love. I don't think either of them is easy to live with, but there's obviously something that has kept them together. And they had great fun together too – everyone loved being around them.

Before Mum gave up drinking nearly twenty years ago, after a few sherries she'd say, 'I don't know why I've stayed with him!'

Knowing damn well that she couldn't survive without him, Debbie and I would respond by saying, 'Well, we're in our thirties now, Mum, so don't feel you have to stay together for the children!'

But even if she did feel something like hatred towards him sometimes, she was far more comfortable when he was by her side. If we were somewhere and Dad was due to join us, she would always be craning her neck looking for him. She obviously adores him, but I'll pay anyone who will get her to admit that!

They still argue about everything. Dad's got a really short fuse, whereas Mum's the sulky one. She can easily go four days without speaking to him, which Dad finds hard to understand because he can barely remember why he blew up in the first place. Now we find it quite amusing. I think it's just a hobby of Dad's and half the time he doesn't realise he's doing it. He'll argue about the tiniest things. 'Dad, it's not important!' we say, when he gets all steamed up. 'You'll have a heart attack if you go on that way!'

They're both very kind-hearted. Yet, while Mum tends to reserve her kindness for her close circle of friends and family, Dad would do anything for anyone. Actually, that's been one of Mum's bones of contention with him. 'I've been asking you to do that for me for years,' she'll complain. 'And yet when so-and-so rings, you drop everything to do it for them!'

I had probably only just been born when Dad dressed up as a woman for the first time. Back then, he was a very good-looking young man, in a pretty way. It all began when Mum and Dad were invited to a fancy-dress party. Mum got dressed up in a leotard, boots, a tie and a bowler hat, so although she looked very sexy, there was definitely a hint of cross-dressing in her outfit. In turn, Dad put on one of Mum's dresses because he was slim enough to fit into it. It was a gold lamé dress with a slit up the side, which showed off his wonderful legs. Annoyingly, men often have good legs, don't they? Next, he put on one of Mum's blonde wigs and Mum made him up. He looked fantastic!

The story goes that a lot of their friends didn't recognise Dad at the party because he looked so good. Somebody was playing the piano and he went up and told a few jokes, staying in character as a female, which went down very well. After that, people started asking him to come to their parties and dress up. By the time I began to be more aware of it, he had formed a group called The Bits and Pieces who would do little charity events. He didn't sing, except for his unique version of Marlene Dietrich's 'Falling in Love Again'; his was a more traditional joke-telling, variety-based act and his gags were quite rude. Still, as I know from the *Loose Women* audience, people love a blue joke; nothing disgusting – just something a bit naughty.

So, from an early age, I was used to the sight of my dad dressed up as Dolly Parton, Shirley Bassey, Marilyn Monroe or Raquel Welch (which is where his drag-act name, Raquel, came from). He absolutely loved it. All these characters spoke Geordie! There was no attempt to do the person's accent; it was really just the physical likeness that he emulated. I don't know where he got his flamboyance from. His sister Cynthia, whom Debbie and I worshipped, was an outspoken person who was very into poetry and amateur dramatics, so perhaps it ran in the family. She used to joke that she did find Dad's transformation quite worrying in one way – the family resemblance meant that it was just like looking in the mirror! Their brother David, the JR Ewing brother, was a totally different character. He was very disapproving. So who knows what lies behind Dad's behaviour?

My own spin on it is that Dad was very frustrated when he had to leave university and go and work in the family business, so he looked elsewhere to express his flair and intelligence. After all, he went from being a potential economics graduate, who could have gone on to do a number of interesting things, to being a sales rep. He needed some kind of expressive outlet and found it in these performances. His work life was unfulfilling, so he threw himself into his social life.

By the time I was a teenager, it had become a regular thing for me to see Dad dressed as a woman. I didn't consider it to be in any way strange. When an insurance man came to the house one day with some papers for Dad to sign, I let him in and asked him to wait. 'He'll be down in a minute,' I said. 'He's just getting ready before he goes off to do a charity night.'

I failed to mention that he was getting dressed up as Dolly Parton, though, so when Dolly walked down the stairs, the poor insurance man nearly had a fit! He started backing into a corner with a look of total horror on his face. Typically, Dad behaved as if there were nothing unusual about the situation and sat down to sign the forms with his legs wide open, probably forgetting that he was wearing a dress. The guy couldn't get out of our house fast enough!

Dad wasn't dressing up in a transvestite way, though. Ninety-eight per cent of transvestites are heterosexual men who feel the need to relax by wearing women's clothes, but that's not what it's all about for Dad. I once asked him if there was anything like that behind it and he said, 'I promise I would tell you if there was.' He didn't have a need to wear women's clothes; he just loved the transformation, the show element of it and the shock value.

I was so accustomed to it as I was growing up that if I was showing photos of my family to someone, I'd be just as happy to show the pictures of Dad in drag as the ones where he was dressed normally. It was just my dad in drag, so what? Debbie, on the other hand, was not so keen on showing those photos. She and I have always been very different. We share the same sense of humour and we absolutely worship and adore each other, but she didn't inherit the wicked gene that I have.

About four years ago, I was asked by a magazine to do a piece about where I grew up. The magazine got in touch with the lovely couple who now live at the house in Woodleigh Road to see if they'd let us look around. It was fantastic to go back with Mum, Dad and Debbie. My husband Tim and son Louis came too.

It was fascinating to look over the house again. Structurally, it was pretty much the same, but it looked so much more modern. I realised that the shrubbery outside the house, which had seemed like a forest when I was little, was only about 10 foot by 10 foot. As we went upstairs, I remembered being terrified of the Old Mother Hubbard wallpaper on my original bedroom wall. For some reason, rather than redecorate the room with something pink and pretty, my parents moved me in with Debbie. We shared a bedroom for the next nine years.

Even the airing cupboard brought back memories – of the day my Number 6 cigarettes were discovered hidden under some towels. I'll never forget Dad holding them up and saying, 'And whose are these?'

I made up something up on the spot. 'They're Susan's,' I blurted out.

'And who is Susan?'

'Er—'

I wasn't going to admit that my best friend Kathryn and I used to go and get cigarettes from the Wine Bin for Mrs Ross across the road, back when shopkeepers sold fags to children if they said they were buying them for an adult. We were about ten years old when we started smoking Consulates and we moved on to Number 6s when we were eleven. As someone who is still a social smoker, aged fifty-one, I rue the day that I ever started!

Kathryn and I had several ways of looking 'grown-up'. One way involved nicking the pointy cones that Mum inserted into her bra to give her some shape. We'd each put one cone up our jumper and drape our coats over the side that didn't have a bump. Then we'd light a ciggie and stand around thinking that people would assume we were adults. After one of these sessions, I went home, thinking, 'Ah ha! I'll hide the fags in the airing cupboard!'

Although I didn't admit the cigarettes were mine, I was grounded anyway. Dad was really quite strict; one look from him was enough to terrorise Debbie and me, which is how it should be. We never misbehaved in company. To this day, Dad goes absolutely mad when he sees other people's children running amok in people's houses and the parents simply laughing it off. 'What has he smashed now? A treasured china ornament? Oh well, ha ha, kids will be kids!'

Mum and Dad only ever wanted the best for us. Debbie and I were mad about horses, so one day, when I was nine and she was six, they surprised us by driving us to Murton House Riding School and signing us up for riding lessons. We lived and breathed Murton House after that, even going there on the days when we didn't have lessons. Our life felt like one long round of gym-khanas, horse shows and winning rosettes. For the next few years, I asked repeatedly, 'Can I have a pony? Can I have a pony?' I put signs on the door saying things like, 'If I get a pony, I promise I'll never ask for a Christmas or birthday present again.'

When I was twelve, I was allowed to go into Whitley Bay on the bus with Kathryn. Sometimes I had to take Debbie too, which is the last thing you want at that age, when you're trying to be grown-up. I used to get a right cob on that I always had to have my snotty little sister in tow. She always seemed to be covered in jam and was constantly telling tales on me to Mum and Dad.

We would go to the tea room at Ryles, the department store, for a cup of tea. How sophisticated! I was that kind of girl; I used to wrap my towel into a turban after washing my hair and sit in front of the mirror, elegantly inhaling and exhaling on a biro, in imitation of my mum. She made everything look cool. Now, of course, I think how uncool it was!

On our way back from Ryles one afternoon, we got to the end of Woodleigh Road and saw a crowd gathered around our garden. I was scared, my heart racing; I bolted up the road to see what the commotion was all about. To my amazement and joy, there was a horse in the garden! Dad had bought it from a pal, Tony Ingham, and it had cost him something like a hundred pounds, which was a lot of money then. All the neighbours had come out to have a look at it.

They were heady days that followed. I lived and breathed that horse, who was called Sam. There was no green-belt area nearby, so he was stabled about three miles away at Dobbinson's Farm and I thought nothing of walking to his stables every day after school. My mum waved me off without a care too; children enjoyed a wonderful freedom back in those days. It's so different now, even though we know that the statistics haven't changed. Just as many children were murdered or snatched then as now, yet I nearly have a nervous breakdown if my son Matthew isn't back when he's supposed to be, and he's twenty. My Mum does too, which is ironic considering how relaxed she used to be about me being out and about!

How blissful life was then. In my memory, the sun was always shining on the hay bales and the evenings were light and balmy.

I've obviously forgotten about the dark winter nights when I trudged all that way to the stables through the mud in my wellies. Although Sam was shared, in my mind he was really mine. Poor Debbie – she was always relegated to the back of the saddle and she had a constant bruise on her fou-fou because I insisted on going too fast! I hardly ever let her have a go at the front. She used to get so frustrated with my bossy, older-sister ways that Mum gave her a cushion, so that when she wanted to punch me, she could punch the cushion instead. To this day, I think that if she still had a cushion like that, she would use it!

Aged thirteen, I would think nothing of getting up at four in the morning to plait Sam's mane and tail, before walking for hours to get to the nearest gymkhana. We didn't have horse boxes – I don't think Sam ever went in a horse box – so I walked some really long distances, up to twelve miles. It took ages, but I didn't care. I was just absolutely besotted with the whole thing. I began to enter better shows and do well at higher levels, especially the jumping section. At one point, I even considered riding professionally.

But then adolescence galloped over the horizon and my dreams of emulating Elizabeth Taylor in *National Velvet* crashed into the fence. Suddenly all I cared about was boys and drama. It was time for Sam to go back to his farm.

Chapter Two

When I was ten, I started to question why we didn't go to church when I knew several of my friends did. Granny's family, on my mother's side, were Catholic and I had been baptised a Catholic. But I think it was only a gesture to please Granny because I certainly wasn't raised a Catholic. Mum and Dad weren't church-goers. Actually, although Granny was religious, she didn't go to church much either. When Mum's sister Jill went off to become a nun, Granny was quite horrified because she felt she was losing her daughter to the convent.

'Well, if you want to go to church, go to church,' Mum said placidly. 'It's just down the road. Go and introduce yourself.' So off I trotted the following Sunday, taking Debbie with me. We went every week for the next two years after that. We found the Bible stories very interesting and loved the church ballroom-dancing events. I was very keen on the boy I was partnered with; he was definitely an incentive for regular attendance.

Being one of those girls who wasn't backwards in coming forwards, I was always interested in boys. I started kissing boys when I was about nine, although it wasn't until I was eleven that I had my first boyfriend, Paul Bean. My sister was going out with Paul's younger brother, Sidney, so we were going out with the

Beans – Mr Bean and his brother. They both had blond crew cuts and looked like proper little scallies. I was madly in love with Paul Bean. I can't honestly tell you that I recall the outcome of the relationship, but I do remember that he was really fit! However, I naughtily snogged somebody else at the church disco when he wasn't there, so I wasn't completely faithful to him.

My churchgoing days ended when I told Mum that I didn't agree with medicine anymore. 'Why's that, then?' she asked.

'The church says it's wrong,' I replied.

'Really?' she said in astonishment.

It turned out that we had taken the wrong turning and ended up at the Christian Science church by mistake! Of course, we didn't know the difference. And all that time, Mum had thought we were going to the Catholic church.

Which meant that I knew absolutely nothing about Catholicism when I started at La Sagesse convent school at eleven years of age. Mum and Dad had thought the local comprehensive wasn't right for me and decided to look into private schools. They picked La Sagesse partly because you got a half-price deal if your child was Catholic. Of course, nobody said anything about being a *practising* Catholic. Oh, the horror of going to chapel and not knowing how to say a Hail Mary! Mary who?

Then there was communion. I'd never taken my first communion, so I just had to copy the others. I didn't have the nerve to say, 'I don't know how to do this.' So it was a case of 'Please don't make me go first! Do you chew this stuff or swallow it whole?' I had to fake being a Catholic and was constantly in detention saying hundreds of Hail Marys that had very little meaning for me. Religion and I have never been very good bedfellows since.

I hated that school, even though it was very highly thought

of. I didn't enjoy being in an all-female environment and it was very strict. We were supposed to wear straw boaters in the summer and I was always in detention for not wearing mine. Within months of being there, I developed a phobia of maths. Even now, I get sweaty palms at the thought of adding up and I still can't do my times tables. It doesn't come naturally to me. I used to vomit before double maths because I was so intimidated by it. When something doesn't compute at all, it's scary. I'd get 86 per cent for French, but just 10 per cent for maths. To make things worse, the nuns just told me off rather than trying to help me.

When I was eleven, Welch's Toffees started to lose money. Dad took over two hairdressing salons in an attempt to diversify, even though he had no knowledge of the workings of hairdressing salons whatsoever. They had proper old hairdryers and smelled of perm lotion. Mum oversaw them for a while and used to make Debbie and me have our hair done there. We've got a clip of old cine film that shows us both looking like Margaret Thatcher! We loved going to the salon for all the gossip and intrigue we could pick up from the customers.

Vincent's Hair Fashions turned out to be quite a short-lived enterprise and as things grew worse at Welch's Toffees, Mum decided to go back to work. Prudhoe Hospital was her first port of call and she was welcomed back there as a psychiatric nurse. She worked with dangerously high-grade patients and she used to come home black and blue sometimes. She worked nights because she was quite nocturnal, and was sometimes running two wards at the same time. Meanwhile, Dad continued to work for Welch's and my parents never revealed to me or Debbie that there were money troubles.

Prudhoe Hospital was quite a way from our house and Mum decided that she was ready to leave the coast. So we upped sticks and moved across the river to a lovely house in the village of Ebchester, near Consett, County Durham, where Mum and Dad still live today. We'd been to see lots of houses and when we eventually drove up to this house, Debbie and I walked in and said, 'We can't afford this, though, can we?' It looked like a picture-book cottage and somehow seemed out of our league. I think it cost around £4,500.

This was quite an unsettling period for me. I now had to travel miles to get to school, but much worse was leaving behind all my friends at the coast. Perhaps this was responsible for my first unfortunate encounter with alcohol, aged thirteen, the night my new best friend Christine and I were asked to babysit her baby cousin. Feeling very grown-up, we decided to raid the drinks cabinet and have ourselves a small gin and tonic. I'm ashamed to say that I didn't know when to stop and we drank the house dry. The next thing I knew, I was in my bed at home with a bucket in front of me.

My parents had received a call from the baby's parents, who had come in to find me collapsed unconscious on the floor. What a fright that must have been! Mum and Dad came rushing down to collect me. They weren't sure whether or not to take me to hospital to have my stomach pumped, but I vomited so much as I was coming round that they thought it was probably unnecessary. I heard my mum say, 'All right, not tonight, tomorrow!' Clearly, my dad was about to give me a bollocking, but I wasn't in a fit state to receive one.

Hangovers are bad enough as an adult, but they're even worse when you are thirteen and have been drinking gin and whisky to the point of collapse. The next day, Dad very calmly told me that I might easily have died. My punishment was to walk the mile down to the house where I had been babysitting and apologise to the baby's parents. It was hell: I was sick every three yards! Every time I drive along that stretch of road, that particular memory comes flooding back. After that, I was grounded for a month. Sadly, it didn't put me off alcohol for good, which that kind of bad experience can do for some people. However, it certainly put me off for a while and I was never a massive teen drinker.

By now I was so miserable at La Sagesse that I pleaded with my parents to let me try for the nearby Consett Grammar School, where several of my new friends went. Eventually they relented. So after two years with the nuns, I moved to Consett, which I absolutely loved. I still hated maths, though. I was terrified of Mr Todd, my maths teacher. He was a great believer in mental arithmetic and always picked on me in class to add something up on the spot because he knew it was my big fear. Consett Grammar was generally much more relaxed than La Sagesse, though.

I went through a skinhead phase just after this, although there is no photographic evidence of it, unfortunately, and Mum always denies it happened. It was purely a fashion thing, just following the pack, as you do in your mid teens, my gang at that time being Christine's friends from the secondary school. When I went out and had a feather cut I thought I looked so cool but my father was totally appalled. 'Go and buy a wig!' he told me.

Mum and Dad wouldn't buy me a Crombie coat initially, so I wore my Sta-Prest flat-fronted trousers with my black riding jacket and a red hanky in the pocket, along with my Ben Sherman shirt with a pleat down the back, electric-pink or electric-green socks and loafers. God, it was so tragic! I wore a lot of heavy black eyeliner and listened to pop reggae, Motown and northern soul. My friends and I were the antithesis of 'the hairies', who liked rock and played air guitar.

Thankfully, there were boys at Consett Grammar, and boys were of huge interest to me. By now, I had snogged with tongues for the first time, with Andrew Thorpe, or Drew, as he was called. We had a right old tumble in a barn that I'll never, ever forget. Then, for my fourteenth birthday, I begged Mum and Dad to go to the pub and let me have my friends around on my own. They agreed to go out for about two hours, but insisted that Debbie stayed at home. She was eleven, so it was a nightmare for me. I remember being on the settee, snogging Tommy Henderson, and as I came up for air, Debbie was standing over me saying, 'What pub are Mum and Dad in? Because I'm telling!' She was a right little snitch. If only I'd known at the time that she'd won a snogging competition with Rory Mourn at her school!

Later that year, I fell in love for the first time, with Simon Robertson, who was the vicar's son and lived in the vicarage in Shotley Bridge. Simon and his friends Rob and Graham were the cool guys in the sixth form at Consett. They always looked so sexy in their biology lab coats. Attracting Simon's attention was extremely flattering because it's not necessarily that cool to be with a fourteen-year-old girl when you're sixteen. I absolutely adored him and there began the first great love affair of my life. Well, apart from my time with Paul Bean, that is!

Simon was quite folky and so I got into folk music too – which really upset my skinhead friends. His mum Audrey was in a group called The Potter's Wheel and I was always going off to the Barley Mow in Newcastle to listen to bearded singers in Aran jumpers with their fingers in their ears. Some of my happiest teenage memories are of sitting in the bay window at Simon's house listening to him play his dulcimer, which he held across his knee. He was madly into Cat Stevens, and so began my lifelong love of Cat Stevens. Any time I hear 'Moonshadow' I'm transported back to being with Simon.

There was a prep room at the back of the biology lab and one day, while I was in biology, Simon walked into the lab and put a rose in my Bunsen burner, in front of everybody. It was quite cool of him to do that in front of a whole gang of fourteen-year-olds and I glowed with pride and pleasure. Unfortunately, he didn't realise that, because he called me 'Pet', his friends had written 'Big Pet, Little Pet' on the back of his lab coat. How embarrassing!

The first time I remember my heart really aching was when my parents took Debbie and me to stay in Rodney Bewes's beautiful cottage in Cadgwith, in Cornwall. I have a couple of photos of me standing near my parents and Debbie, looking forlornly over the sea. I wished the days away, desperately missing Simon. When Mum and Dad found out about a local barn dance and took me there to cheer me up, I just did that teenage thing and sat in the corner, sulking, because they had dragged me away from Simon. I must have been a nightmare. All I could think about was how I would never, ever be so in love again in my entire life!

Debbie and I still have strong memories of that holiday in Cadgwith. We went back there a few years ago, having droned on to our husbands for years about our wonderful holidays in Cornwall. You know how it is when your partner hasn't been somewhere before and you are boring them to death with reminiscences. 'Oh Debbie, do you remember—?' Then I'd say to Tim, 'This is where we went to the barn dance. This is where we watched the fishermen.' Our partners kept saying, 'For God's sake, shut up! Let's go for a pint.'

I vividly remember what I was wearing the day we went

home after that first holiday in Cornwall: a pair of blue, flared, cotton trousers – or loons, as we called them – with a pink pony patch that I'd stitched on the back, and clogs with ridiculously high platform wedges. I was nicely tanned and my hair was up and really wispy from going in the sea a lot. I met up with Simon at Shotley Bridge and was nearly sick with excitement. I can still recall the smell of the aftershave he was wearing that day! I was wearing Charlie.

I didn't actually lose my virginity to him, but we did pretty much everything else. The relationship went on for a blissful two years until I was sixteen. Then Nana, my father's mum, became poorly and I went to visit her. When I arrived back, Simon picked me up in his car, took me to a layby near the infant school at Shotley Bridge and finished with me. That's the first and only time I've ever been finished with. I was absolutely devastated. I hadn't been expecting it at all.

He didn't say, 'I don't love you anymore' or anything like that. It was more like, 'We should move on' or 'It's not working anymore.' I think now that it was because he was going away to college and it was the sensible thing for any eighteen-year-old guy to do in the circumstances, but obviously I didn't have that kind of perspective at the time. I can remember exactly what I was wearing that day as well: a black maxi velour skirt with pink flowers on it that I'd made out of that appalling material you're given in sewing class at school. No wonder he finished with me!

I cried buckets over Simon – not in front of him, but on my own, listening to the Nilsson song 'Without You' in my bedroom. Only it wasn't the Nilsson version, it was a sound-alike cover from one of those *Top of the Pops* albums, the ones that always had a girl on the front wearing hot pants. I had a whole collection of them. I couldn't wait to get each new one when it came out.

I was heartbroken, but as is my wont, I very quickly turned my attentions to Rob Taylor, one of Simon's best friends. It wasn't about teaching Simon a lesson or getting my revenge because that's not in my nature. Possibly there was an element of rebound to it, but really it was because suddenly I was a free agent and I fancied somebody else. I remember lusting after Rob intensely. Most of my day at school was spent looking at the timetable to work out when he would be coming out of the library. My stomach would flip over when I saw him. Being a sixth-former, he wasn't an easy catch.

When I went to see Rob play Puck in the school production of *A Midsummer Night's Dream*, I was just blown away. 'If there is a heaven on earth, this is it,' I thought, as I watched him up on stage, covered in gold paint. Not only did I fall in love with him all over again, but I fell for the production. We weren't a theatre-going family, so watching a play was a fantastic new experience for me. All I had seen until then was the occasional panto and gang show.

'Why don't you come and audition for the next production?' asked Terry Cudden, the drama teacher, when the play ended. It was the first time I had even thought about acting.

The next school play was *Finian's Rainbow*, which coincidentally was also the first play my husband Tim appeared in at school. Without any experience of drama at all, I auditioned and got the part of Susan the Silent, who has to speak through dance for most of the play, until at the very end she says, 'I love you'. Unfortunately, I dried on my one line! There was a long silence and suddenly I realised that it was my cue! Funnily enough, Tim also had a bit of a disaster with his acting debut. He was playing a little black boy, and in those days you blacked up, but he forgot to put any make-up on his legs. So he was black from his head to his waist, and then had these skinny white legs poking out of his shorts!

This sounds so naff, but it felt as if a light had gone on in my life when I appeared in *Finian's Rainbow*. From that moment onwards, I lived and breathed drama at school, completely and utterly. When I went back to Consett Grammar to film a documentary in 2008, I started to cry when I walked into the school hall, which I hadn't seen since the day I left. It still looked and smelled exactly the same! 'Oh my God,' I thought, 'if it wasn't for this hall, the whole trajectory of my life would be completely different.' I felt overcome with nostalgia and gratitude.

I got it together with Rob one evening after he, Simon and I and their friends Geoff and Graham had gone out drinking somewhere in Consett. Back at Rob's house on the Moorside Estate, his dad, Arthur, was out on nights at the steelworks, so it turned into a bit of a party. At one point, I went into the kitchen to make a cup of tea and Rob followed me. That was our first kiss.

I can remember Simon saying, 'Well, it's my fault for letting you go, isn't it?' After that, I was officially with Rob. Still, Simon can't have been that heartbroken because we all remained friends.

I lost my virginity to Rob in his dad's council house, which was freezing cold, with no central heating. It wasn't a major deal to me. If you've done everything else, it's just a natural progression. Afterwards, I thought, 'Well, that was champion!' I didn't regret it because I loved him and we were protected by a condom. I felt blooming freezing, though. When it was over, I remember wanting to get downstairs and have a cup of tea and a crumpet.

It was another massive love affair with Rob. We were madly

in love with each other for the next two years. I felt that my world had fallen apart the day he left for teacher-training college in Leicester, six months into the relationship. I cried racking sobs for days and thought about him constantly. I didn't see him for three weeks and it felt like three years.

The night before he came back, I spent hours getting ready – painting my nails and shaving and tweezing – and when I met him at Durham train station, it was like Trevor Howard and Celia Johnson in *Brief Encounter* all over again. The age of steam was long gone, but in my mind he arrived on a big old steam train and when the smog cleared on the platform, there he was! Oh God, I just couldn't bear being apart from him.

I used to go to Leicester quite a lot and share his tiny bed with him. I absolutely loved going there. Everyone at teacher-training college seemed to have such a great time. There didn't seem to be much learning going on; it was all drinking and having parties in each other's rooms. The only downside of going to visit Rob was that I felt like a child compared with all the students because they were nearly twenty and I was seventeen and still at school. Rob used to involve me, but I still felt like a school kid. I remember endlessly listening to Stevie Wonder's *In Square Circle* around that time.

I didn't tell Mum and Dad that I was having sex, and they never asked me about it. But when I went off to stay with him, I'm sure they didn't think that he had taken a second room in the hall of residence for me. They knew I was serious about Rob and I think they assumed that I was sensible enough to take precautions against pregnancy.

In my last year at school, I played Abigail in *The Crucible* and began to feel that acting was something I could really do well. I instinctively knew what to do when I was on stage. 'If Denise Welch doesn't become a professional actress, I will eat my hat,' said one reviewer in the local paper. I was thrilled, especially as I had never been patted on the back at school for anything before because I was an average student and undoubtedly lazy. Now I was suddenly being praised for my acting skill, which only made me love acting even more.

Even so, I wasn't yet thinking in terms of acting as a career. Consett wasn't a school that produced actors. Years before, Alun Armstrong had been a pupil, but it wasn't a theatre-oriented school like the school Angela Griffin and Sarah-Jane Potts attended in Manchester, where TV companies were always scouting for child actors.

When I went for careers advice, I didn't even mention acting as a possibility. So no one ever said to me, 'Don't be so ridiculous! Wanting to be an actor is just a pipe dream. Go and get an apprenticeship!' which was the case with so many of my actor friends. I wanted to do something in the field of drama, though, so I decided to teach it. I was still very keen on the idea of teacher-training college, not because of what I would learn, but because of the social life.

I knew I wasn't bright enough to go to university. I just wasn't going to work hard enough to get my A levels. By then, I'd done my O levels: English language and literature, French, history and needlework. In the needlework exam (anything to avoid doing another academic subject!) we had to make half a pair of shorts. I failed because, just as we ran out of time, I realised that I'd sewn the leg of my shorts together. At which point my dreams of becoming a seamstress crumbled into the dust. Dad made me retake the two O levels I failed and I scraped through them to get the five I needed to apply for the Crewe & Alsager teacher-training college, where the English and drama course had a good reputation. My friend Jill Hewitson and I wanted to go to Crewe together. (I went to visit her there later and wished I *was* with her, she was having such a good time!) After I went for an interview at Crewe, a letter arrived saying that if I got one A level, I would be accepted on the course. I didn't even consider applying to Leicester, where Rob was studying because I knew their admission requirements were more stringent. One A level was challenging enough.

Meanwhile, Dad, who had been very keen on amateur acting when he was younger, was now getting back into it at a very famous amateur theatre in Jesmond called the People's Theatre, which is run exactly like a professional theatre, except that nobody gets paid. Dad was working with an amateur actor called John Barber, whose son, Paul Antony Barber, was at drama school, and I think this must have given him pause for thought. One day, he arranged to meet my drama teacher, Terry, without my knowledge, and later they sat me down in the school hall for a serious chat.

'I just don't think teaching is your vocation,' Dad said. 'You don't seem to have thought about the actual teaching side of it; you're just looking forward to being at college.'

This was definitely true. 'So what are you saying?' I asked.

'We don't want to push you in the wrong direction, but we both feel strongly that you should try for drama school,' Terry said.

'I've been talking to John Barber,' Dad went on, 'and he tells me that his son Paul is at Mountview Theatre School in Crouch End in London.'

So that was that. I didn't apply to RADA, Central or Webber Douglas – in other words, all the places people usually apply to –

I simply applied to Mountview Theatre School because that was the only drama school I had heard of. I was quite excited by the idea, partly because it might mean that I wouldn't have to take any A levels. I sent off for the prospectus, filled in the application form and the next thing I knew, I was asked to go in for an audition.

Mum and Dad came to the audition with me. I was absolutely in the minority because all the other parents had told their children, 'Please don't be an actor! Please be a teacher!' and mine were doing the complete opposite.

The moment I arrived at Mountview, I felt I'd entered a completely alien world and there wasn't a cat in hell's chance of getting a place there. The first thing I had to do was improvisation, which was terrifying. That was followed by a dance workshop. Since pretty much the only dancing I'd ever done was in my front room with my friends, choreographing routines to Motown songs, I felt very nervous as I went in. Luckily, you simply had to prove that you didn't have two left feet, so I was fine. It wasn't leaping across the room in a balletic way; it was modern jazz dancing.

Then I had to do two speeches: a reading from Shakespeare and something modern. The Shakespeare piece I chose was Lady Macbeth's famous 'Out, damn spot!' speech and the modern piece was an extract from *Five Finger Exercise* by Peter Shaffer. It's always embarrassing trying to perform in a room with two people watching you, but I did my best.

I definitely didn't shine. I came away from it thinking, 'That is the worst piece of acting I've ever done!' The audition finished early and I spent ages sitting on a bench outside, lonely as a cloud, feeling utterly miserable, waiting for Mum and Dad to pick me up. I felt sure that everyone else at the audition had been so much better than me.

Yet, two weeks later, I received a letter that said, 'Dear Jacqueline Denise, we are pleased to offer you a place at Mountview . . .'

I couldn't believe it! I was beyond excited. I even phoned them up to check they had sent the letter to the right place because I thought they'd made a mistake. It was especially thrilling because it was an unconditional offer, so I didn't have to pass any more exams. Phew, no more studying!

Although I was one of the queen bees of the school drama department, this was the first time I'd got any kudos at school. I was actually called into the headmaster's office. 'Congratulations!' he said.

'Thank you!' I replied. I was pleased, but at the same time I thought, 'Yeah, but this is the first time you've ever bothered to speak to me.'

A couple of weeks later, I turned eighteen. Grown up, at last! Actually, I mainly remember my eighteenth birthday for being the first time that I experienced sexual jealousy of my mum. All my friends fancied her! The birthday party was at our house and Mum wore a white catsuit with see-through lace bits. She was only thirty-nine and still had a fantastic figure, so she looked amazing. As my husband says, eighteen-year-old boys adore women of that age. To add to it all, she was wearing a red auburn wig styled into bunches. She was very into wigs – a bit ahead of her time (no pun intended!).

So, as the guys walked into the party and started saying, 'Happy birth—' to me, their jaws dropped at the sight of Mum.

You should have seen the flock of boys behind her as she bent 'to put the potatoes in the oven'. She always denied that she knew what she was doing, but I'm not so sure. Oh, how I wished right then that I had a grey-haired elderly mother who didn't make all my friends drool! But I wouldn't really swap her for the world.

Chapter Three

It was hard to leave home. I was really emotional when the time came. Most of the other students at Mountview were thrilled to get away and be independent, but I found it incredibly difficult being so far from my friends and family, especially Mum and Dad. It was the first time in my life that I had ever felt lonely. I was miserable.

The downside of drama school is that there are no halls of residence, so I had to find my own digs. It was as far away as you could get from my dreams of wild college living and partying. Obviously I was hoping that I would pal up with somebody and share with them eventually, but first I had to find somewhere for myself. Initially, I stayed with a friend of my parents in Richmond. Every day, I scoured the flat-sharing section of the *Evening Standard*, feeling desperately homesick.

I went to see some absolutely grotty places in north London. I'm sure there are lovely places in that area, but I didn't see them because they weren't available to someone on a student grant. Having said that, I was very lucky to get a really good arts grant from Durham Council, who really supported the arts in those days. Grants like that just don't exist anymore; it's heartbreaking the number of letters that Tim and I receive from kids who have been accepted by drama school but can't afford to go.

Eventually, I replied to an advertisement to share with two girls in Muswell Hill. Carol and Alison were a year older than I was and they spoke with broad, almost incomprehensible, Scottish accents. Carol was a big lass, but one of those girls who looks in the mirror and sees somebody who is eight stone. She wore her red hair in a boyish cut and had a penchant for little tops that showed off her midriff.

Alison, who was slight with a pretty face and short, dark hair, was always rushing around with a fag in her hand. She and Carol occupied the ground floor of a big house; Alison lived in a self-contained bedroom-and-living-room and Carol had a big bedsit with two single beds and a kitchen. I shared with Carol.

I lived with Carol and Alison for nine months and although we had a few laughs, I mainly remember the bad times. I had nothing in common with my new flatmates; they worked as secretarial temps and didn't seem to have any particular ambitions. Unfortunately for me, they were also best friends, so if the dishes weren't done, it was usually my fault. Most things were my fault, in fact!

Sometimes I went out with them in the evenings, but only because I thought that's what you were meant to do. If they had planned to go out together and one of them couldn't make it, I felt obliged to fill in. I didn't have the confidence to say that I didn't want to go, especially if it was Carol asking, because I was living in the same room as her. Occasionally, she'd bring back guys and sneak them into the room when she thought I was sleeping. I used to pull my quilt up over my face and bury my head in my pillows to muffle any sounds they might make if they got carried away!

Officially, Carol had a boyfriend, Phil, who was in a medium-security prison on the Isle of Sheppey. Much later, I was told that he was there because he had broken into an off-licence and got drunk inside the shop, instead of stocking up on booze and making a getaway. I have no idea if that is true but it's a great tale! Rubbish thief! Anyway, Carol had two visiting passes to see Phil and, since Alison couldn't make it, she insisted I go with her. I went along purely out of interest because I had never even seen a prison from the outside, let alone been inside one.

'I'll stay in the waiting area,' I volunteered, when we arrived. 'You'll want to be alone with him. You haven't seen him for six weeks.' I was fascinated by my surroundings and quite happy to sit and wait.

'No, no!' she said. 'You must come in and meet him.'

I was really quite astonished at how attractive Phil was. He had long hair and was a bit of a geezer, with a fun sense of humour. To my surprise, he seemed as interested in talking to me as he was to Carol. Well, it's probably any port in a storm if you're a young lad who's been in prison for a while because I was hardly Miss World. Not long afterwards, Carol split up with him and so we didn't visit him again. Bizarrely, though, that wasn't the last I saw of Phil . . .

Meanwhile, I was slowly starting to make friends at drama school, although it was sadly lacking the kind of social scene you get in halls of residence, where you go to the student union bar together and get hammered. We had a college bar, but it wasn't open all the time and the students only really congregated there when there was a production on. Also disappointing, as far as my love life went, was the realisation that many of the boys on my course were gay.

People's parents occasionally came for the weekend, my Mum

and Dad more than others because I missed them and wanted to see them. Most mums and dads would take their kids out for a meal and then to a movie or the theatre, but I was usually taken to the Black Cap drag revue in Camden Town.

I didn't think there was anything strange about it. It was only when I went back to college on the Monday that I realised it was in any way unusual. 'What did you do over the weekend?' people would ask.

'Oh, we went to the Black Cap because my dad wanted to watch drag acts to get some tips.'

'Really?'

I loved drama school for the first year. We had voice classes, acting classes and dance classes; I soaked it all up like a sponge. When my course began in 1976, there were forty-two of us; three years later, only seventeen of us graduated. Some left and quite a lot were asked to leave. You had to prove yourself and if you weren't up to scratch, you were out.

I used to get really freaked out about improvisation, but I was actually good at it. One day, we had to improvise being in a commercial, as part of a lesson on the difference between hard-sell and soft-sell. I was asked to do a hard-sell and on the spur of the moment I invented a DIY sex-change kit called Hormona. First I spoke in a normal voice; then I turned away to drink the Hormona and suddenly my voice dropped so that I sounded like Clement Freud. Don't ask me why, but I won plaudits for this performance!

As time went on, I became very friendly with Rosemary, who wore long flowing dresses and a lot of patchouli oil. Rose became my best friend and she still is today, even though we were the most unlikely pairing – the 'skinhead' (as she called me because of my short hair) and the 'hippy'. Rosemary always had a boyfriend, so

I didn't see her much outside college. I remember going off her at one point because she was having an affair with an American in the third year called Paul Berg; I was really jealous because I fancied him.

Another good friend was Bridget, who I was intrigued to find out was the daughter of a bona fide lady with an inherited title. Also in the gang were Don, Tony and Malcolm, who went on to become George, Bungle and Zippy in *Rainbow*, and Pammy Howell, who was always talking about meeting Mr Right and went on to marry Stephen Wright! I also became pals with a Geordie called Brian, who was on the stage-management course a year above me. I had a bit of a thing about Brian, but it was nothing serious because he had a girlfriend and I had a boyfriend.

I was still officially going out with Rob, but we never sat down and had a discussion about fidelity. I think there was a tacit agreement that we could do our own thing when we were apart. I didn't ever pretend that I didn't have a boyfriend, but I behaved like a single girl and I now know that he approached teacher-training college in the same way.

After loving my first year at drama school and feeling very lucky to be there, I became disenchanted in the second year and kept wanting to leave. I still wanted to be a professional actress, but I didn't know if I could continue the course because I didn't feel I was getting enough out of it and was becoming more aware of the bullshit that was involved. There were some really good teachers who were very inspirational, but there were also a few failed actors who were luvvies trying to live through their students. Some of them taught what I thought was a load of pretentious twaddle, stuff like how important it was to feel the vibrations between your hands, which just didn't make sense to a down-to-earth Geordie like me. Those of you who have seen

A Chorus Line and remember the song 'Nothing' will know exactly what I mean. I felt like yelling, 'Can we just pick up the script and learn the play, please?'

At one point, we had to do a piece from a Greek tragedy. 'It blooming well bores me to tears, this Greek tragedy stuff,' I kept complaining.

It wasn't exactly my thing but I did it and managed to produce tears when necessary. The teacher was delighted. 'It's the classics for you, my girl!' he said joyfully. 'I've always hoped that you wouldn't become a kitchen sink actress.'

'But I want to be a kitchen sink actress,' I said ruefully.

I've never been a luvvie and I was far more interested in kitchen sink drama – natural, contemporary pieces – than the classics. When we did *Hamlet*, all the girls wanted to try for Ophelia, but I had no desire to play her. We were putting on a hip, modern play called *Dusa, Fish, Stas and Vi* alongside *Hamlet* and I was far more eager to be in that. It was never the case that I couldn't do the classics; I just never had a particular interest in them. They didn't rock my boat. The teachers despaired of me because apparently in theatre your aspirations should be to do the classics and occasionally dabble in contemporary drama. Or that's what they said at the time.

During the second year, Bridget and I started living together in Archway. She was going out with Ainsley Harriot, the TV chef, who was an aspiring actor back then, and he often came over. Bridget said that they weren't actually 'going out' together, but they were definitely having a relationship because I heard them! After Ainsley, she went out with Kevin Allen, Keith Allen's brother, who is now a big Hollywood director. Meanwhile, having split up with Rob, I was scouring London for a John Travolta lookalike. Well not really, but I was obsessed with John Travolta.

I must have seen *Saturday Night Fever* ten or eleven times at the cinema and I loved everything about it.

Although AIDS probably did exist in its early form in 1977, none of us was aware of it. They were glory days. All you had to worry about was getting pregnant. Getting a dose of something didn't even seem that bad because the worst that could happen was that you'd have to take some antibiotics. So if you were an eighteen-year-old girl on the Pill, which I was, you didn't even think of using condoms, as they weren't advocated. It was only later that I realised how very lucky I was not to have caught anything.

I've always been able to separate sex from love. In my second year, I used to go out with my friends, who were all single, and dance until three in the morning in a nightclub, and if I fancied someone and they fancied me, I'd say, 'Do you want to come back to mine?' We'd go back to mine, we'd have sex and in the morning I'd say, 'Get yourself a bacon sandwich and off you go!' I was a free spirit on the Pill.

It made my friends very curious. 'But you actually slept with him?' they'd ask.

'Well, yes!'

'But how could you?'

The way I saw it, we had a really good night and nobody got hurt. What was the problem?

'Well, you just don't do that,' my friends would say.

'Tell me why you don't just do that?' I'd ask. I couldn't understand why it was the wrong thing to do. These days, you would say, 'It was wrong because you didn't use a condom.' But we didn't have that to worry about then.

I used to joke with the boys I'd slept with, saying, 'Well, I've lost respect for you now!' as that's what we girls would be told would happen to us.

It seemed ridiculous to me that someone might 'lose respect' for someone after they'd had a great night together. In my fifty-one years, no one has ever lost respect for me after I've slept with them, whether or not it's been on the first night. If we haven't seen each other again, it's either been out of mutual choice or because things have fizzled out. It's never been a case of, 'Ah ha! I've got my way and now I've lost respect for you.' Still, a lot of girls in those days worried about that happening.

Maybe the boys I got together with felt as if they'd met their match. They certainly weren't having to do all the running, and I would make the situation clear. Sex has always been something that can be totally recreational for me. Even now, with the threat of AIDS, I don't see why it can't just be a really fun, recreational, exciting thing to do, as long as you wear a condom. Although I totally and utterly respect people who don't see it that way.

I don't know where my attitude originated, or why. Perhaps I'm a gay man trapped in a woman's body, as some of my friends have suggested! But seriously, it's not like my parents were hippies or I had a free-love upbringing in a commune. It was just the way I was.

I'm not proud of it, but I'm certainly not ashamed of it. I wasn't trying to make a point or prove anything. I didn't think, 'I'm going to be really different and off the wall now and shag people and not care!' That was just how I felt naturally. People may call it promiscuity and maybe it was, but as far as I was concerned, I was just having a good time.

I didn't go out just to pull and bring someone back, but if I fancied someone and wanted to, I didn't see the problem with it. If I was genuinely turned on by someone and there was the possibility of taking him home or going back to his, it seemed pointless to lie around at home instead, feeling totally frustrated, thinking of him feeling totally frustrated in his apartment, when we could have had a great night of sex. No questions asked and off you go in the morning. Sometimes I'd see the guy again and sometimes I wouldn't.

When I was free and single, I found sex with a new partner really exciting. Doesn't everyone?

Don't get me wrong: sex within a long-term relationship is very nice. It's fantastic to have the confidence to be able to take your time, when your partner knows all the buttons to press and there's no embarrassment there. But there is also something incredibly exciting about first-time sex. I would be completely lying to myself if I said otherwise and I think there are a lot of people who think like me, if they're honest.

Nowadays, women are much freer about what they want, I think. Often, they have wasted years when they could have been having great sex because their upbringing has held them back. This seems to be the case particularly with my Catholic friends. You can't get rid of Catholic guilt. Catholics seem to live their lives worrying about what's going to happen to them 'up there'. Now, there is a lot to be said for the way religion gives you a moral basis for living: I'm nice to old people and I love helping charities. But I don't see why I should not have had sex with people, or why that would change things up there, if there really is somewhere up there.

As the year progressed, Bridget and I began to hatch plans to fly to Los Angeles and stay with my godfather Ian La Frenais, who was now living in Beverly Hills. Neither of us had been to America before and, being aspiring actors, the thought of spending the summer in and around Hollywood seemed unbelievably glamorous. But, being a student, I obviously couldn't afford the cost of the flight, let alone living expenses while we were there.

So I needed to make some money fast. A girl at drama school spotted an advertisement for waitresses in the newspaper and we went for an interview.

Toppers was a club in the middle of Soho. The manager, a rake-thin man with a very smooth manner, met us in the bar area upstairs. He hadn't even begun to give a job description when I saw two topless girls heading downstairs, wearing nothing but silver bow ties, micro mini-skirts and high heels.

'Do you have to dress like that to be a waitress here?' I asked, aghast.

'Yeah,' he said.

'OK, well, thanks very much, but we're wasting your time,' I said, getting up to leave.

My friend followed me out into the street. 'Would it really be so bad?' she ventured.

I turned and looked at her, shocked. 'You're not seriously thinking about becoming a topless waitress?' It was OK for her – she was pretty and had a lovely figure. But I had ballooned in weight over the year, partly from being on the Pill, I think. Aside from the tacky aspect of topless waitressing, I felt self-conscious about showing off my body.

'But we both need to earn some money,' she said. 'If we do it for a few weeks, we'll have saved quite a bit. I think it'll be okay.'

One way or another, she managed to persuade me to go back and ask for the manager again. He looked us up and down approvingly. Well, my friend anyway. 'Can you start on Monday?' he asked. I tried to nod enthusiastically.

Toppers was a very plush place, not at all seedy. There was a 'no touching' rule to protect the girls. We'd arrive at 6 p.m., put on our gear (not very much of it!) and stay until 2 a.m. Our job was to welcome the gentlemen when they came into the bar, make a fuss of them and persuade them to buy drinks. Everyone earned a fifteen-quid, flat-rate hostess fee for the night. If you persuaded a man to take you downstairs for dinner, you earned another fifteen pounds. The men always had dinner accompanied by a girl. If you got him to buy champagne, it was yet another fifteen pounds. That meant you could make forty-five pounds in a night, which was a lot of money in 1978.

The whole thing was a big act and it took me a while to get used to the scams. The aim of the men was to get you tiddly, so for every drink you persuaded them to buy for themselves, they also bought you a drink. However, you weren't allowed to get drunk, so when you were offered a drink, you'd ask Mohammed, the barman, for 'a number nine', which was listed as an alcoholic cocktail, but was actually a fruit cocktail.

There was another routine if you managed to wheedle champagne out of someone: you'd go to the toilet with your glass in your hand, giggling as you went, swap it for a non-alcoholic drink and return saying, 'God, I'm so drunk!' Or else you'd tip the champagne onto the carpet. They had a spray to take away the stain and the smell of alcohol. I think most of the men knew that it was all a game, so I didn't feel guilty.

The first time I went topless was horrendously embarrassing. Maybe it would have been better if I had nice tits, though. I remember thinking, 'What am I doing?! I'm going to walk out there wearing a glittery bow tie and no top!' I never got over that feeling of self-consciousness, was never comfortable walking around virtually naked. It was merely a means to an end.

I don't recall there being any bitchiness among the waitresses, although they happily jostled you out of the way to get to the men as they came through the door. When a group of guys came in, you had to try to be the one they'd want to sit with. If they chose someone else, you instantly shifted your focus to the next lot of men who came in. Of course, the girls who had been there a long time knew who the really moneyed clients were and wouldn't let us new girls anywhere near them.

I wasn't naïve sexually, by any stretch of the imagination, but I was naïve about how this sort of world works. It took me ages to work out that several of the girls were hookers and they were making promises to the men as they cajoled them to go downstairs for dinner.

I didn't do very well on the whole; only occasionally did I entice a man to take me down for dinner. My friend was very cute and had the whole package, so she didn't have to try so hard. Then we told another student at Mountview about Toppers and she also came to work there. Jenny was a big girl, but she enjoyed being a big girl; she had a real sexiness about her because she didn't try to hide her voluptuousness.

From the moment she started, Jenny was up and down those stairs like a bride's nightie. Every time we turned around, she would be leading another man down for dinner. She made a fortune because they loved her boobs and curvaceousness. My friend and I only stuck it out for three weeks, but Jenny stayed on long after we left.

When we said we were leaving, the other girls said, 'You're not staying until Christmas? You're mad! The gifts we get at Christmas!' Apparently, some of the men gave out fur coats, jewellery and even cars, but only to the ones who went round the back with them, presumably. I have no idea how much money I made in the end; all I know is that it got to a point where I just couldn't handle that scene anymore. Fortunately, by then, I'd saved up enough for my holiday.

Before Bridget and I flew to LA in August, I decided that I wanted a perm. I wanted to look my best when I swanned around Hollywood. However, at the hairdressing salon, I was warned that my hair was very porous because I'd been dying it various shades of brown and red for years, since I was about fifteen. Henna was all the rage then.

'It'll be okay,' I said confidently, even though I'd never had great hair. It was always very fine.

'I'm not so sure,' the hairdresser said, insisting that I sign a waiver disclaiming my right to sue her. I should have listened to her because, boy, was she right! At first it didn't look too bad because she dried it with a special perm dryer. But when I went home and washed it, suddenly it started to rise and rise. I burst into tears. Why had I insisted on a perm? There was no one to blame but myself.

So when I arrived in LA, on top of being overweight, I looked like Tito Jackson from the Jackson 5 – and, believe me, LA was not the place to be fat with a Tito Jackson perm. Absolutely everything had gone wrong with my appearance and I felt like an alien. God, that perm was ghastly! It took so long to grow out too. I had to wear my hair scraped back for the entire time I was away.

Still, I loved Beverly Hills; it was a fascinating world. We stayed at Ian's beautiful house in Benedict Canyon and Ian really looked after us, so we had a brilliant time. We didn't see much of his wife Doris, though, because she was always off saving whales or adopting people right, left and centre. Doris was and is a wonderfully talented artist and completely bonkers. One day Ian said to me, 'By the way, don't go in the lounge. Doris is wrapped in cellophane.' He said it as though it was the most normal thing in the world to be wrapped head to toe in plastic! It was some kind of detox, I suppose – commonplace today, but really weird back then.

In LA, you are either rich, famous, beautiful, or all three, and sadly I was none of them. We were mixing in a scene that was way above us and the people we were meeting were not interested in nineteen-year-old student girls, especially not the fat one in the corner with the wonky perm. The only boys I attracted were Bridget's cast-offs. It was the first time I'd ever felt invisible.

We went to a party thrown by Twiggy's first husband, the American actor Michael Witney. It was very exciting because the film director Alan Parker was there, along with all kinds of other trendy people. But while Bridget was the centre of attention in the pool, I wandered round saying, 'I'm not normally as ugly as this, honestly.'

At another party, Bridget met a guy who owned a really cool car, a Jensen Interceptor. He and his friend were rich guys; hers was good-looking rich and mine was ugly rich. They took us out for a drive and, unfortunately, we had a spin-out, which was very scary. We were all right afterwards, but a bit shaken up, so they wanted to take us back to the Beverly Wilshire Hotel to 'look after' us. Obviously Bridget wanted to go and I didn't, which turned out to be the pattern of the entire holiday.

I never resented Bridget for being gorgeous – I was probably grateful to have the scraps from her table! But this was my first experience of being the pretty girl's ugly friend and I didn't like it very much. I had always managed to get the boys at school, with a combination of personality and forthrightness as much as looks, I think. To this day, my friend Jill has never got over me getting off with Gorgeous Gordon Gunyan, or 'Stott' as he was commonly known. Jill had fancied him since the age of eleven, but it was clearly never going to happen, so I stormed in. She still brings it up after a few drinks and I say, 'Move on, Jill. I was seventeen then and now I'm fifty-one!' We laugh about it now.

Perhaps because of that first visit, I'll always be slightly in awe of Los Angeles, even though there are so many discontented people there. Still, the trip acted as a kick-start to get me losing weight and looking better, and I certainly made sure that I was slim the next time I went! By then I was with Tim and not looking to get off with boys, but I knew what to expect and made sure I didn't feel inadequate. It also helped that I went as an actress from England, as I felt I had something to offer.

Getting to know Los Angeles was amazing, but I was glad to get back to drama school for the start of the final year. My parents had encouraged me to see it through and I was incredibly happy that I did, because in our third year we took some of our productions on tour to Birmingham and Italy. We even did *Hamlet* on the shores of Lake Como in Italy, which was a great experience.

Before the tour, I had a call from Brian, my pal who had been on the stage management course in the year above me. We had stayed friends after he left at the end of my second year and he was now working at Aberystwyth Theatre. 'There's somebody I think you should meet,' he said.

'Really?' I said, intrigued.

'Yes, I'm working with this actor called David Easter; he's playing Pharaoh in *Joseph*. I've been telling him all about you and he said he'd really like to meet you. He lives just round the corner from you in London.'

'Oh,' I said. 'I've never been on a blind date before. What does he look like?'

'He's quite good-looking. I think you'd like him.'

'OK, then, why not?'

Brian arranged for us to meet in the Mountview theatre bar, so I got dressed up and went along, wondering what this David Easter would be like. In the bar, I waited, and I waited, and I waited, but there was no sign of him. When some other friends from college turned up, I started drinking with them, and eventually I got a bit pissed.

It was obvious by then that he wasn't coming. 'Well, you can go to hell!' I thought, assuming that would be the last I ever heard of David Easter. Fate had other plans for me, though.

Chapter Four

Fortunately, there was a gorgeous first-year student called Charlie Gray in the bar that night. He went on to be the hunk in a famous coffee advert, but at the time he was just Charlie Gray in the first year. His chat-up line to me was, 'Would you like to come back to mine for some Big Soup?' How could I resist? I went back to his, but, needless to say, we didn't open a tin of Heinz's finest. 'Big' was the operative word of the night, but it wasn't in conjunction with food!

So I forgot about David Easter not showing up, until the next day, when the phone rang in the call box in the hall outside the flat I was sharing with Bridget. 'I'm very sorry,' the voice on the other end said, sounding genuinely contrite. 'I was held up and there was no way of getting in touch with you.' There were no mobiles then, of course.

'That's OK,' I said, thinking of Charlie Gray. 'I had a nice evening anyway.'

'What you doing on Friday?' he asked.

I paused. 'Nothing.'

'Well, can I come round?'

'OK.'

I really had no expectations one way or the other when I

answered the door on Friday night. So the sight of David Easter came as a complete surprise. There in front of me was the man of my dreams, a dead ringer for John Travolta! He had Travolta's slicked-back hair, the twinkle, the whole package. The only difference was that John Travolta isn't classically good-looking and David undoubtedly was. I took one look at him and thought, 'Oh my God!' I was smitten from the word go. It was an immediate physical reaction for both of us and we were together from that night onwards.

It's so cringe-making to think of it now, but I couldn't wait to show him off to people because he was so good-looking. Even if you didn't fancy David Easter, you couldn't say he wasn't strikingly handsome. I was certain that he could have had any woman he wanted, so it was flattering that he went for me. David lit up a room when he entered it and could turn on the charm in the blink of an eye. He could be incredibly charismatic when he wanted to be and I found his innate arrogance irresistible. He also had a nervy, twitchy side to him that intrigued me. He seemed very different to any other man I'd met and we had an amazing sex life.

Not only was he gorgeous, but very soon into our relationship, England decided to do its own version of *Saturday Night Fever* (but on a budget of £250,000, rather than £5 million). Starring Gerry Sundquist and Patti Boulaye, it was called *The Music Machine*, and was set at the Camden Palace. The plot revolved around a big dance competition, choreographed by Arlene Phillips, and David was playing the white-suited John Travolta part, a character called Howard Telfer, who was an amazing dancer. The story was ridiculous: everyone thinks that Howard will win the competition, but then a young lad played by Gerry Sundquist comes in at the end and wins against all the odds. It was such rubbish, not least because I have never seen a worse dancer than Gerry Sundquist in my entire life – he had two left feet!

Still, none of that mattered to me because one night at the flat, David walked into my bedroom wearing his white suit, and struck the iconic Travolta pose from the *Saturday Night Fever* poster. I didn't burst out laughing, that's how smitten I was. 'Well, if I can't have John Travolta, I'll have Howard Telfer,' I thought. 'It's the next best thing!'

As David's girlfriend, I obviously assumed that I would be going to the premiere of *The Music Machine* on his arm. But then he told me that his agent had been on the phone and vetoed that idea. He was really sorry, but he was about to sign a record contract and she didn't want him to be seen to have a girlfriend. That old chestnut! She was clearly besotted with him. Anyway, I vaguely remember going to see it when it came out, so it must have had a brief cinema release before it went to video and passed into oblivion.

In the early days, my relationship with David was fantastic. He lived in quite a nice studio-flat in Muswell Hill and very soon I moved in. It was very small, so it was easy to keep tidy. We lived on studenty food like beans on toast and cheese on toast most of the time. Spaghetti Bolognese was probably the most we could muster up. Well, no man has ever been with me for what I put in his tummy!

By now, I'd introduced David to Mum and Dad, who thought he was great and very charming. My granny was especially bowled over by him, partly because he treated her like a teenager. 'Hello, Molly, give us a twirl,' he'd say, reducing her to a simpering, girly wreck. I didn't meet any of his family, though, because he didn't have anything to do with them. All I knew of his background was what he had told me: he was from London, had an Italian father and was related to the actress Greta Scacchi.

After *The Music Machine*, he went on to sign a record deal with EMI and began appearing in all the teen magazines. There were headlines like: 'David doesn't have a girlfriend! As Easter says, "I'm not the kind of guy to put all of my eggs in one basket."' He built up quite a teen fanbase and he was always in *Godspell* playing Jesus, or in *Joseph* playing Joseph or Pharaoh. I spent ages going round the country seeing him in all these productions.

One day, a card arrived from a fan who slavishly followed him around. 'There's a present arriving for you at Paddington station,' it said. 'It's very precious and worth a lot of money. You must be there to pick it up when it arrives.'

Curious, we went along to Paddington at the appointed time. There, waiting for us at the parcel office, was a Labrador puppy! He was just the sweetest thing you'd ever seen and we both fell in love with him. I immediately named him Howard, after David's character in *The Music Machine*. Oh dear, but a flat in Muswell Hill is no place for a dog. I was at drama school and David was off doing *Joseph*, so we didn't have a chance to train it.

Inevitably, after four weeks of this cute little thing weeing and pooing all over the flat, I said to Mum and Dad, 'Would you just take this puppy for a few weeks and train it for us?' Of course, Dad became utterly besotted with Howard and he stayed with them for the next fifteen years.

About six months into our relationship, I discovered that I was pregnant. It was a total accident. Since neither David nor I felt in any way ready to have a baby, especially as he was two years younger than I was, we agreed that I would have a termination. I discussed it with Mum and Dad and they supported our decision, so I went ahead. It wasn't an easy thing to do because I had dreamed of having a baby ever since I was sixteen, but it seemed like the most sensible option. After all, we barely managed to scrape together the money to pay for the procedure, so there was no way we could afford to bring up a child. I had no acting work and David's career was still very uncertain, so we just couldn't provide the stable environment that I wanted for my child. However, although I knew I'd made the right decision, I was pretty tearful when I came out of the clinic. Fortunately, David was very supportive. He kept reassuring me that we had plenty of years ahead of us to have babies, which comforted me.

I had left drama school in the summer of 1979. This was in the time before reality television, before every Tom, Dick and Harriet decided that they could act. I tend to get on the soapbox about the way that happens these days. It's like, 'Hello! I've learnt my craft and spent years honing it, so if I make it look easy, that's because I'm good at it.'

There are undoubtedly naturally talented people who can come into the industry late, but there's also always a woman in Tesco who comes up and says, 'Why can't you get me on *Loose Women*? I could do it with my eyes shut!' Everybody thinks they're a Loose Woman. People seem to think that we toddle into the studio at twenty-five past twelve, put our lipstick on and talk rubbish for an hour, without any preparation whatsoever. In their minds, there's no skill involved in being on a live TV show.

It's the same if you make acting look easy. People often say, 'Well, you were just playing yourself in that, weren't you?' I take it as a compliment, even though it's usually meant as an insult because what it actually means is that you were totally and utterly believable in the role.

If you direct an amateur actor to walk across a room and casually ask someone if they want a cup of tea, they tend to stride over with their arms swinging wildly and unnaturally, and shout, 'CAN I GET YOU A CUP OF TEA, MOLLY?' That's their attempt at being totally natural and there's not a lot you can do to change it.

My personal theory is that you can't teach somebody how to act, but you can teach technique: voice technique and breathing technique. And you can't teach somebody to be funny, although you can give them tools that they can practise with. Generally, I think you can act or you can't. Some people would disagree with me, but I'm sure I've never been proved wrong. I can tell whether someone can act or not the moment they open their mouth. In fact, I can usually tell as soon as they walk in a room, although I couldn't tell you why that is.

People don't go to drama school to learn how to act; they go to learn how to develop their acting skills. It can be really good for giving you confidence, as it did for me. I was positive that I could act, but I didn't know how to get out there and audition, so I needed to learn certain techniques. OK, the teachers tried to get rid of my Geordie accent; in those days, the theatre was all about received pronunciation (in other words, speaking like the Queen, or an old-fashioned newsreader) and they used to hammer your accent out of you. I didn't have a strong Geordie accent, but in hindsight it was helpful that I learned to develop an RP accent when I needed one, even though I've worked mostly as a northern actress. I prefer to work in a dialect that comes naturally, but I can do a neutral accent, should it be required, and have done on many occasions.

People have different opinions on who is a good actor and who isn't. Few people will say that Al Pacino or Jack Nicholson can't act, but it's definitely a question of personal preference. There are a few actors that I just don't get at all, and yet they get loads of leads. I'm astonished that they get work, but to my amazement other people say, 'Aren't they brilliant?' I know I give him a hard time, but my husband is one of my favourite actors.

Some people have to live and breathe a role and take the character home, whereas I approach my work instinctively and am not a method actor. I don't believe you have to murder someone to be able to play a murderer believably! I find some method actors a bit posey, I'm afraid. I believe that I can play a part as well as anybody else, by thinking through who I want to be, learning my lines, turning up and doing it. Still, each to their own.

One of my best friends, Chris Geere, who played Matt Wilding in the third and fourth series of *Waterloo Road*, is very funny about our different approaches to a scene. As he prepares, he'll be saying, 'So, where have I just been? OK, I've just had this argument with the head teacher and I'm going into the classroom now.' The cameras turn over and he'll be focusing hard, saying 'OK, OK . . .'

Meanwhile, I'm saying, 'Did I tell you, he had the biggest donger you've ever seen?' seconds before the director calls, 'ACTION!'

'And Denise got the blooming award and I didn't!' Chris complains afterwards.

In my day, you had to get your Equity card to get into a repertory company, which was the job we were all aiming for. Appearing on television just wasn't even a consideration. Joining Equity meant becoming a member of the British Actors' Equity Association, the trade union for actors, stage managers and models. Until 1981, when closed shop unions were made illegal, you couldn't work as a professional actor without an Equity card.

First you got your provisional Equity card, then you built up forty weeks of work experience to get your full card. Since Mountview Theatre School didn't quite have the reputation then that it does today, you had to work a bit harder for your card than RADA or Central students. There wasn't a flurry of top agents at your graduation show, plucking you from the chorus line, so I don't think anybody on my course had their Equity card when they left.

Most repertory companies had one, or maybe two, cards to give out every year, but there were drama students pouring out of colleges annually, so competition was fierce. It soon became clear that an Equity card wasn't going to land in my lap and since my parents couldn't afford to keep me, I immediately signed up with a temp agency. I did every kind of job while I was waiting to be called up for auditions. I tried being a barmaid, but was sacked several times because I couldn't add up. Those were the days before electronic tills, so I didn't stand a chance. I also tried waitressing and worked at Rank Xerox in London, envelope-stuffing. Oh, how I regretted not having done a secretarial course because the clerical jobs were just so tedious! I was constantly working alongside people I had nothing in common with whatsoever.

I think I probably was a good actor, but I needed audition experience. My agent at the time, a guy called Denis Beecher, was a lovely old dear, but unfortunately he was about ninety-seven years old. He must be dead now, bless him, because he was practically dead when he was looking after me! Denis would send me up for things like *West Side Story*, even though I couldn't really dance, so I would find myself in a lot of cringe-making situations. There can be quite a bit of power-tripping going on when people audition you, even today. For instance, you might go for a commercial casting for an advert in which a woman simply picks up a hairbrush and starts singing into it, while looking at herself in the mirror, but at the audition you'll have to skip across the floor doing double pirouettes and triple axels. All of that went on.

I was out of acting work for the first eight or nine months after I left college. You didn't entirely rely on your agent to get you work back then, so I spent all my spare time writing letters and sending off photographs to theatre companies and directors. Every repertory company and Theatre in Education company was listed in a book called *Contacts* and every week I went through the back of the *Stage* magazine to find out about auditions.

I also auditioned for all the Theatre in Education companies, which were often a newly graduated drama student's first port of call, and a very good one too, because they gave you a better chance of getting an Equity card. Eventually at Watford, Hilary Clulow, the director, liked me and tried to get me a card. Even though her two had already been taken, you could sometimes borrow one from the next year's quota. 'I can't promise you anything, but I'm trying,' she said.

In the meantime, she found me a slightly random job teaching children's dance at Watford Palace Theatre, which had a little drama group for four- to five-year-olds. I can remember exactly two things about that job: teaching a dance routine to Earth Wind & Fire's 'Fantasy', when they would clearly have preferred 'Old MacDonald', and getting David 'John Travolta' Easter to come and judge the dance competition, no doubt wearing his white suit!

There was one particular company that I desperately wanted to work for: Live Theatre Company in Newcastle. I wrote again and again to Live Theatre, but I was constantly knocked back. I'd seen it grow from an acorn into something much bigger over the years, little knowing that one of the founder members was my future husband, Tim Healy. It's still here to this day and we're so proud of it. Renowned for encouraging new writers and writing, it's been well funded over the years.

Never one to give up, I wrote off for yet another audition with the company, for something called *The Rainbow Coloured Disco Dancer*. This time, I was called up to Newcastle. The following day, I found myself in a room full of actors and was asked to audition with Malcolm Healy, a long-haired Geordie actor. It was Tim, of course, and I shall refer to him as Tim from now on, even though I actually call him Malc at home. Why? It's a little bit complicated: his name is Timothy Malcolm Healy, but because his grandfather and his father were both called Timothy Malcolm, they decided to bring him up as Malcolm. However, when he subsequently became a club comic, he used the name Tim Healy, which explains the two names. As he was introduced to me as Malcolm, he's always been Malc to me.

I happened to be wearing a pair of David Easter's black leatherette trousers, cinched in at the waist, and I noticed Tim looking at my bum while I was singing at the piano. He and I were then asked to improvise a scenario in which I was trying to pick him up. After a while, it transpired that we were in a launderette and by the end of the improv, I thought I'd hooked him, only to discover that he was gay, much to the hilarity of the other actors.

When it was over, I thanked everybody and went back to London. Practically the moment I arrived at my flat, the phone rang in the call box in the hall. It was the Watford Palace Theatre, saying, 'We've got you an Equity card!'

This was massive news. 'Oh my God!' I yelled. Champagne celebration! I rushed back into the flat to get some change to call my parents, but before I'd managed to dial their number, the phone rang again. This time, it was Live Theatre Company, saying, 'We'd like to offer you the job and we've managed to secure you an Equity card!' To be honest, I felt quite deflated. To be offered two Equity cards within the space of ten minutes kind of took all the fun out of getting my hands on this rare and precious prize.

I made my decision about which way to go based on David: he was in London, so I chose the Watford job and didn't work for Live Theatre for about ten years. How different my life would have been if I'd gone up to Newcastle! I'm sure I wouldn't have ended up with Tim if I had, though. Firstly, he was madly in love with his girlfriend Jacqui, whom he lived with for twelve years; secondly, when he and I eventually fell in love, it had nothing to do with physicality or being young people. The time wasn't right for us yet.

So my career began with the Watford job and consisted entirely of theatre work. First I did a show at the Watford Palace Theatre called *The Four Spirits*, a Theatre in Education (TIE) production. At Watford, all the TIE work took place at the theatre, which was very rare. Subsequent TIE companies I worked with toured schools, which was a great experience.

Next I worked in Newcastle for Tyne & Wear Theatre in Education company. We devised a show called *Shadows* for children with learning disabilities and it was just brilliant. Dressed in black from head to toe, we played shadows that had escaped from people. In one scene we had to crawl along an arched tube that was lit up and lined with bubble wrap, so that it looked and sounded as if it were on fire. As we crawled along, the bubble wrap made a popping sound like the noise of crackling flames, and the kids totally believed that we were in danger. I've never laughed as much as I did in this production, thanks to the antics of Brendan Healy (no relation) who went on to become a lifelong friend.

Early on, I discovered that one of the worst things that can happen on stage is to 'corpse' or convulse with laughter. You can only really get away with it if you're in the type of play that involves interaction with the audience. For example, Tim recently did an Alan Plater play in which he spent a lot of the time talking to the audience. So if something went slightly wrong, he could say, 'Well, that went bloody tits up!' and still keep the reality of the piece.

However, that approach wasn't going to work when I was doing a play called *The Ghost Train*, by Arnold Ridley from *Dad's Army*, in front of an audience full of old-age pensioners. One of the actors was meant to come on and shoot somebody about halfway through the play, but unfortunately for him, he made the mistake of talking in the wings and not concentrating on his cue. Suddenly, there was silence on stage. It was a genuine pause and meant to be there, but he panicked and thought he'd missed his cue, so he walked on stage with the gun and shot his victim three scenes too early!

Of course, the guy he shot couldn't die because it wasn't his time to die, which meant that he remained standing and speaking while the poor actor who had shot him reversed off the stage as if nothing had happened. I recited the rest of my lines in a really high, strangled voice, as I desperately tried to suppress the laughter bubbling up inside me.

I felt really sorry for that actor because I was always getting into trouble at drama school for talking backstage right up until it was time for me to go on. That was when I was younger, though; I now suffer from terrible nerves before I go on stage.

Your nerves get worse as you get older and you become more well known. You're horribly aware that the audience have higher expectations when you have a bit of a name. You're also more aware of how horrendous 'a dry' can be, when you forget your words. When you're young, it maybe hasn't happened to you yet, but my God, when it *has* happened to you, it's not something you forget.

Working with actors who don't know their lines also scares me. There was one really terrible time when I was doing a Newpalm production of *There's a Girl in My Soup* with this wonderful actor called Gary Taylor. The play lasted about two hours and twenty minutes, with one interval, and my character, Marion, was on stage for nearly every page of the script.

Unfortunately, we only had three days to rehearse the whole play! We rehearsed Monday, Tuesday and Wednesday, learned the lines at home at night, and opened at Bournemouth Pavilion Theatre on the Thursday night. By now, I was an experienced touring actress and confident enough to take something on in a short space of time, but it was still pretty intimidating.

Every actor has the same nightmare about suddenly being thrust onto a stage without knowing what the play is. People are telling you, 'It's your line!' but you don't know what to say. Well, that Thursday night in Bournemouth, when I was in the toilet and heard the call to get ready to go on stage, I thought, 'This is the actor's nightmare come true.'

Just before we went on, Gary said to me, 'Listen, Den, I won't dry because obviously we've been through the lines and I know them back to front. I know them forwards, backwards and sideways.'

'OK,' I said smiling nervously.

'So I know my lines inside out,' he went on, 'but I always like to have a little cushion, just in case anything goes wrong.'

'OK,' I said again.

'So if at any point I say, "Would you like another drink, Marion?" that means I've dried.'

I gulped. 'OK.'

Gary had been on stage for a while when I came on. He was playing a prototype celebrity chef and so he was doing bits and bobs in the kitchen. One of the first things he was supposed to do was bring me a drink, but he didn't even get that far. I sat down and he said the fatal words, 'Would you like another drink, Marion?' before I'd even got my first blooming drink.

I was looking directly at the audience, with a sea of faces staring back at me, and I froze. I didn't have a clue what to say. I'd just walked on, feeling really nervous about remembering my own lines, let alone his, and he'd given me the signal that meant he had dried. When you've been doing a show for a couple of weeks, you might be able to help somebody out, but this was the first minute of the first night!

The silence probably lasted about thirty seconds, but it seemed like thirty years. It reminded me of a horror film: everything seemed to slow down and the faces of the audience stretched and distorted in front of my eyes. 'GET ME OFF THIS STAGE!' I was thinking. 'I AM HAVING A NERVOUS BREAKDOWN!'

In an amateur production, someone in the corner would have shouted the correct line, but you don't get that in professional theatre. Maybe if you shouted, 'Prompt!' someone might help out, but it's practically unheard of to do that. You'd be much more likely to find an excuse to walk off stage, get your line and come back on.

On this particular night, Gary just pretended to do more cooking until the line came to him, at which point he went to fix me a drink. My *first* drink! Did the audience notice? Luckily, they only tend to notice if you let them notice because they buy into whatever you give them. So although I was panicking inside, on the outside I was Marion, a cocky Londoner with big hair and brightly coloured clothes, chewing gum and waiting for someone to say something. Know wha' ah mean?

The high point of that tour was playing the Newcastle Theatre Royal, which had always been my dream because it was my favourite theatre when I was little. Even better, Phil Penfold, a really tough reviewer up there, mentioned me in his review. He didn't know I was a Geordie because I hadn't made a mark as a Geordie actress by then, yet he didn't comment on my accent at all. In a nutshell, he said something like, 'The play was very good and various members of the cast were great, but the real delight was Denise Welch's Marion.' I was so thrilled because I was doing a London accent in my home town and nobody seemed to notice.

No matter what people say, reviews do matter, and they do upset you when they're horrible. Unfortunately, you tend to remember the one bad one rather than the nine good ones.

Next I played, 'Ooh la la!' Simone, the French stripper, in *A Bedfull of Foreigners*, which my relatives would still say was the best thing I did until *Coronation Street*. They loved it.

It was a very light-hearted play and great fun to do, but some of the cast moaned and said, 'One day I hope I'll be working with the Royal Shakespeare Company.' That's not the way I saw it, though. I was just glad to be working.

Sometimes I have a go at some of these young kids I work with now, when they complain that they've been asked to go on tour for twelve weeks. 'What?' I say. 'I'd have bitten somebody's arm off for the chance to do that.' Being on tour when you've got no dependents is great! You're all away together. You can go out with who you like and do what you like; it's fantastic!

Being on tour could be tough, though. It was hard being away from David, although we tried to get together as often as possible. I was still as mad about him as ever and so I was thrilled that I was at home for his nineteenth birthday. I'd been with him for a year now and jokingly referred to him as 'my toyboy' to my friends because of the age difference between us.

He was out doing *Joseph* in Grays in Essex on the evening of his birthday, so I picked up his post for him when I got home. To my bewilderment, there were six twenty-first birthday telegrams in the hall, three of them addressed to Nigel.

'What the hell is this about?' I wondered, as I waited for him to come back. 'Something is definitely not quite right here.'

When he came in, I said, 'How did the show go? By the way, this is really bizarre, but there are six twenty-first birthday telegrams for you. Isn't that weird?'

'Is it?' he said casually.

'Well, I think it's strange. Don't you?'

'I can't believe you're making a big deal about it!' he snapped.

'Look, I'm just saying, you're nineteen and there are six telegrams congratulating you on being twenty-one. I'm surely allowed to ask why.'

'I told you about my bloody family!' he said. 'They get everything wrong. That's why I never talk to them.'

If someone told me that story now, I would think to myself, 'Don't be stupid, it's obvious that he's lying!' But I was so madly in love that I wanted to believe him, and so I did believe him. The Nigel bit he admitted to eventually: his real name was Nigel

Cairns and he had changed it by deed poll to David Easter. But somehow he managed to convince me that six of his relatives and friends had got his age wrong. It turned out that an agent had advised him to knock a couple of years off his age, which was not uncommon in the industry at the time – but I have no idea why he didn't just tell me that!

Chapter Five

David was lovely to me when it was just the two of us: he showered me with love; he was very adoring and tactile; he would look at me and tell me that I was the most gorgeous thing that he'd ever seen and he didn't want for anything else. We spent all of our spare time together. We stayed in a lot and watched television; we would go for walks together, or to the pub, where we sat in the corner, just the two of us. We also went up north to see my family quite a bit. My parents adored him.

David wanted it to be just the two of us all the time. At first, that was all I wanted too, but after a while, I started wanting to involve more people and go out. He couldn't understand it.

'But why do we need to be with other people? Why aren't you just happy with me?' he'd ask.

'I am happy with you! But I like seeing my friends and I want to go out.'

'Why aren't I enough for you?'

Almost from the beginning, I didn't know which David would turn up if my friends were coming round or if we were meeting them somewhere. He could be charming and pleasant or a nightmare. This put me constantly on edge and I always felt he did little more than tolerate my friends. We didn't see his friends because he didn't seem to have many. When I asked him why, he said it was because he'd moved around so much as a child.

One evening, about half a dozen of my friends came round. We had a really nice time, or so I thought. I was pleased to see that David had got on with everyone: they were nice to him and he was nice to them. He had his arm around me as we happily waved them off at the door. I was thinking, 'That was really lovely!'

Just as I was about to say something about how great the evening was, he said, 'God! Why do you have to be like that?'

'What do you mean?' I said, taken aback.

He shrugged. 'It doesn't matter.'

'No, David, what do you mean?' I insisted.

'Well, why did you have to tell that joke?' he said grumpily.

'You mean the joke everybody laughed at?'

'No, no, no, that's where you're wrong,' he said, shaking his head. 'They were laughing *at* you, not *with* you, can't you see?'

I froze. What had I done wrong? Why was he saying this? I felt just awful. Were they laughing at me? Deep down, I knew they weren't, because if I was honest with myself, I knew they were my friends and not David's. But the doubt remained. Hooked on the intensity of the passion we shared for one another, I dismissed such moments, although they still affected me. I started to avoid getting into certain situations.

According to David, everybody I ever worked with was 'a wanker'. I was always the best thing in the play, but everybody else was rubbish, and I was wasted on the production. Of course, he may have thought he was being supportive but he also hated it when I socialised with other members of the cast.

'Can we go to the cast party?' I'd ask, whenever he came to the last night of a play.

He'd sigh. 'Why do you want to go to the party?'

It seemed reasonable enough to me. 'Because I've been working with these people for weeks.'

'But they are wankers!' he'd argue. 'You can tell they don't like you; they're just pretending to be your friends. Why do you want to be with them? They are complete twats. Listen, I've booked us a restaurant down the road. So what we will do is have a curry.'

'But I want to go to the party.'

'OK, you go to the fucking party!' he'd yell, stomping off.

'No, it's OK, I'll come for a curry,' I'd say meekly, rushing to catch up with him. Again, self-doubt crept in. Perhaps he was right. Maybe I was subconsciously making friends with people who didn't like me.

Of course these days I'd stand up for myself but then I always hated the kick-off. He had a fiery side; it wasn't unusual for him to shout 'Fuck you!' and storm out, leaving me to make excuses to my friends. 'Sorry, that was my fault. I had better go and apologise,' I would say, deeply embarrassed. Or, 'David's got a tricky tummy, so he had to go. I'd better go and make sure he's OK.' Then, when we were alone again, he'd revert to his loving, adoring self.

He could flare up just like that and anything could set him off, so I was always tense around other people. If we were at my parents' house and he left a crisp packet or a banana skin somewhere, my mother would quite reasonably tut and say affectionately, 'Come on, buggerlugs, get off your bum and put that in the bin!' I knew he'd do it but would make a fuss about it later.

'She's getting at me all the time!' he'd complain. 'She's got it in for me.' It was easier to avoid the kick-off, so I was constantly trying to anticipate it. If I sensed Mum was going to comment on something like a crisp packet David had left lying, I'd jump up and say, 'Oh, I'll just get that!' I would behave differently now and I expect David would too, but back then we had got ourselves into a pattern of behaviour that was destructive for both of us.

At first, nobody wanted to interfere, so they didn't say anything to me about how we were with each other. On the last night of a play I was doing at the Playhouse in Newcastle, I was once again persuaded not to go to the last-night party, so Mum, Dad and Debbie came along for a curry on the quayside. At one point, I went to the toilet, leaving my pack of cigarettes on the table. Now, David disapproved of me smoking. He didn't smoke or drink himself, so if I had more than two puffs of a cigarette and a glass of wine, he'd be on the verge of calling Narcotics Anonymous.

The packet of cigarettes had vanished when I came back to the table. 'Where are my cigarettes?' I asked.

'What cigarettes?' he said.

'I put my cigarettes on the table!'

'Darling, you didn't,' he said.

'I did!' I searched in my bag and under the table, but I couldn't find them anywhere. Eventually, not wanting to pursue it further while my family was there, I went and bought some more cigarettes.

It was only later on that Debbie told me that as soon as I'd left the table, David had taken the cigarettes and hidden them, in full view of my family. However, I didn't bring it up with him, knowing that there would be a big shouting match if I did. Sometimes it was just easier to let things go. Deep down he probably thought he was helping me by getting me to stop smoking, but the way we were interacting was not healthy at all.

Being a family-oriented person, I begged him to introduce me to his parents and siblings. He was very reluctant; he wouldn't even talk about them most of the time. For a while, he said that he didn't have a mother, when in fact it was just that he didn't like to talk about his mother because she'd gone to prison when he was twelve for embezzling money at a cinema where she was working. He had never forgiven her for that.

'You don't know the circumstances or why she did it,' I'd say in her defence. 'She's not actually killed anybody.'

Finally, I was allowed to meet his mother and stepfather and I got on with them OK. His sister Diane and her husband John were lovely; they lived in Winchester. Then there was Sandy, who was off the wall, but absolutely gorgeous. She and Mike lived in Brighton and had chosen not to have children. His third sister, Paulina, was also an actress. She was hugely ambitious, like her brother, but she didn't get much work, so supported herself by working in the accounts department of a big model agency. David had a brother too, who was 'nothing but trouble', and none of the family had anything to do with him.

To my surprise, I found out from David's sisters that almost everything he had told me about his family background was rubbish. I think when we first met I must have got the version of David's past that his agent had written for him and David never thought about putting me right! There was no Italian blood in him whatsoever. He wasn't from London; he was from Eastleigh in Hampshire. He was not related to the actress Greta Scacchi, who wouldn't know him if she fell over him. And he was actually two years older than he had told me he was.

Of course, he never felt that he had misled me. 'I never said I was from London,' he said. 'I don't know where you got the idea that my father was Italian. That must have been another boyfriend.'

'But you did!' I'd insist. 'Don't you remember? It was the first night we met!'

'You must have something wrong with your memory, Den. Why would I make something like that up?'

'I'm sure . . . and what about your age? You told me you were two years younger than you are!'

He rolled his eyes. 'That was just a wind-up; you know it was! Come on, you never took that seriously.'

Our relationship was, in hindsight, very strained. Maybe we were just too immature to deal with our feelings. Maybe we were driven by lust and mistook it for love. Whatever the reasons, the signs were there for us to see if we had noticed them. At one time he used to preach monogamy at me constantly, drumming into me the importance of being a 'one-man woman'. He just went on and on about it.

'I would never be unfaithful to you. I'd kill myself first. Do you understand how wrong it is to cheat on the person you love?'

'Yes, yes,' I'd say. 'I wouldn't even consider it.'

After this he seemed to be constantly questioning where I was and who I was with. At first it's OK when someone seems madly jealous; you rationalise that it's because they love you so much. But after a while, it became very tiring to have to account for my every movement. Sometimes a quick lie or omission seemed like the easier option.

Whenever our work separated us, I became very adept at phoning him from a call box and giving him the impression that I was out with a gang of girls, when in fact it was a mixed crowd.

'Where are you?' he'd demand.

'We've just come out for a pizza.'

'Are you at a nightclub?'

'No, we're at the pizza place.'

'What's that music in the background? Sounds like you're in a fucking nightclub to me.'

'No, I'm just in the pizza place.'

'Who's there?'

'Sarah, Jane, Julie, Rachel . . .' I listed a string of girls' names. It became second nature never to mention any guys' names.

I began taking the phone off the hook as a matter of course when I went out in the evening, even though what I was doing was perfectly innocent. That way, the next day I'd be able to say, 'What do you mean you were trying to get through to me? I was in all night!'

In fact, as it turned out, it was me who should have been questioning what he was up to. As time went on, there were lots of unexplained absences, excuses that sounded like lies and crap explanations of where he'd been. One day, I came across a card from Pinewood Studios, where he was filming a commercial. There was a casting director there who clearly fancied him and I sensed that there was a flirtation between them. David would always flirt with somebody like that. Actually, even if she weren't a casting director, he would flirt with her.

I opened the card. I couldn't help myself. My mouth went dry as I read it. The words swirled before my eyes and I began to feel dizzy and sick. It said: 'The dinner was in the oven, the champagne was on ice, I was wearing black suspenders, where were you? Love X.'

In a state of shock, I read it again and again. I kept thinking of this woman in suspenders, waiting for my boyfriend to arrive. Angry tears welled up in my eyes and burned tracks down my cheeks. How dare she? How dare he?

'X' was a very powerful casting director at the time, but I just didn't care. I bought a card and sent it off to her. It said: 'Dear X, the thought of you in black suspenders clearly put him off that particular dinner. Love D.' Unsurprisingly, I was never invited to audition for anything that she was casting after that!

When I confronted him about it, David somehow managed to convince me that it was nothing to do with him. The same year, he did a Coca-Cola commercial that was filmed half in South Africa and half in Nice, France. He was that sort of good-looking hunk type: the fit guy in the Coca-Cola advert. One night I came in and there was an envelope from Nice in the mesh letter board in the hall. He obviously hadn't noticed it when he walked past it on his way out of the flat. I opened it to find that it was from a make-up artist he'd been working with.

It's amazing how much school French you remember when you have to. If that letter had been given to me in an O Level exam, I probably couldn't have translated it, but because I suspected that it was from a woman my boyfriend had been sleeping with, I bloody well understood every word.

This time I was convinced that David had been unfaithful and the effect on me was devastating. My knees gave way beneath me and I had to sit down. I felt as if I'd been shot. It was evident to me from what she'd written that they had been shagging for a whole week in Nice. Apparently, he had even promised to see her when she came to England next. He was so stupid! If you are going to give your address to some bit that you have been shagging, you would look at the letter board to see if she'd written to you, wouldn't you? I've heard it said that the best actors are the worst liars and maybe it's true; certainly David was not very good at covering his tracks.

'What's up with you?' he asked when he got home. My eyes were puffy and swollen; it was obvious that I had been crying.

I threw the letter at him furiously. Again, he wriggled out of it. 'She's mad!' he said, quickly scanning it. 'It's all in her mind. I couldn't stop her fancying me, could I?'

Since he was utterly irresistible in my eyes, I could well imagine other women wanting him. But I couldn't get rid of the doubt. My instincts told me that he and this woman had been together; her letter seemed to make it clear that the passion had been mutual. 'Why did you give her your address?' I asked, falteringly.

'I told her to let me know when she was coming to London and we'd have her over for dinner. I told her all about you, Den. But obviously we won't be seeing her now. She's totally mad,' he said, putting his arms around me and pulling me close. 'You're the only woman for me. Don't ever forget that.'

I believed him. He was so persuasive and magnetic that I found it impossible not to. He only had to take me in his arms and look deep into my eyes for me to forget the thread of my argument, or the proof that was staring me in the face. Seeing David on stage also had a similar effect. He was incredibly talented and charismatic, so you didn't want to take your eyes off him. I never grew bored of seeing him perform because he cast a spell on the audience the moment he came on.

In late 1982, I went to the last night of *Godspell* in Northampton and watched it for the eighty-five-millionth time. David had often talked about members of the cast, but there was an unfamiliar name on the cast list when I scanned it. Why hadn't he ever mentioned her? I wondered. Throughout the show, I was very aware of the person who hadn't been mentioned.

When I went backstage, everyone was very nice to me, but there was one girl holding a bouquet and crying her eyes out. Now, people do cry their eyes out on last nights, but she was crying her eyes out and very obviously not looking at me.

'Are you having an affair with that girl, Marina?' I asked David afterwards.

'What fucking planet are you on?' he snapped.

Three weeks later, we were staying at my parents' house while they were away and I was doing a play in Newcastle. David was due in London for an audition and I ironed his red jeans for him before he went. He was planning to stay down there and come back the next day, when we were having my friends Susan and Gordon around for a dinner party.

I was preparing dauphinoise potatoes (get me!) when the phone rang. 'Is that Denise?' said an unfamiliar male voice. 'I'm a friend of Marina's.'

My mouth went dry. 'Oh yes?' I said, trying to keep my voice level.

'Did you know that Marina and David spent the night together in a hotel in London last night?' he said calmly. 'I thought I'd better inform you. I've suspected them of having an affair for some time.'

I felt numb with shock. After putting down the phone, I sat and stared into space, almost forgetting to breathe. Could it be true? Something told me that it was, but at the same time my mind couldn't take it in.

Now, any normal person in that situation would phone up Susan and Gordon and either feign sickness or say, 'I've just discovered that David is having an affair.' But for some reason I went ahead with the dinner party. I think it was because I'd cooked a beef bourguignon and put so much work into it! Cooking and entertaining has never been easy for me.

Susan and Gordon arrived at the house first, whereupon David walked in, full of typical David charm, and I had to go through the whole evening pretending that everything was fine, all the while feeling as if my heart was about to burst out of my body. It was horrible to be going through the motions, when really I wanted to kill David. I've since learned that fidelity is not necessarily the be-all and end-all of a relationship, but when it has been stuffed down your throat that your partner would die before even looking at someone else, it is. The horror was intense.

When Susan and Gordon had left, I told David about the phone call and said, 'If you are having an affair, just tell me.'

His reply was, 'You are fucking mental! I don't even want to talk to you.'

But how could he deny it? He tried to bluff it out as usual, but it was no use. We had a massive row and I cried bitter tears. When I went upstairs later and opened his bag, I found what looked like a girl's hairdryer in it. Incensed, I hit him on the head with it.

I didn't say, 'That's it!' It was more a question of, 'OK, you choose between her and me.'

'I'm choosing you,' he said finally.

'Well, you ring her now and tell her!' I demanded angrily.

So he did, but the next day he phoned her while I was out and said, 'It's all still on.' So they continued to see each other. It was a proper love affair and, my God, did she get her teeth in. Meanwhile, David was being especially loving to me and so I naïvely assumed that it was all over between them.

Then something happened that distracted me from my relationship momentarily. In early 1983, my agent phoned and said, 'The director of *Yakety Yak* wants to see you.'

'What's *Yakety Yak*?'

'It's a musical and it's opening at the London Astoria in nine days' time.'

I gasped. 'A musical? You're having a laugh, aren't you?' I don't think I even heard him say the bit about it opening so soon.

'No, and they really want to see you. Just go down.'

Without knowing the first thing about it, I went along to the audition wearing jeans, a yellow mohair jumper that Mum had knitted me and a denim jacket, with my long blonde hair in a ponytail. I looked very fifties and, coincidentally, the musical was set in the 1950s. I hadn't made the connection – 'Yakety Yak' was a hit song from the fifties.

I was asked to sing, 'Fools Fall in Love', one of the songs from the show. Fortunately, it happened to be exactly in my key. The next thing I knew, I got a call saying, 'You've got the part and you open in the West End in nine days' time.'

'What?!' I'm not a musical performer at all and so it was as much a shock to me as it was to everyone I knew.

The good news was that I was joining a great cast, which included the four McGann brothers, Paul, Stephen, Mark and Joe; Darts, the pop group; Tracy Perry; and Eve Ferret. The bad news was that I had to learn the whole thing from scratch in just over a week. The show had already had a run at the Half Moon Theatre in London, so the rest of the cast were practised in their roles, whereas I was replacing someone who had left suddenly. It was the most intense rehearsal period I have ever experienced.

A couple of days into rehearsals, the director, Rob Walker, phoned me and said, 'Could you lose half a stone before we start?'

He needn't have bothered asking; I went on to lose a stone over the next nine days, and I was only eight and a half stone to start with, which is tiny for me. The weight dropped off me. I was so nervous that I could barely eat anything and found it very hard to keep food down. I was absolutely terrified about opening night. One evening, after rehearsals, I got off the bus in Muswell Hill and vomited into the gutter because I was so tense and wound-up.

It seemed unbelievable that I was in a musical with the McGann brothers and Darts. It should have been a really exciting time, but I was too scared to enjoy it. I'd be standing at the front of the stage at the Astoria with a microphone in my hand, singing some Broadway song with the others, thinking, 'What on earth am I doing here?'

David didn't help; he gave me no support or confidence whatsoever and didn't appear proud of me at all. In fact, he seemed overcome with jealousy, probably because he was a musical artist primarily and a very good one too.

'How on earth did you manage to get a West End musical?' he asked with a sneer.

It was incredibly hurtful. Since I was already feeling like I was on shaky ground, it didn't take much to undermine my confidence even further. I longed for him to encourage me, to reassure me that I was up to the part, but, if anything, he made me feel less sure of myself. He couldn't have played my part but, knowing him, he probably thought he could.

He definitely didn't like the idea of me spending time with the gorgeous McGann brothers. On the afternoon of the dress rehearsal, we were down at the front of the stage singing 'Nights on Broadway', when suddenly the doors at the back of the auditorium slammed open. As David strode down the aisle towards us, the band wound down with a squeaking cacophony and we stopped singing. Everything went silent. 'Oh Christ!' I thought.

When he reached the stage, David pointed to each of the McGanns in turn and asked, 'Which one of you is fucking her?' (Sadly, none of them was.) Can you imagine the mortification of that moment?

I don't remember what happened immediately after that. The guys must have told David to go away (in so many words!)

because the next thing I knew, they were all comforting me. As usual, I made excuses for him. After all, if you are going out with a complete idiot, it reflects on you, so you have to somehow justify why you're with him. 'We've not been getting along and he is very jealous,' I stammered.

'Don't worry about it,' they said. 'Just concentrate on the show.' Somehow I managed to get through the rehearsal, knowing that they despised him.

That night, I went home to the flat in Muswell Hill to find the contents of one of my bags on the road outside and my contraceptive pills scattered all over the front garden. Since there was nowhere else for me to go at such late notice, I gathered everything up and went inside. As I walked into the lounge, David pulled me down onto the sofa and took me in his arms. 'What is it about you that makes me do these things?' he said with a sigh. 'You know it's only because I love you so much, don't you?'

Looking out from behind the curtains and scanning the audience the following evening, I spotted every hip 1980s personality you could think of, including George Michael, Lulu, Shakin' Stevens, Dawn French and Lenny Henry. It was a celebrity gala night and there was little old me from Whitley Bay, singing a number! It was amazing. The Astoria was great then, really cool. It was a dinner-theatre venue, so the audience sat at tables and ate chicken and chips.

Afterwards, Dawn French and Lenny Henry were throwing a bash. Guess who didn't go? Me. Why? Because David felt we needed 'to sit down and discuss things' at Joe Allen restaurant in Covent Garden, on the very first night of my West End debut. So while everybody else is at the star-studded celebrity gala celebrating the musical I'm in, I'm at Joe Allen having calf's liver with David, while he tells me where I've gone wrong in life, how

I'll never survive without him and how everybody is a complete tosser and taking advantage of me.

For once, though, his lecture didn't work. I'd had enough. The next day I phoned Don, who was one of my best friends at drama school and who has been my saviour on many levels. 'I can't stand it anymore!' I told him. 'You have to come and help me move out while David's out tomorrow.' The next day, Don arrived, picked up my stuff and took it to his flat in Tottenham.

I lived at Don's for about three months. It was grotty, but what it lacked environmentally was more than made up for by Don's hospitality. I was unbelievably grateful because I had nowhere else to go. After a couple of weeks, my sister Debbie came to live there too, which was brilliant. She had just left beauty college and was working at a beauty clinic in Knightsbridge doing electrolysis. I didn't miss David. In fact, I dreaded him coming back for me. I used to feel sorry for him when he phoned me, crying and pleading with me to go back to him, but I was determined not to see him. He had such a huge power over me physically that I knew I would find him impossible to resist in person.

Now that I wasn't living with David, I was free to do what I wanted. I had a ball. Everyone in the cast was given West End membership to Stringfellows for the duration of the show and we often partied there after work. Stringfellows wasn't a lap-dancing club then; it was just *the* club to go to and we always had a real laugh there. Often, Debbie would be getting up to go to work just as I'd be coming in from a night out; meanwhile, Don would be making us all crumpets.

I loved to drink and party, but I was very naïve about drugs. When some of my friends recall their teenage years, they talk about trying everything, including coke and LSD. However, none of

Above The Welches of Whitley Bay, 1956. Grandpa is sitting on the left in the back row, with Uncle David in the middle and Dad on the right. Auntie Cynthia is sitting in front of Dad, with Auntie Nora, uncle David's wife, on the left and Nana in the middle.

Right Proof that I was snatched from an Eastern European orphanage . . .

Below Woodleigh Road, Monkseaton. Debbie and I still drive past our old house whenever we feel down as we have such happy memories of being there.

Above 'Urgh! She smells, Mummy!' My new baby sister, Debbie, August 1961.

Above right In the garden, age six. Check out that mischievous grin!

Above Gaie Paris. Me and Debbie posing on holiday with Dad.

Left Dennis Welch, age eleven. Thanks for the basin cut, Mum!

Opposite, top The White House, Ebchester, where we moved when I was twelve. It's still one of my favourite places in the world.

Opposite, bottom Playing Abigail in *The Crucible* at Consett Grammar School, 1973. This was the play that set the trajectory of my life.

Above The entire 1976 entry year
to Mountview Theatre School.
I think I'm the only one still in
the business.

Left On stage with Tony Holtham,
who went on to become George in
Rainbow. Tony and I thought we
were very Fred and Ginger in this
musical revue at Mountview.

Opposite, top left
Bridget and me on Malibu Beach.
Notice how I'm desperately sucking
in my stomach and trying to avoid
showing my frizzy hair to the
camera!

Opposite, top right
Growing out my Tito Jackson perm.

Opposite, bottom
One of my first ever publicity shots.

Above left As Simone the French stripper in *A Bedfull of Foreigners*. I've got no idea where my boobs had gone!

Above My own John Travolta lookalike, David Easter. He was about to turn my life upside down.

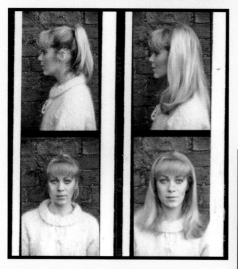

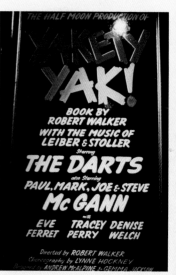

Above Test shots for *Yakety Yak!* I only had nine days to learn all my lines before the show opened.

Right I was so proud when this went up outside the Astoria. Me in a West End musical?!

Above Olivia Newton-John had five
hours in make-up for the famous
transformation from Sandy to vamp –
I had half a page of the script!

Left Sandy and Danny in *Grease*.
Star-crossed lovers both on and off
stage. Leicester Haymarket, 1984.

Above Me and Mum with David after his last night in *Godspell*. Northampton, 1982.

Right Giving it another go. Outside our bedsit in Willesden Green.

Left The night Susan and Gordon came to dinner. That afternoon I'd had the phone call telling me about David's affair.

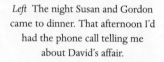

that ever really came my way when I was growing up. I knew people who smoked dope, but dope has never been my thing. It makes me feel sick and I hate stoners. They can be extremely boring.

So when I walked into a room at the Astoria one night before the show and found a couple of people doing lines of coke, I was absolutely horrified. Wouldn't it jeopardise the show to get high before going on? I was furious and told them off, like a real Miss Tweedy Knickers. 'Relax!' everyone said. 'It's fine.' But it wasn't OK in my book.

'Have you ever tried coke?' somebody asked me a few weeks later, when we were having a drink after work before heading to Stringfellows.

'No.' I couldn't help feeling curious, though. I didn't remotely feel that I needed it because I didn't know what effect it had, but I was interested. What was all the fuss about? So I tried a tiny amount. 'Ah,' I thought afterwards, when I felt a bit of a lift, 'I can understand why people do that!' I don't remember being offered it again and I didn't seek it out, but I didn't condemn people for taking it after that.

After three months at Don's, I had saved enough money to move into my own flat in Willesden Green. Life was good: the show was going well and I was having a bit of a flirtation with Kenny Andrews, the black bass singer in Darts, who was 6 feet 6 inches tall and something of a heartthrob. Every night, all the girls in the audience would go mad at two particular points: when Kenny sang his solo, sitting at the front of the stage in a white suit, and when Paul McGann and I kissed. Everybody in the country fancied Paul McGann in 1983; he was on a TV show called *Give Us a Break*. He went on to star in *The Monocled Mutineer* and *Withnail and I*, among other things.

One night backstage, Kenny said to me, 'Hey, baby, would you like me to give you a massage?' I knew he fancied me, so I played the game for a bit and then succumbed. After Stringfellows, we used to go to this after-hours club in Finchley. It reminded me of the speakeasy in *Some Like It Hot* because they used to serve wine in a teapot.

The affair with Kenny went on for about three months, although it wasn't a big love job for either of us. However, as far as my mum was concerned, it was as if I were going out with Barry White. 'Put Kenny on!' she'd say when I phoned her. She loved hearing his deep, velvety voice.

Kenny and I were still seeing each other the night Joe McGann said, 'I'm going to a party at Gary Holton's house in Swiss Cottage. Do you want to come?'

'Yeah, I'll come!' I said.

Gary Holton was a bit of a rock star at the time. He'd been in a big rock group called Heavy Metal Kids and he had a really beautiful girlfriend, who was the sister of Barry Sheene's wife, Stephanie. He was also one of the stars of *Auf Wiedersehen, Pet*, a comedy-drama series about migrant Geordie brickies working in Germany, which had been filmed but not yet aired.

It was a very trendy party. In the kitchen were all the *Auf Wiedersehen* boys and, being a fellow Geordie, I got chatting to them. Among them was Tim Healy, the guy I'd auditioned with at Live Theatre all those years before. Since that audition, I'd bumped into him a couple of times, but there was no spark as far as I could tell; he was just a Geordie acquaintance. 'What are you doing at the moment?' he asked me. I told him about *Yakety Yak* and he said, 'Well, I'll come and see you.' Good as his word, he came to see the show a couple of nights later.

At every performance, just before the finale, we'd pluck some-body out of the audience and drag them up on stage. Since I knew Tim was there, I decided to pick on him. It was quite a laugh because nobody knew who he was yet. 'Watch out for this one, mind!' I said. 'He's going to be famous soon.' Afterwards, we all went to the Music Machine at Camden Palace. That was the last time I saw him for ages.

Then, much to everyone's horror, David came back into my life. He turned up at the theatre one afternoon and asked me to meet him after work. 'Stay away from him!' the entire cast said, but I couldn't resist agreeing to meet him. He still had some kind of hold over me. Seeing him again had set my pulses racing. I could feel myself falling under his spell again and there was nothing I could do about it.

We went for a drink in a West End bar. Tears welled up in his deep brown eyes as we sat down to talk. 'I love you more than anything,' he said, reaching out to take my hand. 'I haven't been able to get over you.'

My heart skipped a beat. He looked so handsome. But things had been so bad between us. I couldn't forgive him, could I? 'But David, I'm seeing someone else now . . .' I said falteringly. 'And Marina . . .'

'It's over with Marina,' he said. 'And it's fine about Kenny. I know he means nothing to you and I can deal with you having a casual affair. But you and I, Den, we're meant to be. We're soul-mates.' He looked intensely into my eyes.

'But . . .' I said, wavering.

'Look, can we please just go back to my place to talk things through?' he begged.

So I went back to his place. No prizes for guessing what hap-pened next. Instantly besotted again, overwhelmed by the intense power of his physical charm, I managed to block the past from my mind. Anyway, David insisted that he had changed. I was the only one for him. There would be no more moodiness or jealousy. That night, he convinced me that life would be perfect if we got back together. A month later, he proposed.

Chapter Six

Despite everything, I was so besotted with David that I was thrilled when he asked me to marry him. I instantly accepted. The next thing I knew, he'd rung my friend Keith and asked him to be best man because he didn't have any friends of his own. Together they went off to get the ring, which was a gold band with three little diamonds. It was nothing flash because he didn't have any money, but I am not somebody who is bothered about the size of my diamonds. He gave me the ring in the yard where Keith worked as a mechanic. It was so blooming typical! Instead of taking me off to Venice to go down on one knee, he did it in some haulage yard in the northeast. Still, I was excited to be engaged.

But then I had to say to my parents, 'I'm engaged to David.' Gulp! They tried to look pleased. I don't think any of my friends or family were happy about it, but I didn't dare ask, in case they told me what they really thought.

Yet, for the first three months after we got engaged, David was the person I had always wanted him to be: constantly charming, never possessive or moody. I was in heaven because I thought he'd changed for good. Now that I'm older, I realise that people like that do not change. They can learn to control areas of their personality, but they cannot fundamentally alter themselves. He was able to suppress certain traits, but only for so long.

I was in *Yakety Yak* for six months, and after I left we went on a wonderful holiday in the sun. While we lounged around on the beach, we talked about the babies we would have once we were married. We even talked about possible names and agreed to call our daughter Georgina. 'When shall I come off the Pill?' I asked him excitedly.

'Whoa, wait a second!' he said. 'There's plenty of time for babies. We need to get our careers established first.'

'Oh,' I said, feeling disappointed. Neither of us had felt ready for a baby when I was twenty and had a termination, but now I was twenty-five and about to get married. It seemed the right time to be thinking about children. However, he refused to discuss it again.

When we came back from holiday, he went up for the part of Danny in *Grease* at the Leicester Haymarket. He looked just like Danny and the part was perfect for him, so it was no surprise when he got a recall. I was also called up for an audition because I'd just come out of *Yakety Yak*, but whereas David had a back catalogue of songs because he was a musical performer, I didn't have anything prepared. 'Oh God!' I thought, 'I'm just going to have to sing a song from *Grease*.'

I asked Don to come along with me for support and he reassured me by saying that at least I looked like Sandy. In the audition, I sang the Rizzo song 'There Are Worse Things I Could Do'. Don was waiting for me when I came out. 'Right, we are ready for *you* now,' the casting assistant told him.

Don looked puzzled. 'I'm not here to audition,' he said.

'Just go in!' I said. So he went in and got the part of Eugene. Then David was offered the role of Danny.

Not knowing that David and I were together, the director, Warren Hooper, said that they needed to see me again because they had cast Danny and wanted to match Sandy with him physically. I didn't say anything until I went for the recall. 'We wanted to see you again because we've just cast Danny—' Warren started saying.

I smiled. 'I know. He's my fiancé,' I said.

He broke into a grin. 'How fantastic!' I got the part.

And so David and I became the young lovers Danny and Sandy in *Grease*. The local TV channel even turned up and did a piece celebrating our engagement. We lived together in a little rented cottage in a hamlet just outside Leicester and life was great. The only thing we argued about was our upcoming wedding. I wanted his mother and stepfather to come; he refused to invite them. I fought to have them there, and eventually won. His sisters came, but since he didn't have any mates, we had to fill out the groom's side of the church with the overspill from my friends and family.

We were married in October 1983, at Lumley Castle in County Durham. It was a lovely venue and a beautiful wedding but, looking back, I realise that I was far more focused on how David and I looked than how we felt about one another. I didn't walk up the aisle thinking, 'I'm so happy that I'm going to marry this man!' What was going through my mind was how lovely people would think we looked. I was really slim with long blonde hair; he was tall, dark and handsome. My bridesmaids were Debbie and my cousin Kirsty. I had so many friends that it seemed easier to stick to family members when it came to choosing bridesmaids.

On the morning of the wedding, I went to the hairdresser's in Newcastle to get my hair done. 'How do you feel?' I said to Dad in the car.

He sighed softly. 'A bit depressed actually.'

'Apparently a lot of dads feel like that when their daughters get married,' I said with false cheeriness. He didn't reply.

Ian La Frenais had flown over for the wedding from Los Angeles and he was in the house with Mum and Dad before we set off to the church. As I came downstairs, he very sweetly said what all godfathers say at a moment like that: 'Oh, you look beautiful!' Then he added, 'By the way, Tim Healy sends his love.'

'Oh, does he?' I said. The guy making our wedding video caught this conversation on camera and it really stood out the last time I watched it back. Most of the rest of the video has a musical soundtrack, and then there's this innocent reference to my future second husband in the middle of my first wedding!

I couldn't meet my parents' eyes in the church. I knew deep down that this marriage was like a dagger to their hearts. However, they had to accept my decision: I was twenty-five and I'd had many opportunities to leave David, but I was dead set on staying with him. It was different with Debbie; she didn't feel the same resistance to the wedding that Mum and Dad did because she was on the cruises and away for six months at a time, so she hadn't witnessed a lot of my relationship with David until then.

We held the reception at the hotel where we were staying that night, before going off on our honeymoon. There were people there who had come from far and wide, as they do for a wedding, and I really enjoyed seeing them all.

At about midnight, David decided that he wanted to go to bed. I was a little tipsy, but totally coherent – I didn't drink as much in those days – and I said, 'I'm not coming to bed! I haven't seen a lot of these people for ages.'

'Darling, it's our wedding night. So let's just go,' he said. But he didn't say it in the way that somebody who desperately wants to take you upstairs and make love to you would say it. It felt like he was purely asserting his control. Still, I went.

It must have been incredibly hard for Mum and Dad but, as a parent, you have to be careful. I've liked all of my son Matthew's girlfriends, but there was one girlfriend whom I felt he pandered to unnecessarily. It wasn't that she ever kicked off like David did, but sometimes she was rude to Matthew, and eventually I felt I had to say something. However, there came a point when I had to stop myself saying any more because I knew that he knew that I knew. It was up to him to make the decision about when to sort it out, which he did when he was ready.

It pains me to think of what Mum and Dad went through because they saw me turn into a different person when I was with David. When he was away, I would leave places when I clearly wasn't ready to leave because he'd said, 'I'm going to ring you at midnight.' I was always so worried about what his reaction would be if I didn't answer. It wasn't that I thought he would leave me. That wasn't the problem. I was simply trying to avoid the kick-off, so even when I was enjoying myself, I made sure I was home in time for his call.

I must have been happy with him for some of the time, although I can't really remember the good times. The bad times obviously outweighed them. The sex was fantastic and I was infatuated with his good looks, but I'm not sure there was much more to it than that. I thought I loved him, though, and I believe that in his own way he loved me.

The year after we were married, he got a regular part in *Brookside*, when it was the hot TV series to watch. He quickly became a huge heartthrob, especially after he was involved in a siege storyline with two nurses. I was really thrilled for him, despite having to deal with my husband becoming a sex symbol.

He did endless sexy cover shoots and everywhere we went sixteen-year-old girls flocked around him. He was charming and flirtatious to all his female fans. I was never allowed to go to the set of *Brookside*, even though he was there for most of the week, every week. He always came up with a reason why I couldn't go. Yet he never once stopped hounding me about what I was doing and where I was going.

Just after he started *Brookside*, I was offered the role of Mrs Manningham in *Gaslight* at the Brighton Actors Workshop, a fantastic fringe theatre company which performed plays at a pub called the Nightingale. I had fallen in love with Brighton when David and I first went there to visit his sister Sandy. It felt like the kind of place I'd be happy to live in, so it was great to be spending a few weeks there. The Nightingale was a profit-share company, which meant that you didn't get paid, but that didn't matter to me. I was just desperate to do the play, which was about a man who tries to drive his wife insane by playing psychological tricks on her.

My friend Rose from drama school rang me just after I got the job. At nineteen, Rose had married Chris, who went on to do *The Sooty Show*, but now Chris had broken up with her and she was in a dreadful state. She needed a distraction, so I asked the director of *Gaslight* if she could play the part of Nancy, the maid, which still hadn't been cast. 'Is she good?' he asked me.

'Very,' I said.

'OK, she's got the part, then.'

Rose was thrilled. 'We need to find somewhere to stay, though,' I told her. 'We can't impose on David's sister.'

Rose had a brainwave. 'My cousin Lester works on the *Brighton Evening Argus* newspaper,' she said. 'Let's ask him if we can stay with him for a couple of weeks.'

I found Lester very stand-offish when I met him; he was all suited and booted and a bit snooty. He didn't particularly like me, either. But as a favour to Rose, he allowed us to stay for two weeks and we went on to strike up a friendship that has lasted to this day, although it has been through many ups and downs.

When Rose went back to London, I stayed on at Lester's. In fact, two weeks turned into a year! Typically, Lester now says it was nine years. He loves to exaggerate. Seeing David in a vest and a pair of black leather shorts sealed the deal, I think. After that, he was happy for me to stay as long as I wanted to!

David didn't fancy men, but he was happy for them to fancy him. He was one of those people who wants attention from either sex. Friday night was gay shopping night at Waitrose in Brighton and if we ever happened to go shopping then, David would grace Waitrose in a singlet and leatherette shorts. 'Why are these bloody poofs always looking at me?' he'd ask, falsely outraged. It was insane! He was driven by vanity and insecurity, the kind of man who would look at himself in his cutlery and adjust his hair when we were out to dinner.

Eventually, we bought a place of our own in Brighton, a lovely little flat by the sea. I was often there on my own during the week, while David was doing *Brookside*, but I didn't mind because I loved Brighton and had some good friends there. It was only when David made excuses about coming back on the Friday night that I felt resentful. I couldn't help getting suspicious. I was always finding scraps of paper with telephone numbers and girls' names on them. Sometimes I would question him casually about them; he always had a plausible answer. But the suspicions remained – of course they did, because I had caught him out before we were married.

As time went on, he turned me into a person I hated, some-one who went through his pockets. I remember my heart pounding the day I found a piece of paper with 'Sheila' written on it, next to a phone number. Obviously it wasn't the first time I had come across what appeared to be a girl's telephone number, but I had never done anything about it before. This time, I rang the number and said, 'Hello, is that Sheila? Is David Easter there?'

'No, he's not here, why?' said the voice on the other end. I hung up.

'Who's Sheila?' I asked when he came in that night.

He scowled. 'What do you mean?'

I waved the piece of paper at him. 'Sheila.'

'Oh, Sheila. Look, I rented a car from Hertz and it broke down and that was the out-of-hours number they gave me . . .' The excuses just tripped off his tongue and I believed every one of them. Well, maybe I didn't believe them deep in my heart, but I wanted to because I was madly in love with him.

These days, I'm the first person to spot a conner. 'Don't fall for him!' I'll say. 'I can see it a mile off.' But I totally understand how easy it is to be fooled. It's amazing; you only see what you want to see and you ignore the rest.

There were so many instances when he gave himself away, but I was naïve, or blind, or obtuse. If a gorgeous girl came into the room and all the other men turned to look, David would pretend he hadn't seen her. 'What girl?' he'd say when I mentioned her afterwards.

'The girl who walked through the room naked with high heels on!'

'Oh, I didn't notice.'

Then I'd find out he had phoned the naked girl and arranged to see her, but somehow I always believed him when he denied it.

I openly admit that I went through his stuff as time went

on. It was awful because it made me feel so devious and sneaky. But it's the only way that you can find things out about somebody who you think is telling you lies. To be fair to me, if I hadn't found anything to arouse my suspicions, I would have stopped doing it. But I always found something that didn't quite fit, whether it was a number or an unfamiliar earring in the car.

We rarely had friends to stay, so I was surprised one day when David told me that his brother was coming for the night. Apparently, he had just come out of prison. He was the black sheep of the family and, as far as I knew, David hadn't seen him for many years.

I was fascinated to meet him at long last, but you could have struck me down with a feather when he came through the door. 'We've met before!' I said.

'What do you mean?' David said, clearly perturbed. 'You can't have done.'

'I came to see you in prison on the Isle of Sheppey with my flatmate Carol,' I said. 'She was your girlfriend at the time.'

'Yeah, I remember,' Phil said, his eyes twinkling. It was an incredible coincidence, but David wasn't impressed. I think he noticed the ease with which Phil and I got on and the twinkle in our eyes! I have always liked lovable rogues, although I would never cheat on my husband with his own brother. Unsurprisingly, David couldn't get rid of Phil quick enough the next day, unable to cope with the idea that we had met before, or that we had such an easy rapport.

Perhaps because *Brookside* kept us apart a lot, his jealousy seemed to intensify. One night, we were in a restaurant, just the two of us, quietly having a meal. I was facing the door and my natural reaction was to look up when the door opened and a couple came in. 'Who are you looking at?' David asked accusingly.

'The couple who've just come in,' I said, thinking nothing of it.

It was like a fuse had been lit. 'Excuse me, mate,' David called over to the man. 'Come over here. I think you'll find my wife wants to fuck you!' Upturning the table we were sitting at, he stormed out of the restaurant.

I was stunned. I didn't know what to do or how to react. It was such extreme behaviour and so embarrassing. After helping to clear up the mess on the floor and paying the bill, I rushed outside. 'That's it. I can't handle it anymore!' I told David when I finally caught up with him.

Then David would start with the tears. Oh, the tears, the tears, the tears. 'I'm so sorry. I don't know why I do that!' he'd say. 'I didn't mean it. It's only because I love you so much. I understand why you want to leave me. But I will change. I'll leave *Brookside* for you.'

'No, I'm leaving you!' I'd declare.

But every time I left him, he wooed me back by saying that he loved me and would change for me. I think he always thought that he would get me back. Flowers would arrive every three minutes. Somehow he convinced me that things would be different, and for a short time they would be. It got to the point when my parents became absolutely fed up with me turning up at their house with my suitcases and then going back to David again.

He had clearly had a messed-up childhood. But I know other people who have come from incredibly difficult backgrounds and yet they are wonderful husbands and fathers, so it's not necessarily an excuse for the way he behaved.

I had been faithful up to this point, partly because I was never allowed out and partly because I was too scared to stray. But that changed about a year after we got married, when I did another play in Newcastle called *The Gambling Man*. David and I had been having a really bad time, so it's probably not surprising that I was drawn to Brendan Price, the lead actor in the play. Brendan had been in a series with Patrick Mower called *Target* and he was really fit. He was good-looking and charismatic, just my type. It was lust at first sight for me.

Brendan wasn't so sure. 'But you're married,' he said.

'Yes,' I said, 'but we're not that close at the moment.' Still he resisted.

I stayed at my parents' house while I did the play. One day I was upstairs in the bath when the phone rang. 'It's Brendan Price for you!' Dad shouted. I ran downstairs.

I noticed a change in tone the moment I heard Brendan's voice. 'Hi, you know you said that you'd teach me to do a Geordie accent?' he said. 'Well, I just wondered if you fancied going to Whitley Bay for the day tomorrow.'

'OK,' I said.

'By the way, I've decided that your marriage is your problem, not mine,' he added.

I laughed. 'Good!'

When I came off the phone, Dad said, 'Make hay while the sun shines!' I took that as Dad giving me his blessing. I didn't discuss it with him; he just knew.

So off I went to Whitley Bay to start this affair with Brendan. In those days, I was very looks-oriented, so it didn't matter to me whether we were particularly compatible. When you grow up, I think looks start to become less important, but that's how it was for me then. I wasn't necessarily looking for a serious relationship, anyway.

I had fun with Brendan, but I was still obsessed with David. It really upset me that the day I passed my driving test, David was the one person who didn't phone me to congratulate me; it was Brendan who was pleased for me. David was working in Edinburgh and was due back the following night, but he didn't turn up or call. As the night wore on and I waited for him to appear, a huge knot formed in my stomach and I became beside myself with worry. It may sound odd, because I had been seeing Brendan, but David was still my main focus. Finally, my dad said, 'It's up to you what you do, but I've come to the conclusion that this guy is a complete shit.' David arrived the next morning, full of excuses for why he hadn't called. I found out later that he had been with another woman.

The next day, we had a massive row at Mum and Dad's house. He was right in my face, shouting and screaming, and the noise woke Mum, who was asleep upstairs because she was on nights at the hospital. She got up and came to find us. 'Hey, enough!' she said, standing between us.

David pushed her away. 'Leave us alone!' he screeched. 'You've always wanted us to split up!' He turned to me. 'And you're obsessed with your fucking family.'

I was speechless with shock.

David turned to Mum again. 'You're mental!' he yelled. I was appalled. How could he speak to her like that?

'Get out!' Mum said, trembling with anger.

'Sorry, Mum,' I wailed, collapsing into tears. I led David out of the house and away from Mum, horrified by what had happened.

David gave me a lift to the theatre on his way back to *Brookside*. On the way, I told him it was over between us. I couldn't handle his behaviour anymore, or the fact that none of my friends or family liked him. First, he tried to argue with me. Then he apologised for being rude to Mum. But I'd had enough. We went on arguing until we were outside the theatre, when I got out of the car and slammed the door.

About half an hour before I went on, there was an announcement over the tannoy. 'Denise Welch, there's a phone call for you at the stage door.'

It was Dad. 'Hi, darling,' he said. 'I would never usually do this to you before a show, but I just need to say that if you want to continue being with David, it's your life, and your mum and I won't interfere. But you must understand that he will never, ever set foot in this house again. Just as long as you know that.'

'I've split up with him,' I said miserably. 'I'm so sorry about what he said to Mum.'

'I know you are. It wasn't your fault. But you must know that if you get back together with him again, what I've just said will still stand.'

'OK,' I said.

Two weeks later, I left the theatre to find David outside in the car, crying. 'I can't live without you!' he sobbed. 'I realise what a twat I've been. What I did to your mother was terrible. Please give me another chance. Please, please, please!'

'No, David,' I said.

'And I know all you've ever wanted is a baby, darling,' he went on. 'I've been really selfish. So if you want a baby, we will have a baby.'

This floored me because I was desperate for a baby. I had been broody ever since I could remember, and I was twenty-seven now and my biological clock was ticking. But David had always said that it wasn't the right time. I realise now that this was because he couldn't fit parenthood in with all his extra-curricular shagging, but obviously I knew nothing about that side of his life then.

I thought I had left him for good, but he knew exactly which buttons to press to lure me back. He had returned to show me how much he loved me and what a huge mistake he had made. He had changed his mind about having a baby! It put a whole new perspective on things.

'Well . . .' I said. He looked at me with his deep brown eyes and I melted again, despite myself. It was awful. He could be-witch me within seconds and I wanted to believe him so much. My longing for a child felt overwhelming. I didn't want to wait any longer; I wanted it to happen as soon as possible. Maybe we could work things out after all, I told myself. Perhaps all the years we had spent together had been leading to this moment and he would finally be a good husband. Within seconds, I had convin-ced myself that he would change when he became a father; he would finally become the person I wanted him to be.

Obviously, we couldn't go to Mum and Dad's house that night, so I rang my friends Susan and Keith, who were the only people that we saw much of in Newcastle at the time. Keith, of course, had been David's best man.

'Can we come to you?' I asked Susan. 'David's not welcome at my parents' house.'

'Of course,' she said, true friend that she was.

Susan and Keith are very much early-nighters, so they were in bed when we arrived and they'd put the sofa bed out for us. 'I came off the Pill when we split up,' I told David as we got into bed, 'so we're not protected.'

'I'm sure we'll be fine,' he said confidently, 'but if you get pregnant, that'll be wonderful!'

The following week, I played a tiny part in *Auf Wiedersehen, Pet*. I was a character called Jean, in an episode called 'Marjorie

Doesn't Live Here Anymore'. Ironically none of my scenes were with Tim. My TV roles were very few and far between at that time, but I lived in hope of getting a bigger break. Still, my work in the theatre was interesting and varied and I was doing quite a few radio plays, often working for a director called Tony Cliff at Radio 4 in Oxford Road, Manchester. I still love doing radio; I just adore the whole process. It calls on very different techniques and skills to theatre or television, and I love the challenge of making the dialogue jump off the page. It gives you the chance to create something that every listener can envisage in a different way.

Three weeks after my bit part in *Auf Wiedersehen, Pet*, I did another radio play in Manchester and stayed with my mum's sister, Auntie Julie, in Wilmslow, just down the road from where I now live. While I was there, I realised I'd missed my period and did a pregnancy test. It was positive! I was shocked, but excited. 'I've got to tell David!' I thought.

I rang him at *Brookside*. 'Can you come home early?' I said.

'Why?' he said suspiciously.

'I've just got something to tell you.'

'What is it? Tell me now.'

'No, I don't just want to tell you on the phone.'

'Why, is it bad news?'

Everything was always such a hassle! 'No, it's not bad news. I just want you to come home.'

He arrived at Auntie Julie's a little later. Auntie Julie and Uncle Dennis were in the main lounge and he and I went into the dining area. Coincidentally, there was a copy of the *Sun* newspaper on the dining table and on the front cover was a picture of the actor Gary Holton, who was currently playing Wayne in *Auf Wiedersehen, Pet*. Sadly for him, he had just been outed as a heroin addict.

However, Gary was the last person on my mind as I geared up to tell David my news. 'What is it then?' he asked, narrowing his eyes.

'I'm pregnant,' I said, smiling shyly.

Suddenly it was as if a wall had come down. To my horror, David pointed at the picture of Gary Holton on the front cover of the *Sun* and said, 'It's probably his. Did you shag him when you were doing *Auf Wiedersehen, Pet*?'

'What?' I gasped. Was I going mad? I felt like Mrs Manningham in *Gaslight*. Our relationship had been fine for the last month; there had been no deterioration whatsoever since he'd said that it would be great if we had a baby. Now he was accusing me of being pregnant with someone else's child. It didn't make any sense. I was devastated and confused.

'You made love to me at Susan and Keith's house and said, "If this results in pregnancy, that's what I want",' I blurted out.

'Yeah, but that was a month ago. You were probably fucking him a week later, so how do I know it's my baby?'

'How do you know it's your baby?' I echoed. 'What the hell are you talking about?'

'Well, I don't know that it's my baby,' he insisted.

My head swam. I felt sick. I just didn't know what to think. I was so desperate for him to be happy and for everything to be nice, but he was turning it into a nightmare. What on earth had made him change his mind about having a baby, when he had agreed to it a month earlier? Why was he questioning whether it was his? I couldn't understand it. I gulped and blinked back the tears that were welling up in my eyes. 'It'll be fine,' I told him, trying to be brave. 'You'll get over the shock of it. I'm sure lots of people feel shocked when they first hear.'

I hadn't told Mum and Dad that David and I were back

together and in my bones I knew not to say anything about the pregnancy, to them or Auntie Julie and Uncle Dennis. Instead, I decided to tell Sandy, David's sister. I was really fond of Sandy and I'm still occasionally in touch with her.

'Sandy, I'm pregnant,' I told her, once I was back in Brighton the following week.

'Wonderful!' she said. 'What does Nige think?' (His family still called him by his real name.)

'He's taking a bit of time to get used to it,' I replied. 'But I was thinking that perhaps he might come round if we talked about it openly with you and Mike.'

So that weekend, we went to Sandy and Mike's for dinner and Sandy made a delicious spaghetti Bolognese. Sweetly, she had put some perfume next to my place at the table, a bottle of aftershave next to David's place and a little pair of booties in the middle of the table. As we sat down, David wordlessly took the booties off the table and put them under his chair.

Now, Sandy wasn't the kind of person who would say, 'Right, you are clearly not happy about the pregnancy, so let's discuss it.' Instead she said, 'So, is there something we should talk about, Nige?'

'No, Sandy, there isn't,' he said, and the conversation ended there.

I was heartbroken. This wasn't comparable to when I had conceived when I was twenty and we weren't even living together. This baby had been conceived within marriage, within a loving relationship (or so I thought) and with his consent. Yet it was clear that he didn't want me to go ahead and have his child.

I didn't sleep that night, or the next. 'OK,' I thought, 'I can either have this baby on my own because he clearly doesn't want to be part of it, or I can have a termination.' I kept turning the options over in my head. I wasn't so worried about being a single parent because I would have the support of my family to give the child a loving upbringing and continue working. It was the thought of being tied to David for the rest of my life that upset me.

If I went ahead and had the baby on my own, I was anxious about the possibility that he would suddenly step in when the child was about three or four and say, 'Daddy's here!' I had a premonition that it would fall in love with its absent father and I would end up waving my child off to wonderful Daddy at the weekends. I couldn't bear the idea of doing that. Some of my friends who are single parents have brilliant relationships with their exes. They've put their children first and I think that's what you have to do. But I've got other friends who slag off their children's father in front of the kids, which makes me sick, no matter how awful he has been. I didn't want to find myself in that position.

Without telling anybody apart from Sandy and Mike, I found a termination clinic in Brighton and went along on my own for the obligatory counselling session. I said that I had thought long and hard, it wasn't an easy decision and I wasn't making it lightly, but that I didn't want to be a single parent. They agreed to do the termination.

When I came round from the anaesthetic afterwards, David was by my bed, stroking my hand. 'Do you still love me?' he said, looking intently into my eyes. The sad thing was, I sort of did, although I didn't say so. I stared at him blankly. 'I love you so much,' he went on. 'But it's better this way because we weren't ready for a baby yet. You'll soon realise it was for the best.'

I couldn't believe what I was hearing. What made it worse was that all the other women in the ward recognised him, so there were suddenly all these women scurrying around Pat Hancock from *Brookside*, asking for his autograph. I'd just aborted our child and they were all saying how marvellous he was. It was horribly ironic. The rest is just a blur.

Chapter Seven

On one level, I didn't want my marriage to end. That's why I can understand how women become caught in a trap with men who are either physically abusive or mentally abusive, like David was because their charming side is so powerful. But I couldn't justify staying with him this time. I realised that he wasn't going to change.

A few days after the termination, he had to leave Brighton and go back to *Brookside*. 'It's over,' I told him. 'I can't be with you anymore.' He tried to change my mind, but I kept saying, 'I can't. I can't.'

Then it came to the moment when he had to leave. 'Well, see you then,' I said, closing the door behind him. When he'd gone, I collapsed on the floor in floods of tears and cried my heart out. Half an hour later, the phone rang. It was my friend Lester. 'I've got two tickets for the Hippodrome in London tonight!' he said.

'I can't possibly go to the Hippodrome,' I sobbed.

But Lester wouldn't take no for an answer. 'I'm coming to get you,' he said.

That night, I was suddenly overcome by the most amazing sense of freedom. David and I had split up many times before, but somewhere deep inside I had always believed that we would get back together. This time was different, though. I knew it was finally over. I guess there comes a point when somebody does something so bad that there isn't any way of going back. I knew I was much better off without him.

Of course, the relationship left its scars. After David, I felt very confused about what I wanted. Still, I knew what I didn't want and what I wouldn't put up with. I wouldn't put up with someone telling me what to do and I wouldn't stay with a man who didn't like me for who I was.

One thing still bothered me, though. I could never understand why he had suddenly flipped when I told him I was pregnant. It was only by accident that I discovered the reason behind his change of heart, a long, long time afterwards, through Dusty, a friend of David's sister Paulina. I had always adored Dusty, and so had David, so when he called to tell me that he had cancer, I was really upset. 'Oh, Dusty, I'm so sorry,' I said.

He was partly calling to put wrongs right. 'I just want to say how sorry I am for covering up for David,' he said and went on to confess that he'd let David and another woman, a model, stay at his house when they came to London.

'Oh dear,' I thought, 'I can't let him know that I didn't know!' So I said, 'Listen, Dusty, you were somebody who was always there for him and I would expect one of my dear friends to do that for me in a similar situation.'

Everything began to slot into place when I put down the phone. Thinking back, I recalled how David and I used to look through magazines and joke to one another about who we fancied. Around the time that I became pregnant, he had a real thing about a top model who was really quite big at the time. She was very beautiful.

It so happened that the week I appeared in *Auf Wiedersehen, Pet*, just after David and I had got back together that final time, David's sister Paulina had rung and asked if I'd like to go and have lunch with her at the big London model agency where she worked.

'I'd love to,' I said. The next week, we had a takeaway in her office. Coincidentally, halfway through the meal, this gorgeous woman walked in to get her wages. 'Oh my God!' I exclaimed, almost choking on my food. She turned to look at me.

'Sorry,' I said, quickly swallowing down my mouthful. 'I'm Denise. It's just that my husband, Paulina's brother, thinks you're fantastic.'

Her face lit up. 'Oh yeah!' she said to Paulina. 'You've told us about your hunky brother.'

'Look, do you have one of your handout photos that you can sign for David?' I asked. 'It would make him very happy.'

'Not a problem,' she said, autographing a photo card for me. David laughed about it when I took it home; we both laughed. Then he called her up and started shagging her.

Of course, this had all happened, unbeknownst to me, in the month between me conceiving and finding out I was pregnant. So when I told David I was pregnant, he was already shagging this beautiful model. I was completely over him by the time Dusty phoned. And now I'm actually thankful he was having this affair, otherwise things might have been very different. We might have gone through with the pregnancy and God knows how it would have turned out.

What did hurt was that David met someone called Tina not long after we split up and had a baby daughter with her really quickly. I was hurt, as you can imagine, when I found out that he had called the baby Georgina, the name we had chosen. He then met another girl, who had won a date with him in a competition, and he had another baby with her.

Last year, I worked with a cracking young actress called Rachel Cairns in *Waterloo Road*. In the scene we did together, my character, Steph Haydock, finds her lying on the floor in the toilets, having fainted. The scene took ages to film, so I was kneeling beside her for hours, holding her head up. At one point I said, 'My ex-husband is called Cairns: Nigel Cairns.'

'Nigel Cairns?' she said. 'My dad's called Nigel Cairns.'

Just then, the director said, 'Action!'

Calculating that Rachel was about the same age that David Easter's other child would have been, I completely went to pieces. I dropped her head and began to shake violently. 'What's your mother called?' I said weakly.

Thankfully, we immediately established that it wasn't the same Nigel. 'My dad's never heard of anybody else called Nigel Cairns,' she said, amazed.

I was fortunate to have some very good friends around me when David and I split up. Lester was an absolutely fantastic support, as was my other best gay friend, Steven Smith, a hairdresser in Brighton. At the time, Steven was living with Martin, who was the incredibly successful financial director of an Oklahoma-based company.

When their friend dropped out of a skiing holiday to Klosters in Switzerland, Steven phoned me. 'Bob was coming with us,' he explained, 'but he's poorly, so we'd love you to come in his place, especially as you're a bit down. It's all been paid for.'

'I'd love to come!' I said. 'As long as you don't mind if I don't ski.' Since I have never had any interest in sport, apart from watching Wimbledon, I had no desire to ski. 'So while you two go off on the slopes, I shall be more than happy to have a massage, potter about and look at all the beautiful people,' I added.

I fell in love with Klosters the moment we arrived. The resort was beautiful, the atmosphere was amazing, the hotel was fantastic and everybody was attractive. I felt so lucky: I was an impoverished rep actress and suddenly I was being treated to a life of luxury. 'If you change your mind about skiing, I'll pay for you to have a private instructor all day long,' Martin very generously offered.

I wasn't sure at first. I hadn't skied before and I'm not an adrenaline junkie in any shape or form. Still, how could I pass up an opportunity like that? So, for the next five days, I spent eight hours a day having one-to-one skiing instruction with a totally fit Swiss man called Florian. I loved it! I learned how to ski really quickly and was parallel skiing by the second day. Of course, it helped that Florian was very easy on the eye. In fact, I was determined to persuade him to come 'après-skiing' with me. How typical am I? It's a total cliché: BRITISH WOMAN ON REBOUND FROM HUSBAND SEEKS SOLACE IN GORGEOUS SKI INSTRUCTOR! He must have had it a million times and was so not bothered.

Meanwhile, Martin and Steven were being very sensible and going to bed after a very swift après-ski, so that they could be on the slopes bright and early every morning. So, of course, by nine thirty at night, I'd be sitting there, picking my nose, thinking, 'How boring is this!' Which made me even more determined to see more of Florian. On the third evening, I instigated a meeting with him at the hotel bar, and what happened next put a proper smile on my face. After that, I loved the days *and* the nights! All in all, it was the kind of fabulous holiday that puts a spring back into your step.

I had to laugh when I got home and heard what had happened to my sister Debbie. She was working for a Greek cruise line and she had arranged for Mum and Dad to have a week-long cruise at a discount. Her one proviso was that Dad would not dress up while he was on the ship. She hated the way he always took his dressing-up kit away on holiday. To this day, Dad loves nothing more than to go on a trip and meet a gang of Brits that he and Mum have a laugh with; then, maybe on the penultimate night, he will transform. Da da! Raquel comes downstairs and they all wet their pants laughing at how hilarious he is. Brilliant holiday.

'I'm being serious, Mum,' Debbie said. 'I've got lots of friends on this ship and I don't want Dad to bring his dresses, even for a joke, because it won't be at all amusing.' She made Mum promise, adding, 'The Greeks can be funny about anything like that.' Ironically, she went on to marry a Greek who thinks it's hilarious when Dad dresses up, but that's another story.

Fast forward to Captain's Night. Dad disappeared from the table with tummy ache. After about half an hour, Debbie said to Mum, 'I'm just going to check to see if he's OK.' As she walked along to his cabin, who did she pass coming the other way but Shirley Bassey! She was nearly sick. The horror!

Totally mortified and unable to bear the idea of going back to the dining room, she walked straight past him to the cabin, where she fell on the bed and cried buckets for about twenty minutes. He had done precisely what she had asked him not to do! Eventually, she summoned up the courage to go back and face everyone, only to find Dad up and dancing with none other than the captain. There was subsequently a competition to name the king and queen of the cruise and Dad was crowned with both titles. They bloody loved him!

*

Back in Brighton, I received an interesting phone call from Steven. 'The vice president of Martin's company is coming over to England,' he announced. 'He's the president's son and it's Martin's job to entertain him.'

'And?'

'So we thought we'd get a group of girls together, go up to Stringfellows and show him the town. Why don't you bring your sister Debbie?'

So Debbie came down and we got a group of eight girls together. At the time, Martin had a fabulous Aston Martin and a Bentley, and we set out to show this vice president a good time.

Sidney was about ten years older than me and had a distinctive limp, which I was fascinated to hear was the result of childhood polio. He had lovely chocolate-brown eyes and was very charming, but I generally find Americans to be charming, and he didn't make much of an impact on me. There definitely wasn't a vibe between us. In fact, he spent all evening talking to my sister and I thought, 'Get in there, Deb!' It was a brilliant evening. We all went up to Stringfellows and got absolutely hammered.

Three days later, after Debbie had gone back to the northeast, Sidney called me. 'I hope you don't mind, but I got your number from Steven and Martin,' he said. 'I'm over here for three weeks and I wondered if you'd like to have dinner with me.'

'Of course, that would be lovely,' I said, simply thinking that it would be a nice thing to do.

But it was better than nice; it was great. People say that Americans don't understand irony or get the British sense of humour, but that's rubbish. Sid and I laughed our way through the meal and we totally got each other. So when he asked me if I'd accompany him on a few business dinners, I was more than happy to say yes. I didn't consider them to be dates; I was just doing Steven a favour by helping Martin's business partner out.

It was great fun, anyway. Sid didn't take these business dinners very seriously and we would often find ourselves in the corner like naughty children, crying with laughter. One night, after a few vinos, it developed into something else. Sid was attractive and he was always dressed nicely, but it was really a classic case of laughing each other into bed. It was just fabulous. I fell madly in love with him and we had an amazing whirlwind romance, me and this millionaire.

After a couple of weeks, he phoned me and said, 'What are you doing at the weekend?'

'Not a lot,' I replied. 'I've got a couple of things I might do, but nothing particular. Why?'

'I just thought we could go to a little local restaurant, nothing flash,' he suggested.

'Great, I'd much rather be with you,' I said happily.

He phoned me back an hour later. 'That was a bit of a test,' he said.

'In what way?' I asked, intrigued.

'Well, I'd actually like to take you to Nice for the weekend. It's a business trip, but it would be a lot more fun if you came with me.'

'I'd love to come!' I said, without a moment's hesitation.

'Can I pick you up tonight and we can talk about it over dinner?'

'That would be lovely!'

A few hours later, the doorbell went and I looked out of the window to see a Rolls Royce outside my flat! Sid's driver, Brenda, was in the front and he was in the back, holding two glasses of kir royale. I felt like I was in a scene from *Arthur*!

Just then, my friend Susan rang me. 'Susan, I can't talk,' I said excitedly, 'because my current boyfriend has just arrived to pick me up and he's waiting outside in a Rolls Royce with two glasses of kir royale.'

'You've been watching too much *Dynasty*!' she said.

'No, really,' I said. 'I'll tell you about it tomorrow.'

What was so wonderful was that I then got into a Rolls Royce with someone I loved dearly; I really adored his company and we were madly attracted to each other. Brenda drove us to a beautiful restaurant overlooking the sea and it was so romantic and gorgeous. When people say that money doesn't matter, I agree that it doesn't, if you don't fancy the person. I could never be with anybody purely for money. That's just depressing. However, when you do fancy someone and they've got money, without a shadow of a doubt it makes a difference.

The next morning, we flew to Nice and checked into the most fantastic hotel. Again, we found it hard to sit and have dinner with his business associates because we were constantly crying with laughter about everything. It was the same when we went to dinner at someone's beautiful mansion on the coast on the Saturday. It was big money, proper money, but as Sid was very casual about it, I felt very relaxed, even though it was a world that I was totally unaccustomed to.

By now, he had told me that he had a girlfriend back home, officially at least. He called her the Dragon and clearly didn't love her, but the family approved of her, which was important. I didn't care. As far as I was concerned, we were just two people who were very much in love.

His allotted three weeks in England were up when we got back from Nice. I was devastated and so was he. But then he called home to say that there was still pressing business for him in the UK, which was partly true. The three weeks became a month.

One night, we were out with one of his business associates who mentioned something about going to Paris. 'Oh yes, we have to go to Paris next weekend,' Sidney said. 'Would you like to come?'

'Do you want me to come?'

'You know I want you to come.'

So the next weekend we went to Paris. On the way there, I said, rather pathetically, 'I just want you to know that I've got £72 in my purse. I would just love to say to you, "Let me pay for dinner at the Ritz", but I'm afraid I can't.'

'Honey, don't worry about it,' he said tenderly.

That night in bed, he asked, 'Does the fact that I'm rich make any difference to you?'

I looked around our sumptuous room, from the elaborate cornicing on the ceiling to the silk hangings around our four-poster bed.

'It's an interesting question,' I said. 'I suppose it does, inasmuch as you are enabling us to be in love in Paris in this fabulous hotel and experience an amazing jet-setting lifestyle. Also, being successful and from a privileged background makes you the person you are, and I'm attracted to that person. But if you didn't have any money, I'm sure we'd still be in love. We would be living on my rep wages in my flat in Brighton, but we would still be having a great time. And if you told me tomorrow that we weren't going on any more foreign trips, I wouldn't suddenly end it.'

The affair grew more intense as the weeks went on. I even took him up to the northeast to meet Mum and Dad, who adored him. But soon my friends began to feel concerned for me because they could see how much in love we were, and yet Sid couldn't stay in England for ever. Meanwhile, he kept delaying his departure, to the point that I'd almost forgotten that he was going back to Tulsa; it felt like he was never going back. Whenever I did think about it, I didn't mention it, in case he said, 'Actually, you're right, I'd better go back right now.'

Then came his *pièce de résistance*. My twenty-eighth birthday was coming up on 22 May and he said, 'What do you want to do for your birthday? I'd like to take you somewhere you've never been. Where would you like to go?'

'Well, I've always wanted to go to Venice,' I said tentatively.

He smiled. 'OK, let me deal with it.'

The day before my birthday, just before we were due to leave for the airport, he turned up with a package from a shop I loved in Brighton. I'm not someone who is exclusively into designer clothes, but I did love this particular shop. Inside the package, there was a black pencil skirt with a coordinating box jacket, white with big, black polka dots (remember, this was the 1980s!). It was gorgeous and it must have cost a fortune.

'Thank you! I love it!' I said, throwing my arms around him.

'Try it on,' he said, and so I did. 'Keep it on,' he added.

'I'm not keeping it on,' I said. 'I'll take it with me.'

'Honey, keep it on,' he said.

It was far too nice to travel in and I said so. 'Look, I'm telling you now, I'm not wearing it to the airport!'

'If you love me, you'll keep it on,' he wheedled.

How could I argue? His charm won the day. 'OK, I'll keep it on!' I said in mock exasperation.

The taxi arrived to take us to the airport. Lester and Steven were in it. 'Why on earth are you here?' I asked.

Lester laughed. 'We came to wave you off!' he said.

I sighed dramatically. 'You can't miss out on anything, can you?'

We arrived at Gatwick and drove to a Portakabin on the far side of the airport. As we got out of the taxi, eleven of Steven's and my closest friends emerged from the cabin, all waving their passports. 'What the—?' I said. Steven looked equally bemused, but Lester was grinning.

It turned out that Martin and Sidney had chartered a plane to take us all to Paris for dinner! As it was Steven's birthday the day after mine, they had decided to have a joint celebration. Through Lester, they had got in touch with people like my friend Rose and Steven's mum and told them to meet us at the airport. It was just amazing! It really was like being in *Dynasty*, but with someone that I loved! Sid wasn't blasé about it at all, either. He seemed genuinely thrilled for me, although he had probably done this kind of thing a million times before. In all the excitement, I completely forgot that we were meant to be going to Venice. It was only later that I remembered.

I was a bit scared when we set off because I wasn't a great flyer and it was quite a small private plane, but I was OK once I was sitting with the pilot, drinking champagne. When we arrived in Paris there were four limousines waiting to sweep us off to a private room at Le Grand Véfour, a restaurant in rue de Beaujolais. Everything was so beautifully organised. Even the menus were personalised with our names. Then out came a birthday cake decorated with two swans and 'Steven and Denise' in swirly iced writing.

I turned to Sid. 'This is amazing,' I said. 'Thank you so much.'

'Isn't it great?' he said.

'I would have liked to go to Venice as well, just with you,' I said, although perhaps I shouldn't have done.

He grinned. 'Darling, we're going to Venice after this! The plane's waiting for us; we can leave whenever we're ready.'

I nearly screamed! I felt so lucky. Back at the airport, we waved our friends off (much to Lester's dismay), got back in the private plane and flew to Venice.

Now, I had stayed in some nice hotels with Sid, but when we walked into the Excelsior Lido, I burst into tears. Overlooking the canal and the gondolas, it's hard to imagine a more beautiful or elegant hotel. I was totally overwhelmed. I think Sid probably quite liked that. You want that reaction when you've gone to so much trouble, don't you?

We had a fantastic weekend of sun and sex. We did all kinds of wonderful things, like exploring the canals in a gondola and wandering through the cobbled streets. Money was no object, so we could just stroll around and do whatever we liked, on a whim. I don't mean shopping. There was no 'Ooh, let's look in that jeweller's window!' He knew he didn't need to impress me or buy me expensive presents.

Aside from the fact that jewellery has never been a big thing for me, money buys experiences, as far as I'm concerned. Some people spend £2,000 on a new table, but I'll go without the table if I have to choose between a table and a holiday. As somebody once said to me, 'Come the revolution, they can take everything away from you apart from your memories.' So I'd always rather invest in experiences and people than material things.

The day after we arrived, we went to the hotel pool. It was full of beautiful nineteen-year-old girls rubbing oil on the shriv-elled backs of sixty-five-year-old men. Now, I love an older man and I would not have kicked Howard Keel out of bed when I met him, at seventy-two, but there was something sad about the certainty that these girls were going to have to give the old men a blow job when they got back to their rooms.

As I pointed out to Sid, I could have chosen that path. I could easily have met a rich old man while I worked at Toppers. Almost any vaguely pretty girl can go and sit in the foyer of the Hilton and pick up somebody like that; anybody can have that life. But where's the joy in staying at the Excelsior Lido, knowing that you've got to give someone's grandpa a blow job when you go back to your bedroom? What's the point? To have dinner in lovely dresses? I'd rather live in a council house with someone I love, although there's a happy medium, obviously.

Of course, we laughed at everything. It was brilliant just watching it all go on. Also, I was feeling really good about myself and happy with the way I looked, so I had a wonderful sense of everything being just right.

There's a moment that I'll never forget: I had left my sun cream in the room, so I looked around for a way to improvise. Earlier, I'd ordered some salad and the waiter had brought an elegant glass olive-oil pourer to the table; now I picked it up and dripped olive oil on my skin to keep it moisturised. Sid was transfixed as he watched me smooth the oil on my arms and legs. 'That's the sexiest thing that I've ever seen anyone do,' he said delightedly.

Gradually, I became aware of what his life was like back in America with Poppa, the president of this multimillion-dollar international firm. Clearly his father ruled the roost and controlled most aspects of his family's lives. But we rarely talked about Sid's girlfriend, the Dragon, although I knew he was phoning her.

Every minute I spent with Sid was magical. I was really turned on by his intelligence. Oh God, he was amazingly interesting! Yet he wore his knowledge lightly and didn't bamboozle me with big words.

He was so clever that he had wanted to train to be an astronaut, but the polio prevented him from doing so. Nevertheless, he had held a high-powered job within NASA at one point. I tried desperately to get information about NASA out of him. Pillow talk! He told me that there was a room there that only six people were allowed to enter, and he had been one of them. I could have shagged him to death and he would never have told me what that room contained. 'Everybody in the world thinks they want to know everything, but they don't really because it would freak them out,' he told me. I have no idea what he was referring to, whether it was extra-terrestrials or something entirely different, but I was fascinated all the same.

Of course, the end was nigh when we got back to England, and soon it came to the time when he was going to have to go back to America. It was devastating. As the day of his departure approached, he started to say that he wanted me to join him there and marry him. He didn't actually say, 'I want to marry you.' It was more a case of going to America and ultimately marrying him.

'If I came to America, what would happen if I wanted to continue my career?' I asked him.

'Well, I would buy you a little repertory company,' he said, and he meant it very sweetly.

I was thrilled at this evidence of his desire to please me, even though it wasn't a practical solution! But I had one proviso. 'You have to finish with the Dragon first,' I said.

'I will, I will!' he kept saying. 'But I can't do it over the telephone,' he added, understandably. 'I've been with her for a long time and she's expecting me to marry her, so I have to go back and tell her in person. You must give me time.'

'OK,' I said, blissfully imagining our life together in America.

'Are you mad?' my friends all said. 'He lives in the middle of nowhere. It's the Bible-bashing capital of the world! You'll end up like Pammy Ewing!'

I blocked my ears. 'I don't care. This is what I want to do!'

While all of this was happening, I was called up for an audition for a play called *Trafford Tanzi*. Set in a wrestling ring, it's about a woman who becomes a female wrestler and eventually challenges her wrestling-champion husband to a match, with the loser being required to do the housework. It was a three-month job in Swansea and my agent wanted me to go for it.

'I'm not going to get it!' I protested. 'It's an open audition, so the whole world will be there. Plus, I'm not an athlete, not even a gymnast, and you're saying that I'll have to wrestle?'

'Don't worry, Mitzi Mueller, the European Women's Wrestling Champion, is going to train you all.'

'And that's supposed to make me feel better?'

In the end, I went along just to please my agent. Fortunately, when I arrived, I bumped into Rob, one of Rose's best friends, who was auditioning for the role of the referee. I had always been aware that Rob had a little bit of an eye for me, but it didn't matter. He was lovely and I adored him because he was just great fun.

At the audition, there were all these mats on the floor: you literally had to run and 'take a drop', or throw yourself over and land flat on the mat. Amazingly, I managed this a couple of times, then I did a reading and a bit of a song. Well, I only got the job! The job that I didn't want and was never going to get. How was it possible? 'This can't be right. Are you sure?' I asked my agent a hundred times.

Then Rob rang me to say that he'd been offered the role of the ref. 'Have you heard anything?' he asked.

'Yes! They want me to play Platinum Sue!'

I asked Sid for his advice. 'I think it would be a great idea if you did this job,' he said, very sensibly. 'It will keep you busy for three months while I go back to America and lay the groundwork for us. When you're finished with the play, you can come over to Tulsa and we'll see how it goes.'

The day he left, we were both in floods of tears. Brenda, the driver, tried desperately to console us on the journey to the airport. When we arrived, Sid went through passport control and then came back and then went through again. I was distraught when he finally left. Brenda took me back in the Rolls Royce, handing me handkerchiefs every two seconds. 'You really do love him, don't you?' she said.

'Oh my God, I really, really do love him!' I sobbed.

Two weeks later, I missed my period.

Chapter Eight

'I think I might be pregnant,' I told Sid the next time I rang him from a phone box on a windswept seafront in Swansea. For some reason, I hadn't done a test. I don't know why. Maybe I didn't want to know.

'Oh my God! Honey, are you OK?'

'Yes, I'm OK, but I've missed my period,' I said.

'Listen, I'll pay for anything that has to happen,' he said, without hesitation. He didn't ask if I'd done a test. 'If you need money, just let me know.'

My heart sank. So that was how it was. Even though we were supposed to be in love with one another, it was a given that I would have a termination. There wasn't to be any discussion about it. There was nothing to discuss.

His reaction changed things for me. I'm not saying that I wanted his baby right then, or that I had any intention of turning up in America with a wailing child, saying, 'Hi, I'm Sid's girlfriend!' And it wasn't as if he went cold, as David had done. He was still very lovely and charming. 'I wish you were here, I wish I was with you,' he kept saying.

But he could have handled the situation with a lot more sensitivity. He could have asked me what I wanted to do, before instantly offering to pay for an abortion. 'I'll send you as much money as you need,' he said. It was very disappointing. I bit my lip. My dreams of spending my life with Sid were crumbling.

'What about the Dragon?' I asked, the next time we spoke.

There was a pause. 'Honey, listen, this is a complex situation,' he blustered. 'It's much more involved than you understand. I'm planning to tell her, but I have to make sure it's the right time.'

After that, I asked him the same thing every time I phoned: 'Have you finished with the Dragon?'

'Honey, listen, you just have to give me time,' he kept saying, 'because my dad—'

Later I heard from Steven that Sid's father had asked him why he was taking so long to come back from England. 'Pop, I've met an actress,' Sid apparently said.

'Leave her at the airport, son,' Poppa said dismissively.

Steven and Martin were convinced that I would hate Oklahoma. 'You wouldn't be happy there,' Martin told me repeatedly. Apparently, even if Sid's father had accepted me, which was unlikely, I would have been expected to be a society wife, regardless of what Sid or I wanted. I suspected that if Sid had his choice, he would opt out of that life, but he was completely and utterly controlled by his father. The Sid I knew would have been happy to live in a shack on the beach if we could have been together, but his life in America was something else entirely. His family really were like the Ewings, and his dad was Jock! His position as vice president of a massive company came through his father; he was nothing without him.

So I would have produced three little boys who would have been expected to appear at dinner in sailor suits; Sid would have patted them on the head and they would have recited something they had learned at school; then the nanny would have taken them upstairs while I prepared a dinner party for twenty of his business friends. And all I would have been expected to talk about was who I was going to play tennis with at the country club the next day.

Oh my God! I couldn't cook and I would have had a nervous breakdown if somebody had said, 'Do a dinner for twenty people.' In those days, I wouldn't even have been able to choose a menu, let alone cook it. Actually, nowt's changed!

As it turned out, I wasn't pregnant, and as the weeks went on, I realised that my friends were right: it was just a dream to go and live in America with Sid. 'I'm not going after all,' I told Mum. 'I don't think it's the right thing to do.'

Mum looked at me as if she had been stabbed! 'Why not give it a try?' she coaxed, although she always denies it now. To be fair, she wasn't only thinking of her retirement in a multimillion-pound house in the States; she and Dad genuinely thought Sid was wonderful!

Things just petered out between Sid and me. There was never a big ending; it just faded away. After a while, I stopped calling him and then there was no contact until ten years ago, when I got drunk with some pals and decided to try to reach him when they'd gone. On the spur of the moment, I called his company and he eventually came on the phone. There was obvious trepidation in his voice and I could sense by the way he spoke to me that he thought I was going to say something like 'I'm ringing to tell you about our child . . .'

Once we'd established that wasn't the case, we had a nice conversation. He told me that he hadn't married the Dragon, but somebody else with three children whom he had adopted. He said that he'd been in Brighton about a year before and had walked past a shop and seen my face on a magazine cover. He'd thought of contacting me, 'But I read that you were married, so I decided not to go there . . .' It was probably for the best.

Doing *Trafford Tanzi* in Swansea definitely helped me to get over Sid. Physically, it was the toughest thing I've ever done in my life. During the show, Lindsay Coulson, who was playing Tanzi, had to take thirty 'bumps' and I had to take ten. It was bloody hard! And I had to do a Welsh accent, in Swansea! I had to practise the accent all the time because the trouble with Welsh is that it's very close to Geordie.

As time went on, I became close to Rob, Rose's friend. He was a good pal to me during the pregnancy scare with Sid. Then one thing led to another and we started having a relationship, once *Trafford Tanzi* had finished. At the time, Rob was between homes, living the repertory actor's life. Since I was still based in the flat in Brighton that David and I had bought, I said, 'Well, why don't you come and live with me in Brighton?'

It was a snap decision and probably the wrong one. I hope I don't hurt Rob's feelings by saying this, but we moved in together far too quickly. It was a choice we made based on practical considerations, rather than something we had really thought through, which was a mistake.

For a while it was great. Then he went on a cruise as part of a theatre-at-sea project, where actors performed plays on cruise ships. I was really upset when he left in late summer because my work commitments meant that I wasn't able to join him until November. We counted the days until we could be together again and eventually I joined him on the *Canberra* for a fortnight. We had a lovely time, but when he finally came back to Brighton, I realised that I no longer felt the same way about him. It was awful because every time I tried to broach it, he would just well up. So because I didn't want to hurt him, the relationship continued.

Bless his heart! He is such a lovely person, and he was so good for me, in so many ways. But I knew that it wasn't going to last. We never had any money, which made things difficult. He was prepared to do anything to support us – he even got a job as a chambermaid in a hotel at one point – but his attitude to money used to make me furious. If someone rang up and said, 'Would you like to come for dinner?' he'd tell them, 'Sorry, we can't come because we've got no money, so we can't even bring a bottle of wine.'

'Don't tell people that we can't afford a bottle of wine!' I'd snap. It wasn't that I was grandiose or had ideas above my station, but I hated admitting that we were so poor. He could never see it, though.

Christmas 1986 was the first Christmas that I didn't go home to my parents because I was appearing in pantomime for the first time, playing Jack in *Jack and the Beanstalk*. I was in digs in Bury St Edmunds, and it was too far to go home on Christmas Day because I had two shows on Boxing Day. I was staying in a family house and my hosts kindly invited me to join their family Christmas, but I didn't know them and wouldn't have felt comfortable. So when Lester and his boyfriend Paul invited me to spend the day with them in Brighton, I was thrilled. It was still a journey, but not as far as going home.

On Christmas Eve, I started feeling really fluey, but I was determined to go anyway, even when I got up on Christmas morning to the most terrible weather. So I set out for Brighton in the old Hillman Avenger that Rob had bought me for about £250, the one that Tim always refers to as being 'two-tone and rust'. It was freezing cold inside and out because, among other things, it didn't have a heater.

I was halfway to Brighton when a stone landed on my

windscreen and shattered it. Suddenly, I couldn't see anything and I swerved off the road onto the hard shoulder. It was incredibly scary. I was lucky not to hit anything.

In the freezing cold rain, shaking like a leaf with fear and fever, I tried to punch out the broken windscreen glass. But I couldn't dislodge it. So, since it was in the days before mobile phones, I trudged off to one of those yellow phone boxes to call for help. For the next two and a half hours, I sat in the back of the car, feeling terrible, shivering in my coat, waiting for someone to come and help me. When the mechanic eventually arrived, he charged me £110 to fit a new windscreen. I remember it so well because it was my entire wages! I had to hand over my little brown wages envelope intact.

I burst into tears when I arrived at Paul and Lester's house. I felt incredibly poorly by now. Nothing they could say or do made me feel better, so it completely ruined their Christmas too. I felt so dreadful that I couldn't even enjoy my dinner and went to bed early.

The next day, despite still feeling very poorly, I got up early to drive back for my matinée. On the journey, the brakes went and I had to pull over again. Since I had no money to call anyone out, I had to drive the rest of the way at about one mile an hour, pumping the brake. I just about got to the theatre in time. Then, during the matinée, I was halfway up the beanstalk when I fainted and fell to the floor. Curtain down! I ended up in hospital with pleurisy, almost hallucinating. 'The beanstalk . . . I have to get back to the beanstalk!' I kept moaning, so the nurses told me afterwards. That was definitely the worst Christmas I've ever had.

The relationship with Rob lurched on for another year, although we were apart a lot. I knew how intense his feelings for me were and I didn't want to be responsible for the hurt I would cause him when I left, so I kept it going for far longer than I should have. I used to think that maybe I'd have to meet someone else before I had the confidence to leave him, even though that seemed the cowardly way out. I suspect that he knew what was going on in my mind because it's pretty obvious when somebody is not reciprocating your feelings, but he'd possibly arrived at that stage where he didn't want to know.

We were still together over the Christmas of 1987, when I went to see him in panto with Les Dennis, who has since become a friend. Again, I was going to end it. I drove up in the old two-tone-and-rust Hillman Avenger, rehearsing how I would word it. But in the end I didn't say anything; I just couldn't bring myself to do it.

The next day was New Year's Day and I drove on to the north-east to spend some time with my family. That evening, I had been asked to go for dinner with my friend Max Roberts and his then girlfriend, Annie, at their house. Max was the director of Live Theatre Company at the time.

I felt really tired and low when I got home. I kept thinking, 'Why didn't I do it? Why didn't I tell him? I'm just making it worse for Rob. I'm making it worse for myself.'

I phoned Annie to say, 'Look, I'm really sorry, I'm just so tired. Would you mind if I didn't come?'

But before I could get the words out, she said, 'Where are you?'

'I've just got in,' I said.

'The bloody dinner is ready and we're all waiting. Come on! Get in the car!'

'I can't say it now,' I thought. 'They're all waiting for me!'

'Who's there?' I asked.

'Robson Green and Shelly [Robson's girlfriend at the time], me and Max, and Tim Healy.'

Oh God, Tim Healy. 'What's he doing there?' I said.

'What's the problem with you two?' she asked. 'Because I've just said to him that we're waiting for Denise Welch and he said, "What's she coming for?"'

Tim and I had known each other for ten years now, ever since I'd met him at the audition for Live Theatre Company. But since he'd shot to fame in *Auf Wiedersehen, Pet*, he seemed to have become very guarded and was much less friendly than he had been before. Although I didn't know it at the time, this was partly because overnight fame had not been easy for him. For a while, it was a bit like being one of the Beatles, from what he's since told me. To this day, the legacy of the programme is massive, so it's easy to imagine how mad it was when it first exploded. It was hard to handle and he became disillusioned.

Added to the pressures of fame was the sadness he felt when his girlfriend of twelve years left him almost as soon as he became famous. She had been with him through all the rough times, but couldn't handle him being well known, with all the attention and autograph hunters. Tim and Jacqui had been madly in love and he was lost without her. I didn't know any of this at the time, though. I just thought he had become grumpy and miserable. Meanwhile, he thought I was frivolous and fluffy – 'Never without a glass of wine and a fag in her hand,' he used to say. As if!

It didn't help that he had seriously pissed me off the previous year, while I was in a play called *The Geordie Gentleman* at the Newcastle Playhouse. It was a Geordie version of Molière's *Le Bourgeois Gentilhomme* and I'd be the first to admit that it was awful. But it had a great cast that included Miles Richardson, Ian Richardson's son, the marvellous Richenda Carey, who was in the

West End production of *Calendar Girls*, Tyler Butterworth and a comedian called Bobby Patterson. It was directed by John Blackmore, whom I found hugely inspirational.

Although it wasn't very good, we had a scream doing it. I corpsed more in that show than I ever have, before or since, because Tyler Butterworth is one of those people who can make you laugh so much that you can't actually breathe. He once made my sister so hysterical while we were in the car that she tried to crawl out of the window and get away, just to stop laughing. He would whisper things to me on stage that made me ache as I tried to keep a straight face. It was terribly indulgent and so unprofessional, but it was hilarious. Then Bobby Patterson would stand in the wings, knowing that I had to look off stage at one point, and get his bits out and do a chicken impression with his willy. I was constantly speaking in that high, strangulated voice that I do when I'm trying not to laugh.

One night we heard that Tim Healy had come to see the play. 'Oh has he?' I said. 'How honoured we are!' Then we heard that he had left before seeing the second half. This infuriated me because when somebody like him comes to a show, the cast always gets to hear about it. Therefore, if they leave before the end, the cast will also get to hear about it, as Tim would have known only too well. OK, I have done the same thing once or twice, but only when I know for sure that the cast don't know I'm there. If I've been spotted, I stay to the end, even if I want to stab myself in every orifice while I'm watching it! Actors would always much rather you come round and say, 'Not my cup of tea,' than just leave.

'Well, that is Tim Healy all over,' I thought at the time. 'What a twat! "Let them know that I turned up; let them know that I left." I'd like to see him get up and make something out of a Geordie version of Molière's play!'

Anyway, I wasn't anticipating having the time of my life at that dinner party, I can tell you.

Mum and Dad were having a party that night. Just before I left, my sister said to me, 'Where are you going?'

'To Max and Annie's,' I said.

'Please come back tonight!' she begged. 'Please don't leave me with Mum and Dad's drunk friends on my own.' So I promised I'd be back by midnight, Cinderella-style.

It was a lovely, relaxed evening at Max and Annie's; everyone was in jeans. When I arrived, Tim made me a black velvet, which is a delicious mixture of Guinness and champagne. Then he made me another. He was about to mix up a third when I said, 'No, I've got to stop. I promised my sister I'd be back for midnight, and I really did promise.' (I think I could control myself better in those days than I can now!)

'Don't worry, we'll get you a taxi,' everyone said.

Then it was time for dinner, which Tim had cooked, much to my surprise. What's more, the food was fantastic. Suddenly he was showing a side of himself that I didn't know, because of course I didn't know him at all. You know those little things that your mum has brought you up to do, that you are super-aware of in other people? And if they do something different to the way you've been taught, it can actually start to annoy you? Well, it may sound silly, but when we sat down to eat, I immediately noticed that he held his knife and fork in the right way!

After dinner, we played a game of Trivial Pursuit and it was a lot of fun. I still didn't think that I remotely fancied Tim, but he struck me as a completely different person now, cocooned by his close friends. Max was one of his best friends and he had mentored Robson into the business, so he felt totally at home with everyone. He wasn't the guarded man I had met at parties; he was happy, relaxed and funny.

At about quarter past eleven, I said, 'Listen, guys. I'm having a really good time, but I have to go.'

'I'll drive you,' Tim offered.

'No, I'll be fine,' I said, thinking of all Mum and Dad's friends at home, who would be decidedly merry by this time.

'Honestly, let me drive you,' he said.

I sighed. 'Look, I'm really grateful. But if you do, I should warn you that my mum and dad's friends will be there. They will be a bit pissed, you are off the telly and they will be mithering you. So, as long as you are fine with that . . . Of course, you can just drop me at the door if you like, but if you come in, I'm just telling you what they will be like.'

'No, that's okay,' he said.

As I was saying goodbye to everybody, he went upstairs. About ten minutes later, he came back down, having changed into a suit, which he wore over a t-shirt. I said nothing, but obviously I noticed! We got into his car, which was a lovely white Jag. He always says now that I said, 'Oh, and you've got a car phone too!' But I swear I didn't. It drives me mad because why would I have said that? For God's sake, I'd just been out with an American millionaire; a car phone wasn't going to impress me! The other thing he always says is that he pulled me out of a squat in Brighton, which is also patently untrue! It was actually a lovely little seaside flat, but it always gets a laugh.

When we got back to my parent's house, I asked him if he wanted to come in. 'Yes,' he said, and the moment he got through the door, all my parents' friends fell on him, just as I'd warned him they would.

They were lovely, but they had all had a drink, so they said some pretty cringey things, like, 'Oh Tim, we hear you play the guitar! Give us a song.' He was brilliant and happily played the guitar and sang for everybody.

Of course, now when I go to a do and my Auntie Margaret asks for a photo with one of my well-known friends, it doesn't matter at all. But back then I was really embarrassed about it.

A little later, I went off to mix some drinks. Tim was sitting in a rocking chair nearby. I turned round and caught him studying me quite intently. He is not very good at concealing what's going on inside, so I could see what was going through his head: 'Do I trust this person? I've met her family now. She's not how I thought she was.'

After what I'd been through with David, I was also thinking hard. 'Why am I drawn to this person?' I wondered. Physically, he was totally different to anyone I'd ever been with before, so I couldn't understand what the attraction was.

At one point during the evening, I went to the toilet. When I came out, he was waiting outside, unaware that I was in there. Just like that, he pulled me into the bathroom and kissed me. 'This is all too weird!' I thought.

After a while, people started queuing outside and banging on the door, saying, 'Who's in there? What are you doing?'

'We're just talking!' I yelled from the other side of the door. Honestly, it was like being sixteen again, except that I was thirty.

When he eventually left, he said, 'So, do you want to come for dinner at the flat in London?'

'That would be lovely,' I said.

A week later, I took the coach to London. Being a penniless repertory actress meant that the coach was most often my form of transport because the Hillman Avenger was terrifically unreliable. It used to take five or six hours to get to Victoria by coach, but at least I could be sure of getting there. Tim had filmed a commercial in Sheffield that day and he must have broken the sound barrier, let alone the speed limit, to get from Sheffield to his flat in time to cook me dinner.

I was dead impressed by his flat, especially as he had designed the interior himself. It was on the top floor of an old Victorian house in Shepherds Hill, on the boundary of Crouch End and Highgate. It had a 30-foot living room with a Spanish-style kitchen at the end, three bedrooms and the most beautiful bathroom with a roll-top bath and two Victorian-looking gentlemen's sinks. It was a proper bachelor pad, but it was gorgeous: lived in, but really well put together. It certainly wasn't the typical Geordie actor's flat that I'd expected.

He cooked me pasta carbonara, which I later discovered was his date speciality. He was obviously up for sex, but I didn't do the full Monty, only because I was a bit confused by the whole thing. I can't have stayed very late because I went back to Brighton that night.

When I got home, the phone rang. Tim had written me a song and he played it down the phone. It was very romantic. He properly wooed me and I really enjoyed being wooed. Most of my relationships before that had begun with an explosion and then we'd settled down to see what happened next. But this was totally different. It was a slow burn for me.

Not long after our first date, he came down to Brighton to visit me. While we were wandering around town, I spotted a wonderful bag and boots in Russell & Bromley. Now, I'm not the sort of woman who likes a man to buy me things, but I was thrilled when Tim slipped back into the shop and bought them for me after we'd left, just because I'd admired them. I think I was touched by the gesture more than anything. As I say, he really did woo me.

I knew now that I had to end it with Rob as soon as possible. He must have sensed it too because the next time I saw him, he said, 'You've met somebody, haven't you?' Perhaps he had noticed that I'd hidden the bag and boots and had put two and two together.

My normal reaction would be to deny it and say, 'No, I haven't!' But instead I just came out with it and said, 'Yes, I have.' I had to do it for my own sanity because not saying anything was making me feel unbalanced. It was just so horrible. I had no idea that I'd met my future husband; I wasn't thinking that far ahead. I just knew I needed to end it with Rob. We were at an age when we were thinking about our futures and Rob saw me as his future, so it wasn't fair.

I would hate him to read this and think I didn't love him, because I did love him, but his feelings for me were stronger than mine for him and if I'd let the relationship go on for any longer, it would only have been worse when we did inevitably split up. However, I never wanted it to happen that way.

He was absolutely devastated. 'I have to go,' I said. 'I can't stay.' I couldn't stand to see the pain that it was causing him, so I went to stay with Lester and Paul that night. Rob took a long time to recover, I later heard. I don't see him anymore, but I have a couple of friends who do and they say he is incredibly happy now, thankfully. He is married with children and it's all fine. I'm so glad.

Ending it with Rob didn't mean I was going to fly into Tim's arms and live happily ever after. It wasn't necessarily serious for either of us at the beginning, although we both knew that there was a strong attraction there. For me, there wasn't the initial wow factor that I'd had with my other boyfriends and I was curious as to what was luring me in. Perhaps it was partly because his story was so interesting. It fascinated me that this incredibly successful actor had begun his working life as a welder and I found him very intriguing. Plus, he had a wicked sense of humour and really made me laugh.

Chapter Nine

'Did you go for me because I was well known?' Tim likes to tease me.

'What, like I'd never met any well-known people who wanted to get off with me before you?' I say in outrage. After all, I could have gone down to Stringfellows and got off with somebody well-known any day of the week, if I'd wanted to! For goodness' sake, Bobby Ball from Cannon and Ball was always chasing me! He's now a mate and we've laughed about it since.

I was drawn to Tim because he was funny and successful and came from a family who had nothing, but surrounded him with lots of love. Brought up in a very working-class family in Benwell, Newcastle, he was the son of a Londoner and a Geordie. He worshipped his dad, also called Tim, a brilliant tool-maker, who was born in Plumstead and spoke a mixture of Cockney and Geordie. His mother, Sadie, worked in the tax office. Tim senior and Sadie were joined at the hip and did everything together, including amateur dramatics, which is how my Tim's love of theatre developed. From an early age, he felt very comfortable being up in front of an audience.

When Tim left school, his dad insisted that he took up a welder's apprenticeship at the Caterpillar Tractor Company in

Birtley. Tim senior wanted the best for his son and welding was a reliable, secure way of making a living. But my Tim didn't enjoy welding; in fact, he hated it. When he decided that he couldn't stand it anymore, he applied for the job of Head of Entertainment at Langley Castle, without his parents' knowledge. Before he knew it, he was MC-ing big medieval nights at the castle, where wenches served up the banquets and Tim ran around playing court jester. There were also vampire-themed nights, where he dressed up as Dracula, went around biting all the girls' necks and got in and out of coffins with them. I was once asked where the oddest place that Tim or I ever made love was. A coffin was the answer, although I hasten to add that it wasn't with me!

Next Tim tried out stand-up comedy. He also started acting and joined a fledgling theatre company. It was a struggle financially, but at least he was doing what he wanted to do, even though it was a world away from what was expected of him. Although his dad didn't exactly disapprove of this change in direction, he didn't think he would ever make a go of comedy or acting. It wasn't that Tim senior didn't have faith in him, but people from their background just didn't become actors. Still, as long as he wasn't coming to him for money, good luck to him, although why he didn't stick to a secure job like welding was beyond him.

Tim senior had a little blue Fiat and my Tim used to borrow it to go and do his gigs. His dad's dream was always to have an MG BGT and Tim used to say to him, 'One day, when I'm famous, I'll buy you one'. But, sadly, when that day finally came, his dad wasn't there to benefit. Having worked in the smoky atmosphere of the Royal Ordnance Factory for most of his life, he gave his retirement speech at the age of fifty-nine and promptly dropped down dead. It was a heartbreaking loss for the whole family.

As much as she loved her boys, Sadie was inconsolable when Tim's dad died. Tim remembers how she would go to work, come home, feed him and his brother John, who was five years older than him, and then sit silently and watch the television, fiddling with her hands. The boys tried to comfort her. 'We're still here, Mum!' they reassured her. But she missed their dad so desperately that life was empty for her when he was gone.

Sadie lived to see the first two episodes of *Auf Wiedersehen, Pet* hit the screens, and then she died. It was as if she had simply gone on living to see that Tim would be all right, before giving up the ghost. He was in his mid-twenties when she went, and he felt totally lost and devastated. No doubt this tragic double loss contributed to the guardedness that I noticed in him in the years before I got to know him properly.

Sadly, I never met Tim's dad or Sadie because they died far too young, several years before I got together with Tim. It's so sad because he absolutely adored them, and I'd love our kids to have met their grandparents, especially because they both resemble the Healy side of the family. 'But don't worry, you'll grow out of it!' I often joke with them.

Tim and I experienced a hiccup or two in our relationship before things began to go smoothly between us. About a month after we got together, I was doing a play at Live Theatre Company called *Kiddar's Luck*. Robson Green and I were playing husband and wife and Joe Caffrey was playing our son. Actually, I was playing a couple of parts: Robson's wife and Mrs Dillop, who came on in the second half. I love playing more than one role. It's when you can really shine as a character actress. Perhaps that's why my idols are people like Pat Coombs and Hattie Jacques and I admire Julie Walters so much.

Tim couldn't come to see the play in production, so he came to dress rehearsal instead. There were only a few people watching, so I was very aware of him leaving in the middle of the second half – and absolutely furious to discover that he'd gone off to have a whisky in the bar. 'How dare you?' I stormed. 'I remember when you left *The Geordie Gentleman* too!' I really kicked off.

Tim was shocked. He had never seen this side of me before, the fiery side that I've inherited from my dad. 'I was going to come back in,' he protested. 'I just took five minutes to have a whisky!' He didn't see anything wrong with it because it was just a rehearsal after all.

'Don't you ever dare leave a play I'm in again!' I yelled. I was going to end it there and then because I felt it was a total lack of respect and support. I couldn't bear the thought of him going out because he wanted a whisky. (Says me, who then went on to become an alcoholic extraordinaire!) Perhaps I was particularly outraged because he had done it before. OK, fine, the pub had beckoned after one half of *The Geordie Gentleman*; that was understandable. 'But not when you are with me, Sonny Jim! People have paid a lot of money to see my Mrs Dillop!' It was our first wobbly moment, but we got over it. Of course, I couldn't have a bigger fan than Tim, as it turns out, but maybe I needed a bit of reassurance in those early days.

Kiddar's Luck was a great play and all the Live Theatre people came to the first night, along with everyone from the cool and trendy scene in Newcastle. In those days, Live Theatre tended to be fairly left-wing and everybody wore a lot of black. It's not like that so much now, but it had a political leaning in those days. I didn't necessarily share that leaning, but it's the way things were.

In the bar after the play, I received some very nice compliments, as generally happens on your first night. Suddenly everything went quiet and people started whispering, 'Who's that? Who's that?' I turned around to see none other than Marilyn Monroe sauntering towards me. She was wearing a tiny skirt and knickers which said 'SAUCY' on the front. 'Hello, Dad!' I said. 'Nice of you to make the effort!' My friends thought it was hilarious.

At the time, Tim was doing the second series of a sitcom called *A Kind of Living*, with Richard Griffiths and Francis de la Tour, so he was often away in Nottingham. I was still living in Brighton, but increasingly I began to stay in London with him. One day, Tim wrote me a card saying something like, 'Well, since your bras are all over the place, you might as well become a permanent fixture.'

So I left Brighton, put the flat up for sale and moved in with him. 'But this is only a stopgap to going somewhere else,' I warned him. 'I don't want London to be my permanent home.' Much as I love it as a city, I never really liked living in London, not as a student, nor in later years. Tim was very happy there, but he agreed to think about moving north.

This sounds so corny and naff, but the moment I realised that I truly loved Tim was the Sunday night he phoned me from the northeast and told me to watch *Highway*, with Harry Secombe. I turned the television on just as Harry Secombe was saying, 'Well, I'm up in Newcastle and I've got the wonderful Tim Healy here, who is going to come on the boat with me and sing.'

Tim sang the Bread song 'Everything I Own' and dedicated it to his dad. It was incredibly heartfelt and poignant; it moved me to tears. As I watched, I thought, 'This man is really genuine. He's a proper person and a fantastic singer.'

When he came back, I said, 'You were brilliant on *Highway* and I really, really love you!'

We always had a really good time together, but, as I've said, it was a slow burner for me. After what I'd been through with David, I was cautious. I knew what I didn't want, but I still didn't know what I wanted. It wasn't a case of 'Oh, I'm looking for a little Geordie guy who's a good actor and can cook.' I had no idea what I was looking for, so it was going to have to find me rather than me find it.

At first, it was enough that I felt comfortable and safe with Tim and he made me laugh. 'You fit,' he used to say when he put his arm around me, because he was just the right height for me. It felt like a good match.

Crucially, he was socially acceptable, which David never was. This was definitely something I knew I wanted. It was really important to be with someone I could be relaxed with when we were out with friends. I couldn't bear the thought of worrying that I'd overhear someone talking about Tim and saying, 'Who the hell is that wanker?' So I was thrilled that everyone loved him. Whenever he was chatting to people and I went up, he'd be making them all laugh. It felt so liberating not to be feeling anxious about who he might be upsetting, who he wasn't getting on with, or what flak I'd get when we got home. He wasn't the jealous type either, which was a huge relief.

Things weren't quite so easy for him, however. I was determined that nobody would ever try to change me or tell me what to do again, EVER. So in the early days, I found it hard to compromise. So a perfectly reasonable request of 'Darling, it's 6 a.m. and I think you should perhaps put your clothes on and stop dancing on that table' was met with 'Hey, don't tell me what to do!'

On the other hand, whereas Jacqui hadn't enjoyed people coming over for an autograph and making a fuss of Tim, I loved all of that. He was very into the celebrity golf circuit and I enjoyed going with him to meet people like Stan Boardman, Howard Keel and Gareth Hunt (I know, but I hadn't met many famous people in those days!). It was heaven. We always had a brilliant night on the Saturday before the golf tournament on the Sunday. 'I just love it that you get on with everybody,' Tim would say. It was refreshing for him that I was sociable and enjoyed mixing with show-business people.

Clearly I'm not one of these people who says, 'I wouldn't want to be married to an actor! I hate industry people.' I've got loads of friends outside the industry, but I love my industry friends. I adore comedians and actors and it's perfect for me to be married to an actor because we understand each other.

Tim introduced me to football players, snooker players, singers and all kinds of interesting people. It's funny to think now that I was welcomed by everyone as 'Tim's girlfriend'. As far as they were concerned, I didn't have an identity outside of my partnership with him. Fairly often, I'd walk along the hotel corridor past the celebrities I'd been socialising with the night before and they wouldn't remember me. Then they'd see me with Tim again and say, 'Denise! What a brilliant night we had last night!'

It didn't bother me. I was just happy to be supportive to Tim. It's funny, I'm often asked whether I get sick of people coming up to me in the street, the supermarket, or at the airport; I don't ever get sick of it, but I find it hard to remember what life was like before it started happening, until I think back to those celebrity golf weekends.

One night in Newcastle, we had dinner aboard the *Tuxedo Princess*, which was a big floating disco boat on the Tyne; it also had a restaurant that was quite highly thought of. Halfway through dinner, Tim looked at me and said, 'So, are ya gonna marry us, or what?'

My immediate response was to laugh and say, 'I can't because I'm not divorced yet.' But I knew then that I wanted to be with Tim, so I followed that up with, 'Yes, of course I will.' We didn't make any plans for when it would happen; we just agreed that we would marry in time, after my divorce came through. 'My God, you must have given that some thought,' I teased him later. 'Let's take her on the boat and say, "Will you marry us, or what?" No taking me up in a small aircraft to look down at the pebbles laid out to spell a proposal. None of that!'

By now, I had been on and off the Pill pretty much since I was sixteen. So I felt a bit worried when I read in a magazine that sometimes it can be two years before you get pregnant after coming off the Pill, especially if you've been on it for a long time. Since Tim and I definitely wanted a family, and I was thirty and he was thirty-six, I suggested that I stopped taking it. 'I think it's probably time I came off it, anyway,' I said. He agreed.

The next thing I knew, just six months into our relationship, I began to feel a familiar sensation. No, it couldn't be! Could it? It hadn't crossed my mind that it would happen so quickly. I thought it would take much, much longer. The magazine article had said two years, not two weeks!

While Tim was at work, I went to the chemist and bought a pregnancy test. As I sat on the toilet lid in his lovely bathroom, waiting for the result to appear on the test stick, it struck me that in three minutes' time, my life could change irrevocably, for ever. This time, there was no decision to be made. If I was pregnant, I was going to have a baby, unless something went wrong naturally.

'If I'm not,' I thought, 'it's not the end of the world because we've not planned it. But if I am, won't it be fantastic?'

After what had happened with David and Sid, I had dreamed of a day when I would tell my partner that I was pregnant and he would be overjoyed, whoever he was. Fortunately, I knew that Tim would be thrilled. He would be as over the moon as I was. Wouldn't he? The doubt started to creep in, another legacy of what had happened with David. 'But what if it's not fantastic?' I thought. 'What if he changes his mind?'

So was I pregnant? All I had to do was walk a few feet over to the test to find out! How amazing that a tiny distance like that can change the rest of your life, just a few feet. Finally, I took a peek and there it was: a faint blue line. It was positive! I was overjoyed and incredibly excited. I desperately wanted to have Tim's child.

When Tim came back from work, I handed him the test stick. 'I'm pregnant,' I said. He instantly burst into tears of happiness.

He made me phone the company who made the test to ask if the result was still valid if there was a little zigzag on the side of the blue line. Did it still mean I was pregnant? Eventually, I went out and bought another test to be sure. Again, it was positive. 'But I'm probably only a fortnight pregnant,' I warned, 'so we mustn't tell anybody.'

The very next day, Tim's best friend Ronnie rang up to say, 'Congratulations!'

'You weren't supposed to tell anyone!' I chastised Tim.

'I'm sorry,' he said, grinning from ear to ear. 'I just couldn't keep it to myself.'

Since the cat was out of the bag, I decided to tell my parents.

I had never discussed with them the idea of having a baby without being married, so I wondered how they would react. I desperately wanted them to say, 'That's fantastic!' I wanted everyone to be as pleased and happy as I was.

I phoned them that day. 'I didn't want to tell you this so early on,' I said, 'but Tim has already told Ronnie . . .'

They were absolutely overjoyed. 'Eeh, that's wonderful, pet!' they said. The question of whether or not we were married didn't come into it at all; the important thing was that they saw Tim as somebody who was going to look after me. I'd had other boy-friends they had liked and they had adored Rob, but I think they knew that Tim was the one for me.

A couple of days later, Tim was doing some exterior shots in London for *A Kind of Living*. When I went to see him on set, I realised immediately that everybody knew I was pregnant. Tim had been told not to tell anybody, but he had told *everybody*!

Then, at about 9 a.m., I noticed a distinct change in atmosphere on set. People suddenly started behaving a little bit oddly towards me.

'Why is everyone being so strange all of a sudden?' I asked Tim.

'I don't know what you're talking about,' he said, not looking me in the eye.

He went off to film a scene and I made my way to the butty wagon to have a sandwich and a cup of tea. 'What do you think of that then?' someone said, handing me the *Sun* newspaper, which was open at the centre-page spread.

I looked down at a photograph of a girl posed provocatively across a settee, with the tip of one finger in her mouth. She was wearing a froufrou dress and staring seductively at the camera. Above her, the headline said, 'MY WILD NIGHTS WITH TIGER

TIM, by Angie Gold'. As soon as I gathered that she was referring to a liaison with Tim before he and I got together, I began
to laugh. By the time I'd read the article, I was doubled up, in
stitches.

It said things like 'Tim took me up to his Hacienda-
style apartment.' Hacienda-style? Was she thinking of the arch
between the long lounge and the kitchen? 'The fridge was stocked
with champagne and lovely food.' Hmm, I couldn't imagine that.
She probably meant a half-empty champagne bottle and a bit of
old, mouldy cheese. 'Tim was a cross between Casanova and James
Bond rolled into one.' Oh! I practically wet myself laughing.

The TV crew collectively breathed an almost audible sigh of
relief. They'd thought I'd be horrified when I saw the piece, but
I found it absolutely hilarious. 'Casanova and James Bond?' I guf-
fawed. 'More like Dick Emery, you mean.'

I read on. Next it said something like 'We made love in the
bath. His lovemaking was so intense that my head was banging
against the taps. Eventually I had to put a Band-Aid on the back
of my head.' Oh my God!

'Hello, Tiger Tim!' I called out when Tim came off set, and the
jokes continued all day. As we drove home, several lorry drivers
spotted him and honked, making obscene gestures and calling
out, 'Wahay!'

'I'll give you a bit of extra steak tonight, Tim, wink wink,'
the butcher's shop assistant said. It seemed that absolutely everyone we met had read about Tiger Tim's amazing exploits.

Although Tim was embarrassed, at least she had given him
a good report. It would be horrifying for a man if a woman did
a kiss-and-tell on him and said that he had a willy like an acorn
and was absolutely rubbish in bed. Instead, she'd said that he was

Casanova and James Bond rolled into one, which isn't going to do anyone's ego any harm, is it?

For me, the defining moment with Tim had been when I saw him dedicate a song to his dad on *Highway*. This was now the moment that cemented his feeling that I was the one for him. Instead of kicking off and getting angry about this story, I'd laughed and made it into a joke. Mind you, if she'd been talking about banging her head on the taps while we'd been together, it would have been a completely different story!

A few months into the pregnancy, Tim and I went away for a celebrity golf weekend on the Isle of Man. Since Tim and I hadn't been together all that long, I hadn't met a lot of his pals, but now was my chance to get to know his good friends Pam and Ian Sharrock. Ian was the major heartthrob in *Emmerdale* at the time, playing a character called Jackie Merrick. His Yorkshire-born wife, Pam, was four foot eleven and very bubbly.

Tim hadn't had a serious girlfriend since Jacqui, so Pam and Ian assumed I was just a casual fling. Pam says that she remembers thinking, 'Oh, Tim's come along with some blonde bit.' I was the complete antithesis of Jacqui, in every way, shape and form, so they thought he was definitely rebounding. But when Pam found out I was pregnant, we bonded. She had given birth to her first child nine months before and we laughed about her leaking nipples because she'd come away without him. She went on to pour her heart out about the problems she'd had when William was born with a hole in his heart. After that weekend, Tim and I spent loads of our time with Ian and Pam; she and I went on to become the best of friends.

I remember feeling a bit odd when my divorce from David came through. Several people have told me that even if you've had the worst marriage in the world, there is something really upsetting about getting the decree nisi. It feels like a failure and you find yourself mourning something that could have been so different, or that you'd had such expectations of.

David and I had to speak to each other that day; it was something to do with the decree nisi, I think. While I was waiting for him to phone me, annoyingly someone kept ringing and blocking the line. I couldn't hear who it was, because his voice was coming through in staccato bursts: 'He-mi-ca-yo-plea-ar-ma-it-yo-ip-ti-Norm—'

'I can't hear you,' I said. 'I'm sorry, I'm waiting for a phone call.'

Then it would happen again. 'Hi-no-ap-pli-Norm-an—'

By the time Tim came in, I was seething. 'Someone keeps ringing and doing my head in! I can't hear what they're saying! Someone called Norman?'

Well, it was only Norman Collier, one of the funniest comedians in the entire world, who has made a stage act out of pretending that the microphone isn't working. Tim found it hilarious, because he'd obviously been doing it to wind me up.

'Why are you upset about the divorce coming through?' Tim asked later. 'I thought you'd be thrilled.'

I paused to think. 'Part of me is thrilled, but there's still a sense of loss, I suppose.'

Marrying Tim felt very different to marrying David. We had to hold the legal ceremony in a register office in London because I'd been married before; the church blessing came afterwards. The service was on Tuesday, 18 October 1988 and our witnesses were my sister Debbie, Tim's good friend Ian Oliver and Ian's mum Bunty. I wore a red Cossack-style suit and a black hat.

The register office was in Wood Green in London and it was a bit grotty, with peeling paint on the walls. I remember thinking, 'We'll just go straight in and out because we have to, and the blessing will be the beautiful part of the ceremony.' I told my parents that it was just a formality, so they could come if they wanted, but the blessing in Birtley on the following Sunday was the important day.

Yet despite the crumbly wallpaper and the boring woman in a suit presiding over the proceedings, the service was really powerful. 'This is how you are meant to feel on your wedding day,' I thought emotionally. It was lovely. It just felt right.

Because Tim had never been married before, we wanted the blessing to be as much like a proper wedding as possible, and it was. It was held in St John's Church in Birtley, where Tim's parents had got married and were, sadly, also buried. Although I was four and a half months pregnant, I wasn't showing, so I wore a long, off-the-shoulder ivory gown. It was the first dress I saw: went in, tried it on, job done. That's how I shop to this day. I didn't have a veil, but I wore a headpiece and the men all wore morning suits.

We held the reception at Linden Hall, near Morpeth in Northumberland. It was a really beautiful venue. All our friends and family were there, around 250 people. It was a wonderful day and I organised the whole thing in six weeks! People kept saying, 'It can't be done!' but I managed it, and nothing was left out. It was a Sunday, and there were fewer people getting married on a Sunday in those days, so that helped, but I'm baffled as to why it can take some people three years to organise their weddings. I booked the church and the reception. I told them what we wanted to eat, found a disco and sent out the invitations. Tim got his friends together to make up a band. I'm not sure what else there is to do that could possibly take three years of planning!

We had a bit of a random honeymoon. I had to arrange it very quickly and we ended up going to Tenerife, which isn't my favourite place. I'm not sure quite how it happened, but we stayed in Johnny Briggs's apartment. I was never particularly close to Johnny (aka *Corrie*'s Mike Baldwin), simply because our story-lines didn't cross very often, so it was very nice of him to lend his Tenerife apartment to us. As I say, I'm not mad about Tenerife, but we had an OK time.

Some people hate being pregnant: 'My ankles are swollen, my hair's greasy and I've got spots,' they moan. But I adored every minute of my pregnancy and glowed throughout. My skin was great. My hair was great. I loved the whole thing. Unlike a lot of women, I never reached a point of thinking, 'Please, get this thing out of me!' It was all fantastic.

I was full of wonder at having a little person growing inside me. I loved lying in the bath, watching him move around in my tummy. The whole miracle of life and birth was wonderfully incomprehensible to me. It was especially amazing when I went along to the recording of *A Kind of Living* in Nottingham, because as soon as Tim came on the set, Matthew would start rummaging around inside me.

As the pregnancy progressed, I started to feel a homing instinct for the north. I had only ever felt that living in London was a temporary option, so we began to look around for somewhere else. Since Tim was often working in Nottingham and Carlton Television was very active back then, we focused our search on the Nottingham area.

I didn't care if I worked or not while I was pregnant. The idea was that I would go back to work once the baby was born, although it didn't matter one way or the other financially because Tim was doing all right. We put in offers on a few houses, but, fortunately, they didn't work out. Moving to Nottingham would have been totally wrong in the light of what happened next, although we didn't know it at the time.

I then realised how much I hankered after the northeast, so we employed a relocation agent who found a few places, including a house called the Hemmel in High Mickley, near Stocksfield. It only had three bedrooms and I wanted four, so we didn't go to see it for a while.

The next time we were in the northeast, we were sent the spec for this house again. It looked lovely, so I said, 'Let's just go and have a look.'

I fell in love with it the moment I walked through the door. It was called the Hemmel after the place that corn was stored on a farm, so the downstairs lounge was a big, round room with a pointed roof called a gin gan. This, I found out later, was the collective name for the farm machinery that was attached to cattle who walked around in a circle grinding the corn that was then stored in the Hemmel. In Northumberland, there are several of these gin gans. 'I love it!' I said.

'Oh, I hate it when people do that to me because they get so disappointed with the upstairs,' said the lady who was showing me round. It was easy to see why because the upstairs area was just a corridor with three bedrooms off it. All the same, I just knew I had to have the house. So we put in an offer.

In those months, I was a happy-go-lucky person, living a blissful, stress-free life. Everything was looking rosy; there was nothing to suggest that anything could possibly go wrong in the immediate future. I was madly in love, all our friends and family were happy about the pregnancy and we had some money in the bank.

And now it looked like we were moving back to the northeast, much to my delight.

When it came to choosing a hospital, Tim was initially determined that we would do everything on the National Health, in true Labour-supporter style. I was fine with that until I went to our local NHS hospital, which was a grim, depressing, Jack-the-Ripper kind of place where they kept losing my notes and tried to treat me several times for the same minor infection. I felt I couldn't have my baby there if there was any other option, so I went private. I was so lucky to have the choice. Tim wasn't overjoyed, but my happiness was paramount.

I was nine days overdue with Matthew, but when the contractions started, I still didn't think this was it. Tim took me to the hospital just in case. First-time father anxiety! They sent me away because it was still too early, but the moment we got home, the contractions started to come every five minutes, so we went straight back to the hospital again.

My contractions were coming thick and fast now and I was in a lot of pain. In the natural childbirth classes that I'd attended at the hospital, they had promised me that pain relief would be available, but now they tried to convince me that, as I was going to be nearing the second stage very soon, I should try to do without. At one point I was shouting, 'Could somebody please hit me on the head with a spiked mallet?'

The pain relief I was finally offered was to sit in a warm birthing pool – which helped, although not much – whereupon Tim said, 'Do you mind if I go out for a quick fag?' Just after he had left, the bulb went out in the birthing-pool room, and I was left vomiting in the bath, shouting 'Help!' I can laugh about it now, but it didn't seem funny at the time.

I was then taken back into my private room, where they

broke my waters while I was lying over a large bean bag, watching television, determined not to miss the final instalment of *Dynasty*, in which Fallon had been captured by aliens! By now, I was incredibly excited. Fingers crossed, it wouldn't be long before I was holding a tiny baby in my arms. I had longed for this moment for many years and, after all the heartbreak and disappointment of the past, my dreams were coming true at last.

The second stage of labour should normally last no more than an hour. This is the stage where, in movies, people are told to push. However, I had no natural bearing-down reflex whatsoever and, whereas I know now that there should have been some sort of intervention, I was left to go through my second stage for eight hours. I later learned that you shouldn't be allowed to go anywhere near that long in the second stage.

I eventually gave birth to Matthew, trendily squatting on the floor in candlelight. 'Maybe if you took your tights off, this would be a bit quicker,' Tim said. Again, I can laugh about it now, but at the time I wanted to punch his face in! I very soon gave birth to a beautiful eight-pound baby boy, at which point Tim, ever the joker, said, 'I suppose a fuck's out of the question?' Grrrr!

Phoning my parents and telling them about their first grandchild was one of the happiest moments of my life. I had Matthew on the Saturday and on the Wednesday I took him home. When I left the hospital, the nurses told me that I was one of the easiest new mothers that they'd come across. 'You weren't anxious at all!' one of them said brightly. There was no inkling that the calm I felt in those few days was about to end.

Thankfully, Matthew was fine and I bonded with him the moment he was born. He was gorgeous and I was overwhelmed with love for him. I distinctly remember thinking that I couldn't understand why some people had problems bonding with their babies. I spent hours and hours just staring at him, transfixed by every detail, from his cute little face to his tiny, perfect toes. My baby! He was the most beautiful being I'd ever seen in my life and holding him in my arms overwhelmed me with a strength of love that I had never experienced before. It was an amazing feeling. I was thrilled. He didn't feed a lot at first, but I was told not to be overly concerned because his weight was normal and so were his blood sugars.

Then, as we were driving home from the hospital, I said to Tim, 'I feel really weird, as if I'm outside looking in.'

'You're probably feeling tired, pet,' he said.

But it wasn't tiredness, it was something else altogether, and it was about to turn my world upside down.

Chapter Ten

My heart began to race. I sat up and tried to breathe in and out calmly, but my heartbeat just sped faster and faster, until I began to panic and sweat. 'What's happening?' I thought nervously. My breaths became shallower by the second. It was horrible; I'd never experienced anything like it. It just came from nowhere.

You know when you nearly crash in a car and your heart pumps and races? Afterwards, you calm down and the feeling subsides. But this feeling didn't subside. My heart pumped faster every time Matthew made a noise, even if he just made a tiny movement. I was terrified because I had no idea what was causing it.

Twenty-four hours earlier, I'd felt disoriented on the way home from hospital. I'd gone on to experience an intense bout of the baby blues, as almost every new mother does. It was normal to be emotional; I expected it and I was prepared for it. But I wasn't prepared for this.

It was only my second night at home and I barely slept a wink. I was totally worn out by morning. Even worse, my boobs had gone from Jane Mansfield's to Twiggy's; they were empty and floppy. The lactation process had stopped during the night and I had no milk to offer Matthew.

'Thank God the midwife's coming,' I thought. 'She will be

able to tell me what's happening. She'll probably say that this is perfectly normal.'

But the midwife reacted with shock when she saw my boobs. 'That's very unusual!' she said. 'I've only seen it happen when there's been a bereavement, when the mother loses her husband or the baby dies.'

I was horrified. It was the last thing I wanted to hear. I felt like an alien. My heart started pounding again. 'I suggest you go out and get him some bottles,' she added, unhelpfully.

Thank God Tim was there to help! She sent him off to get some bottles and sterilising equipment and soon Matthew was happily sucking down formula milk.

Mum and Dad arrived the next day, totally overexcited about seeing their first grandchild, and I was able to have a good cry on Mum's shoulder.

'Let's get you out for some fresh air,' Mum suggested.

I still wasn't feeling anywhere near normal, but I agreed to take Matthew out for his first walk, while Dad and Tim went off to play golf.

'I feel like I'm in a dream,' I told Mum as we sat having a coffee.

'You don't feel depressed, do you?' Mum said. Being a psychiatric nurse, she was alert to any sign of depression.

'I just feel really weird,' I replied. 'Nothing seems real.'

'Oh dear,' Mum thought. We set off home again; it was about a half-mile walk. On the way, I went into a newsagent's shop. The radio was on and the first news of the tragic disaster at Hillsborough was being reported. It was 15 April 1989.

'I've just heard on the news that ninety-six people have been killed at the Hillsborough football stadium,' I told Mum when I came out of the shop.

Mum looked horrified. 'Oh God, that's terrible!' she said.

'How did it happen?' she asked, once we were home.

'No, Mum, that was a dream,' I said.

'Pet, you told me about it as you came out of that shop just now,' she said.

'Stop trying to make me go mad!' I snapped. 'I told you, it was a dream.'

At that, Mum knew the writing was on the wall. Within half an hour of getting back to the flat, I was looking at Matthew as though I didn't know who he was. Lester and Paul came round to coo over the baby. They were trying to make me laugh, but I couldn't even force a smile. I kept thinking, 'Please leave me alone. I want you to go!'

After they had left, a terrible blackness and an indescribable feeling of despair crept up on me. Within about twenty seconds, I felt suicidal. I desperately needed to put an end to the unbearable way I was feeling, and the next minute Mum found me trying to climb out of the window of the flat. I don't remember much about what happened next, but I know that Mum pulled me back and immediately called the hospital where I'd had the baby. Two medics came to see me, but I don't think they'd ever seen anybody in that state and they really didn't know what to do. When Tim came back from playing golf with Dad, they were standing around my bed. My twenty-year nightmare struggle with depression had begun.

The next day, Mum took me to the hospital, where I saw the doctor who had delivered Matthew. He took me into a darkened room and started to play amateur psychologist with me, trying to blame my condition on things that had happened in my past. He suggested that perhaps I was feeling this way because I hadn't got over the terminations I'd had. Of course, it wasn't anything to do with that, but what he said made me feel confused and upset. Could he be right? I had no idea what had caused me to plunge into depression and I was looking to the medical profession for answers. That was the start of people trying to analyse my childhood and erroneously link it to my depression.

Tim was under a huge amount of pressure with his work at the time. He was doing two jobs at the same time – *Boon* and *Casualty* – and he was being driven through the night between the two locations in Birmingham and Bristol. Added to this, he had a newborn baby and his wife was terribly poorly. While every other new mother was saying to her partner, 'Bye, darling, see you later!' I kept phoning him in a hysterical state, sobbing uncontrollably and pleading with him to come home. 'I'm going to commit suicide!' I told him continually. 'I'm going to jump out of the window.' I was seriously worried that I would be driven to end my life because I was desperate to put a stop to the misery and blackness. I can only imagine now how these phone calls made Tim feel, poor thing.

In *Casualty*, he was playing a man who'd had a heart attack. Well, he was so exhausted from being there for me that when he walked into make-up, they put a bit of powder on his nose and said, 'That's you ready then!'

'But I'm supposed to have had a heart attack,' he said.

'Well, you look like you have!' they replied, because he was so drained and ill-looking.

Mum had only come down for a few days, but because Tim was away, she decided to stay. She took unpaid leave from the hospital and nursed me. To this day, I'll never forget the scent of the Balmain perfume she wore then. It's incredible how smells are so evocative and even now, despite being well, if I walk past somebody wearing it, I have to get away as quickly as I can. One whiff of it can start my heart racing again because it was the only perfume Mum had with her for the whole five weeks she stayed with me.

The scent of Ivoire de Balmain reminds me of that awful time more than anything else, when I went from being a together, happy thirty-one-year-old woman to someone who spent all day in a dressing gown on the corner of the settee. I didn't want a shower or a bath; I had no desire to do anything, or be there at all. I would look at Matthew in his carrycot and feel no emotion whatsoever. I remember saying to Mum one day, 'Why is that baby here?' It must have been heartbreaking for her and Dad.

Some women get puerperal psychosis after they've given birth. It's a very extreme condition that triggers them to do all kinds of crazy things, even to the point of killing their babies. I have absolute empathy when I hear those stories and I feel so sorry for the mothers affected.

It makes me shudder when people say things like, 'She had beautiful twins, a successful business and a loving husband. How could she have walked into the sea with those children? She must be evil.'

'No,' I think. 'She probably had post-natal illness.'

Electroconvulsive therapy (ECT) is an amazingly effective treatment for those women. Most people who suffer from puerperal psychosis and are given ECT are cured within six weeks and never have a recurrence of it. However, people with severe post-natal depression like me often don't recover at all, so although puerperal psychosis is more extreme, there is often a quicker release from it.

I was desperate for help. The doctor who had delivered

Matthew had recommended I see a cranial osteopath and I was keen to go, but first Mum said, 'I'm going to take you to your GP.' I didn't want to go because putting my clothes on was too monumental even to contemplate and leaving the house was too terrifying. But Mum insisted that I did.

In the taxi on our way to the doctor, my depression was so black that I opened the car door and tried to get out as we were pulling away from some traffic lights. 'Oi!' the taxi driver shouted, and Mum leant over and pulled the car door shut. I honestly don't know what was going through my head at that moment – whether I really wanted to die or had the idea that if I hurt myself, the physical pain would distract me from my mental anguish, that I'd end up in hospital and somehow wouldn't have to deal with the way I was feeling.

I was signed up to a practice where there were lots of doctors, so I didn't have a specific GP. The GP we saw was very unsympathetic. 'I had five children, dear, and I didn't have time to get depressed,' she said disapprovingly. Can you imagine? She was saying this to someone who had just tried to throw herself out of the car on the way there, someone who had been a normal, functioning person two days previously. I tell you, my mother would kill that GP if she met her again!

I came across this outdated attitude several times, always from older people. In their day, post-natal depression didn't have a name, but if you think about it, we've all heard someone whisper, 'Auntie Muriel went a bit funny after the birth.' I remember my granny saying it about one of her relatives. Of course, it went untreated back then.

For years, Mum had worked as a psychiatric nurse at a hospital for people with mental disabilities and there were people there who had been admitted for post-natal depression and then became institutionalised because of lack of treatment. It really upsets me to think of the women from earlier generations who had my illness. The thought of their suffering haunts me.

The reason I'm still here today is because my family never, ever doubted it was an illness. They never once thought it was an indulgence, as some people do. As if someone with depression actually has any control over it! It's not like you're thinking, 'God, this is so much harder than I thought it would be, so I just won't bother with it.' Depression is not an indulgence.

My friends, bless them, would phone and say, 'We're going to come round and take you to Brent Cross and get you a lovely new dress!'

But that approach was hopeless. They didn't seem to realise that I wanted nothing more than to feel well enough to have a lovely day out at Brent Cross, my local shopping centre at the time. I wanted my depression to be circumstantial, but it just wasn't the case. Unless you have had clinical depression, it's very hard to understand it.

Next I went to see a psychiatrist. He had an incredibly patronising smile. 'Nobody told you it was going to be easy, did they, Mrs Healy?' he said, as if I was merely finding motherhood much more tiring than I'd expected it to be. He also tried to make links between my depression and my childhood and went on to ask me questions like 'Did you spend too much time in the bath with your dad?' It was so irresponsible. When you're as poorly as I was, I think that kind of suggestion can put false thoughts or memories into your mind. I can't say it made me worse because I couldn't have been any worse at that time, and at least he prescribed antidepressants, which I desperately needed.

The worst time for you to have clinical depression is when you have a newborn baby. Suddenly you have this dependent child and you feel totally incapable of looking after it. I was really poorly the week after I saw the psychiatrist. All I did was sit on the corner of the settee in an almost catatonic state. Fortunately, Mum had enough experience and was savvy enough to know that it was crucial for me to keep up the physical contact with Matthew. So although she was hands-on with everything else, she made me do his feeds.

Every four hours, Mum would encourage me to go and do his bottle. Since the living room in our flat was about 30 feet long and the bottles, milk and steriliser were in the kitchen right at the other end, it was as if she had told me to go and climb Mount Everest. It felt like the most mammoth task imaginable, but Mum insisted that I did it. I would move down the room on automatic pilot, just wanting to die every step of the way.

After I'd sorted out his bottle, I would hold Matthew and feed him, feeling no emotion whatsoever, not love, not hate. It was just something that I had to do; I was like a Stepford wife. Of course, it was so important for Matthew that his mum was giving him his bottle. He needed the smell and the feel of me; it was essential to the bonding process.

I lost a stone and a half in a week and a half. I wouldn't eat anything; I felt I *couldn't* eat anything. Mum tried to get me to drink Complan, but I couldn't swallow anything down. I didn't even want to smoke or drink. 'I just want a pill to make everything go away,' I kept saying. I wanted someone to inject me and make me go to sleep. I constantly begged Mum for my next lot of pills, the antidepressants I'd been prescribed. They hadn't started to take effect yet, but at least they helped to induce sleep. 'Please can I have my tablets?' I'd plead. I used to spend all day praying for the time when Mum would give me my medication.

'No, you can't have them until eight,' Mum would have to say. I'd plead with her, but there was nothing she could do.

When I went to sleep, I had normal dreams, but when I was awake, life was a living nightmare. It was the reverse of night terrors. It was as if my whole life was in reverse. Every morning I'd wake up to the blackness, after a perfectly normal night. As I opened my eyes, the depression would descend.

Meanwhile, I was like a child. 'You love Matthew more than me; I know you do,' I'd say to Mum disconsolately.

She had to sit with me and stroke my hand all day. She constantly had to reassure me. 'Darling, I could never love anybody more than you. I love you more than anything.'

Years later, when I became more active on the post-natal depression scene, if you can call it that, I learned that a childlike need for your mother is one of the symptoms of the illness. It was so hard for Tim. I think it made him feel inadequate. In some ways, I needed him, but I needed my mum more, to reassure me and say, 'You're my baby.' It was totally irrational because I had happily lived away from home for eleven or twelve years until then. I was cuckoo, and yet I was aware of everything that was happening, down to the last detail.

One day, Tim arrived back with a moustache, which he'd had to grow for work. I hadn't seen him for a week and was appalled when I caught sight of it. I thought it was part of a horrible plot against me. 'Why is everybody trying to change everything?' I kept asking. My surroundings had a totally surreal feel to them. I knew I was in the flat, but it didn't seem like the flat I knew. Having Mum and Dad there obviously contributed to that feeling because they lived in the northeast and it wasn't usual for them to be around. Poor old Tim had to talk to me with his hand over his mouth until he was able to shave his moustache off.

Then came the added pressure of my sister Debbie coming back from six months away, working on the cruises as a beauty therapist. Of course, she couldn't wait to see the baby and I desperately wanted to be the sister that proudly presents her darling newborn. I knew that Debbie had been told what I was going through and wasn't expecting me to be like other new mothers, but I so badly wanted to come up to the mark. So in the days leading up to her return, I kept thinking, 'Oh no, Debbie's coming back!' when normally I would have been desperate to see her.

Assuming that he would be a brain specialist, I still wanted to try seeing the cranial osteopath that my obstetrician had recommended. But when I eventually saw him, he diagnosed my condition as being down to devils and demons in my head. He lay me down, passed his hands across my head and kept repeating, 'Mmmm, aaah, mmmm'. He was someone else Mum wanted to kill! After seeing him, she decided that it would be better to take me back up to the northeast for a while because she felt I would be better off there.

I experienced a huge sense of relief that I was leaving London and going home. As soon as I reached my parents' house, I began to feel calmer. It must have been a respite for Tim as well because he was no longer coming back to a suicidal wife whenever he had time off. He could live life a little, knowing I was safe up in the northeast, being looked after by my parents.

Back home, I went to see the doctor. Bless him, he didn't know much about depression and he admitted as much. Many doctors don't know much about mental illness to this day, except to prescribe antidepressants.

As the months went on, I began to have periods of feeling more lucid. It started with the occasional good day, when the blackness wasn't as severe. Then there would be a few good days, but they were always outnumbered by the bad days. Finally, Tim and I started to prepare to move to the Hemmel, the house in High Mickley that I had loved so much when I was pregnant. I was in a complete daze when we moved; I can barely recall it. I was just going through the motions. I did everything because I had to do it.

Soon afterwards, Tim suggested that we left Matthew with my parents and went to the Lake District for the weekend. I so wanted to be the wife who was ready for a weekend away with just her partner, now that the baby was six months old. I went, but when I was there I just wanted to go home. Not to the baby, just to go home. I felt so awful.

When I had a good day, Tim would be so excited. Then the next day it would be back to the blackness. It was so hard for him, especially as we had only been together for just over a year. He had known me as a flirty, happy person and then he suddenly lost me; he lost his wife. Yet he never, ever criticised me, even when I irrationally blamed him for things.

He has since said that subsequently he has warned partners of people who have some sort of mental illness about this. 'You will be blamed for everything,' he tells them.

If I couldn't find something, or something had been moved, if a plan went awry or he wasn't back on time, I'd screech and squawk and accuse him of not being supportive. This was partly because if I'd got my head around a particular plan and then it changed, I'd panic and worry that I wouldn't be able to cope with the change.

How did he cope with my behaviour? He was incredible from the start, even though it was a nightmare for him. He would go out into the garden and scream at the top of his voice, he now tells me. Then he'd come back in and say, 'You're all right, petal. Want a cup of tea?' He was amazing, especially considering how little he was getting back from me. Unfortunately, because of my illness, most of the time I felt no emotion whatsoever. Depression robs you of your feelings. I used to explain to people who didn't understand depression that if somebody had come to the door and said that I'd won £17 million on the lottery, or that my family had been wiped out in an aircraft disaster, I would have felt nothing either way. It is so debilitating and so isolating, firstly because people don't understand it and secondly because you are cut off from the world due to your lack of emotions.

My illness didn't stop me being a good person and it didn't turn me into a bad mother either. But it did affect how I was as a wife because I tended to take everything out on Tim. He couldn't help but notice that, however ill I was, I could answer the phone and make a supreme effort to sound OK. I could 'happily' say 'Hiya!' and chat away to a friend or colleague, despite feeling terrible inside. I think he wished that I could make the same effort with him, even if it was only from time to time.

But it's different with your partner, isn't it? Although I didn't ever blame him for my illness, there were times when I complained that he wasn't being understanding enough. Every time I cried, every time I threw things or curled up in a ball and shut myself off, he bore the brunt of it. Yet to this day, the one person I need when I am really bad is Tim. I always know that he'll be there for me when I'm poorly and will look after me. I still feel I have to put on a front with other people, but with Tim I can just be ill.

I was so lucky that Tim and my mum were there to tell me every day, 'You will get well. You will get well.' I feel so sorry for people who suffer from depression and don't have a supportive family network. I needed them to be there because I was frightened of what I might do to stop the pain if I was alone.

It was important for me at the time to focus on the fact that, outside of my illness, my life was great. So I can understand why people who have this illness while they're living in a horrible flat in a tenement block with a horrible partner jump off the roof. It's bad enough to be in that situation without being ill, but with the illness as well, I can totally understand why life wouldn't seem worth living. The pit of blackness!

Matthew was a good child. He wasn't a fussy baby. When he was seven months old, Tim managed to persuade me to go and see a play at Live Theatre Company in Newcastle. My cousin Kirsty came over to babysit and I was having a good day, so I was happy to leave him with her. Everybody said, 'Don't rush home. She will call you if there is a problem.'

But when we got home, Matthew was hysterical and Kirsty was walking around with him in her arms, trying everything to calm him down. 'I didn't know what to do,' she said helplessly. 'I didn't want to call.'

I reached over and took him from her. The moment I held him in my arms, he instantly stopped crying. It was a defining moment, a moment of deep bonding. Not that it made me well again, but it was significant that my child went from hysterical sobbing to calmness when I took him from her. I felt very connected with him, despite my generally detached state.

Not long afterwards, I went away to a golf do with Tim and got absolutely legless for the first time since I'd had Matthew, not really for fun, but because I wanted to blot everything out. I woke up on the Sunday with a huge hangover and a strong sense of not wanting to go home to the baby. It's hard for me to say it now, because I love my children dearly, but it was almost as if

I didn't want to see Matthew or smell him because he reminded me of why I had become ill.

However, I never resented Matthew, partly I think because we had bonded so well right at the start, when he was born. I couldn't forget how much I'd wanted him and how much I loved him. As much as I longed to feel the way I'd felt before the depression descended, I couldn't imagine a life without my child. It was very confusing to have so many conflicting feelings, but getting drunk had, for a few hours at least, taken away the pain. Looking back, I think that's the point at which I began to drink too much on a regular basis. Alcohol was a powerful painkiller for me, despite the misery of the following day's hangover.

For eighteen months, my mornings were always bad. I woke up in a bad way every day. But sometimes, as the day went on, I could feel the depression lift, almost physically. The Hemmel had original beams holding up the roof and when I was feeling OK, it was almost as if the depression would rise up and hit the beams.

Spike Milligan's book *Depression and How to Survive It* is the best book I've ever read on this subject. It puts in layman's terms how depression feels, not how psychologists say it feels. I felt so much recognition when I read the book. Here at last was someone who had been through it too! I devoured every page. 'God, you know just how I feel,' I kept thinking.

I can look back on old video footage of people coming to see us at the Hemmel and of me in the garden with Matthew and I'll know in an instant how I was feeling on each particular day, whether it was a good or bad day. I can vividly remember how I felt every time someone took a photo, whether I was genuinely laughing or feeling terrible and trying to disguise it.

There was so much pressure on me. I felt I should be like the women you see on the front of baby magazines, looking happy

Above On my way to indulge in a bit of après-ski with Florian. Klosters, 1986.

Above right Please don't make me join a series set by a beach in Cyprus and starring loads of good-looking men! OK then, if I must . . . *Soldier, Soldier*, 1993.

Right My double-A side 'You Don't Have to Say You Love Me'/'Cry Me a River' went straight in at number 23 . . . and straight back out!

Left Hey Deb, I'm getting married. Why don't you wear your comedy zebra-print pantaloons?! Outside Wood Green register office after our legal ceremony.

Opposite Love's young dream. Tim and I had known each other for a long time before we realised we were meant to be together. Here we are on the day of our wedding blessing, St John's Church, Birtley, 1988.

Right Just having had a baby is no excuse for this hairdo! Matthew was born on 8 April, 1989.

Below Our first proper home. The Hemmel, Northumberland.

Above left Matt's christening,
August 1989. These were the darkest
days of my life and yet look at
my beautiful baby. Depression is
a cruel, cruel illness.

Above I felt like my life was
one big act. This was another of
those days when I was smiling
for the camera but torn to
pieces inside.

Left My boys. Tim had many
a day when he had to look after
me as well as Matthew. I don't
know what I would have done
without him.

Top I do love TV work, but my true passion has always been for the theatre.

Above Hilda Ogden eat your heart out . . .
A Nightingale Sang, August 1989.

Left I was delighted when I won Best Actress for my role in *The Rise and Fall of Little Voice*.
Royal Exchange Theatre, 2003.

Above Marlene Dietrich (or 'Dad' as she's known to me) at the Consett Working Men's Club. They got all the top stars!

Right We look scarily alike here!

Opposite My wonderful mum and dad, and my beautiful sister Debbie with her husband Peter. My family will always play a huge role in my life.

Above Me, Mum and Debbie on holiday in Paris for my fortieth birthday, 1998.

Below Ian La Frenais. The Godfather.

and pretty and smiling adoringly. That's how you are supposed to look when you have a baby, so I felt deeply inadequate. There were always people outside pubs with their babies, enjoying a glass of wine or beer. As I passed by, I'd think, 'I want to be that person!' I felt really bad for Tim. It was so hard for him, especially when he went to the park and other people's husbands were there with their babies, saying how wonderful it all was. Having a wife with post-natal depression was particularly hard in a place like Newcastle, where it's all about the lads.

It's hard to believe just how much the understanding of depression has advanced in the last twenty years – not just post-natal depression, but depression in general. It wasn't talked about much twenty years ago, so Tim didn't have anybody to confide in or discuss it with. People tended to say, 'We all get depressed. What has she got to be depressed about?' They looked at the lovely house we lived in and all the other trappings we had and furrowed their brows. What on earth could possibly be wrong? Too often people equate depression with circumstantial stuff, with being fed up or upset after an unfortunate turn of events, like losing a job or someone dying. But that's not depression: that's being sad or low or emotionally traumatised. I'm not underestimating that kind of pain, but it doesn't mean that you are clinically depressed.

I think that some of Tim's friends thought I was just being self-indulgent. 'She's been like that for months. Tell her to pull herself together.' I heard that phrase so many times: 'Pull yourself together!' Hence the title of this book.

The periods of feeling OK slowly began to grow longer. Maybe I'd have six good days and two bad days, then five good days followed by another two bad days. I was crippled by the bad days, though. They were terrible and dark and heavy.

Work was the last thing on my mind, but about four months after it all started, Max Roberts, the director of Live Theatre, called me to ask for a favour. Max was one of our best friends, but he too found it hard to understand what I was going through. It wasn't that he didn't sympathise; it was just alien to him.

Max was staging a production of a wonderful C. P. Taylor play called *And a Nightingale Sang* at the Queen's Hall Theatre in Hexham, starring Val Maclean, Jimmy Nail's sister, a stalwart of Live Theatre. 'Val has slipped a disc in her back and she can't go on, so we wondered if you would come and read the part from a book on stage tomorrow night? It's just for one night.'

I immediately went into a sweat of anxiety, but the actress in me said, 'I've got to do it'. I had to prove that I could still get up on stage, even though I felt terrible. Getting to the theatre is a blur, but I do remember putting a picture of Matthew on the mirror in the dressing room. I had an hour to rehearse and then I went on and read the part from a book, feeling absolutely awful.

Afterwards, a woman paid me one of the biggest compliments I've ever received, by saying, 'I thought it was a wonderful touch, how your character was holding a Bible all the way through the play.' She actually thought that it was meant to be part of the action!

As soon as the curtain came down, my depression took over again. It hadn't gone away while I was on stage, but I had managed to focus on getting through the play, which was a breakthrough. I wondered if this was the way it was always going to be from now on. 'Am I going to have this illness for ever?' I thought. 'Will I constantly live and work under a cloud?'

Chapter Eleven

In 1991, when Matthew was about two, I wrote an article for the local newspaper about post-natal depression. My agent didn't want me to do it. 'Don't start talking about it,' he said. 'It may affect future work. People might think you've gone mad.'

'Sorry, but I feel I must,' I said. 'Because if this can happen to me, it can happen to anybody.'

After the article appeared, I was contacted by the producers of *The Time, The Place*, a morning discussion programme presented by John Stapleton. It was Anglia TV's answer to *Kilroy* with Robert Kilroy-Silk, but while *Kilroy* tended to centre on political and social issues, *The Time, The Place* focused more on human interest stories.

I appeared on an episode that dealt specifically with post-natal depression and featured a mix of psychologists, psychiatrists and members of the public who had been through it. Among them was the well-known gynaecologist and endocrinologist Dr Katharina Dalton, who is most famous for coining the term 'premenstrual syndrome'. She advocated treating PMS and post-natal depression with natural progesterone.

Dr Dalton said that 80 per cent of women who have severe PMS will go on to develop post-natal depression, but accepted that I broke the mould because I had never suffered from PMS. I went on to appear on several discussion shows on the subject and I always asserted that you would never have been able to predict that I would suffer from post-natal depression. If you had put all my friends in a row, everyone would have agreed that I was the last person it would happen to.

Most of the psychologists I met argued against me, though. 'We can always spot someone who will be a likely candidate for post-natal depression,' they said.

'You couldn't have spotted me,' I said.

'I think you will find that we could,' they insisted.

It was irritating because they couldn't accept that I was the exception to their rule. I wasn't trying to diffuse their argument or contradict their vast knowledge, but the fact was that I loved every single minute of my pregnancy, I had never had one day of psychiatric illness in my life and there was nothing about me that indicated that I might be prone to it. So I was simply saying, 'You can't possibly make a correct prediction every single time.'

Katharina Dalton's theory was different. She was convinced that people who bloom in pregnancy are much more likely to develop post-natal depression. This was based on the fact that when you are pregnant, you produce fifty times more progesterone than you do normally; obviously, once you have given birth, it takes some time for the hormone levels to rebalance.

Most women will experience the baby blues and be very weepy in the days after having a baby. All it takes is for somebody to say, 'What a lovely baby,' for you to burst into tears. But after a couple of days you come out of it, hopefully. However, for some women, the chemical chaos has a much bigger impact, perhaps because they are producing so much more progesterone when they are pregnant. The subsequent drop in progesterone levels is so extreme that it doesn't right itself. As a result, it produces a far more pronounced attack of depression or imbalance than the average bout of baby blues.

Dr Dalton was on the programme with a woman called Anna Reynolds, who had written a book called *Tightrope*, an account of how she had killed her mother while suffering from post-natal illness. After she was sentenced to life imprisonment, her appeal lawyers contacted Dr Dalton to help them argue that her actions had been triggered by a massive drop in progesterone. There seemed to be no other explanation because her relationship with her mother had been fine until she began to suffer from post-natal problems. It would never even have entered her head to harm her unless she had been extremely ill. There was no history of a strained relationship and she had never had any psychiatric problems.

The state refused to pay for Reynolds's tests, and so Dr Dalton took it upon herself to pay for clinical trials because she was so affected by her story. She wasn't trying to be one of these Lord Longford do-gooders who befriend murderers; she was interested in the case because it was central to her area of research and expertise. The tests showed that Anna Reynolds was almost completely deficient in progesterone and oestrogen, which explained why she had had a complete meltdown. Women cannot function without progesterone and oestrogen; they are totally necessary for our wellbeing.

Dr Dalton's approach was to treat post-natal illness with progesterone, and she reckoned that she had really high success rates. Of course, I was desperate for this treatment, but she was unable to administer it legally without a referral from my GP.

My GP was incredibly understanding, and said, 'I have very little idea of the link between a person's psychological state and their hormone levels. I wish we had done this at medical school, but we didn't. However, I'm willing to learn.' I was lucky to have such a sympathetic ear because it wasn't uncommon for doctors to dismiss the relevance of hormones and say that post-natal depression was a myth.

He sent my blood off for tests. A week later, I went to see him for the results. 'I've never been more astonished in my entire medical career,' he told me. 'You are almost entirely deficient in progesterone.' He happily referred me to Dr Dalton, who treated me with a course of natural progesterone. Unfortunately, it didn't really have much of an effect on me because what I actually needed was oestrogen, as I later discovered.

The medical profession definitely needs to do much more research into hormones. Doctors know a certain amount now, but they don't know it all. Medical students need to be taught that there can be a link between hormonal disorders and behavioural disorders or psychological problems. It's important that they learn about cases like that of Anna Reynolds, that they know someone can lose their mind while suffering from post-natal illness, but can recover through hormone treatment. Of course, if men had babies, there would be a post-natal illness clinic on every corner, or the population would die out!

Things have changed so much since I was first poorly. When I was given books or pregnancy magazines containing information about post-natal depression, the contact details for the Association for Post-Natal Illness never included a phone number. There always seemed to be somewhere you could call if you or your child had a physical problem: 'If you have a child with eight noses, then phone 0898 . . .' Meanwhile, people who needed help with post-natal depression were advised to write off for advice and information. But you can't put pen to paper when you are ill with depression. Writing a letter is like climbing Mount Everest! Fortunately, they now have a post-natal illness support line, which enables you to talk to somebody who has recovered from what you're going through, when you are well enough to speak about it.

It really helps to know that other people have been through what you're going through. Discovering that a childlike need for your mother is a symptom of the illness made a big difference to me because I began to understand that there was no rational reason for me to be so needy of Mum. It wasn't connected to my childhood or upbringing, as some cranks had tried to suggest. It was just a psychological manifestation of a physical imbalance.

Ironically, just when I was going through the worst time of my life, my TV career took off. Matthew was not even a year old when I had a call from *Byker Grove* asking if I would like to play the part of Polly, a tart with a heart and mother to Donna, for eight or nine episodes. It was very exciting because I'd hardly done any television.

Two nights later, Jimmy Nail turned up at the house with another offer. I knew Jimmy through Tim; they had worked together on *Auf Wiedersehen, Pet*. 'I've written a TV series with your godfather, Ian La Frenais,' he told me. 'It's called *Spender* and I've written a part with you in mind. I'm not in a position to offer it to you right now, but you'd be playing Frances, my character's ex-wife. Would you be interested?'

'Well, I've just agreed to do nine episodes of *Byker Grove*,' I said. 'But otherwise, yes, of course I'd be interested.'

Tim was really concerned because he didn't want me to take too much on, but I didn't see any harm in going to see the director of *Spender* to discuss it. At least both *Spender* and *Byker Grove* were being filmed in Newcastle, which made things a lot easier.

Meanwhile, Tim was also in demand. A month before this, he had taken part in a charity event in London celebrating the work of the playwright Harold Pinter. He played a Londoner in *The Dumb Waiter* opposite Peter Howitt, then known for his role in *Bread*, now a well-known director. I met him and his girlfriend, Helena, through Tim and they saw me through a lot of my dark days.

Harold Pinter had gone backstage to tell Tim that he was marvellous in the role. When Tim thanked him in his Geordie accent, Pinter was absolutely taken aback. He couldn't believe that Tim wasn't a Londoner. 'One of my friends is looking for a cockney to play a part in an Australian TV series and I'm going to tell him about you!' he said excitedly.

Subsequently, Tim was offered the lead in the series *Boys from the Bush*, playing a whingeing Pom QPR supporter in Melbourne. His character was married to an Australian and had Australian children, but he hated everything about Australia and moaned about it the whole time. The timing was perfect because it was back when *Neighbours* and *Home and Away* were huge.

It was a six-month contract, so obviously he wanted us to go to Australia with him. However, I had this job offer pending for *Spender*. I was really torn. I rang Jimmy. 'I haven't heard back from the director,' I said. 'Either someone tells me that I've got the job tonight, or I'm going to Australia.'

A little later, Jimmy rang back. 'You've got the job,' he said.

Tim didn't try to persuade me to change my mind, even though it meant he was going to be away from Matthew. It was very generous of him and I appreciated it. Sometimes I now wish that I had gone to Australia with him because maybe it was what I should have done as his wife. But, then again, I don't think I would have had a career if I hadn't done *Spender*. It was a career springboard, and that's what I needed at the time.

So Tim went off to Australia for six months and I stayed at home in England. It was tough being apart from him, but it was a really busy time. Having not done much television before, suddenly I was filming *Byker Grove* and *Spender* at the same time.

I was still having good days and bad days. But, whether I was up or down, I was always able to con people when it came to my work. I think that's partly because I'm a good actress. No matter how much frivolous stuff I've worked on or how many people in the profession think that I shouldn't be taken seriously because I can send myself up on *Loose Women*, I'm still confident in my ability to act. It's the one thing I do know.

I couldn't have done a workload like *Coronation Street* or *Waterloo Road*, though; I would have gone under very quickly. Fortunately, it wasn't relentless in that way because neither of the parts were leads. I was needed for two days, perhaps, and would then not have to go in for four days, and then do half a day, with a day off, and then another two days.

Byker Grove was over with quite quickly because it was only nine episodes. It was great fun and I really enjoyed working with Jill Halfpenny, Donna Air and Ant and Dec, who were about twelve at the time. I used to help them with their homework, so they all blame me for not getting great exam results. In fact, when I was on *This is Your Life*, Ant and Dec came on and said, 'Denise did our maths for us, which is why we had to become pop stars!' I had a lot of good times making *Spender*, too, which lasted for three series, aired between 1991 and 1993. Although my illness never fully went away, I went through significant periods of feeling better.

My character, Frances, was Spender's (Jimmy Nail's) estranged wife and she lived separately with their two girls. She was always saying, 'More pizza, anyone?' This is still a jokey bone of contention between Jimmy and me because she was perpetually in the kitchen or upstairs cleaning the bathroom. I pleaded with him to give her something more interesting to say or do. 'Can she please say something other than, "Would anyone like a cup of tea?"'She still loved her ex-husband, of course, and every guest artist on the show wanted to get off with him too! Jimmy and I had our ups and downs. I've only ever had a tantrum and walked off set twice in my life: once on *Coronation Street*, when a Director told me 'not to worry my pretty little head'. (I may be blonde, but I'm not stupid!) The other time was during the filming of *Spender*. I'm not a flouncy actress at all, but Jimmy was being a nightmare and finally he drove me to the point where I thought, 'I'm not working with him anymore!'

Jimmy is a complex character. He was brilliant in *Auf Wiedersehen, Pet* and he's a good writer and a very clever man all round, but that doesn't always come over. He could be too hard on himself sometimes and then his intensity would rub off on me.

One day I managed to lose my cool over something really silly. For *Spender*, he had a jet perm, whatever a jet perm was, and one day he wouldn't come back on set because it wasn't right. Much to my irritation, when he eventually walked back on the set, the jet perm was exactly the same as it had been when he had walked off. He still wasn't happy about it and I said, 'That's it! I'm not wasting my time over this.' I walked off set and headed to my dressing room to cool down. Half an hour later, I was cajoled back to the set to continue the scene.

The next day, the make-up people told me that poor Jimmy had insisted on having his hair washed with his back to the mirrors. Apparently, he'd said he was never going to look in a mirror again because Denise had made him feel like such a fool about his hair. He may laugh about this now because we are dear friends; I hope he does.

Although I was loving my work, Tim and I hated being apart. I think it was especially tough for him because he was the one on the other side of the world. The massive time difference didn't help. I'd often have to call him at night to catch him in the morning over there. Of course, he'd want to speak to Matthew, but by then Matthew was in bed. So I'd call when Matthew was having his cornflakes, only to find that Tim was on a night shoot and couldn't talk. It was a nightmare.

After two months apart, I had a fortnight off work in June and decided to go to Australia because I missed him so much. Very kindly, the BBC paid for Matthew and me to go business class. (Not in a million years would that happen now!) I had been feeling OK for a while, so I thought the journey would be manageable. But then, the night before we were due to fly, I started feeling terrible. The thought of being so far away from home with a two-year-old child was intimidating. If anything went wrong, it was a twenty-four-hour flight to England. I began to panic.

Suddenly I didn't want to go. The pressure was terrible. If I could have waved a magic wand to make it all stop, I would have done it in an instant. Yet how could I back out now? Tim was so looking forward to seeing us. It was just horrendous.

I made myself go to the airport and get on the plane. If I hadn't been with Matthew, I would have taken a sleeping pill and slept through the whole flight, but obviously you can't do that when you're with a child. Thankfully, the cabin crew helped me out. We flew Malaysia Airlines and, my God, the staff were amazing. They could tell that I wasn't very well and they looked after Matthew for at least four hours, two hours of which he spent in the cockpit with the pilots, playing with a stick-on wheel. The stewardesses had him for the other two hours, which was just so generous of them. It made a huge difference.

Eventually, we arrived in Melbourne. We'd had a heat wave in England, one of those crazy spells when you could fry eggs on the M1, and I was expecting Australia to be the same. I scanned the airport for surfers in shorts, but it was the middle of winter, and Melbourne in the winter is freezing and grey, like Manchester. It was miserable. So much for my thoughts of a holiday in Summer Bay!

Tim was waiting for us with his friend Mark, who played his nephew in the series, and Mark's wife Melanie. Melanie was really looking forward to meeting me. Ten years younger than me, she had heard a lot about this wife of Tim's. Unfortunately, I was so poorly by then that Tim had to arrange for me to see a psychologist the minute I got off the plane. Melanie thought it was all very odd. She just didn't understand because at that time she had no idea how badly depression can affect a person. 'But I've organised for us to go to a barbecue,' she said. 'Let's just go out!'

Although Tim was delighted to see Matthew, the trip was tough on both of us because I was in a real state and mentally incapable of anything. Bizarre things bothered me, like the smell of the carpet in Tim's apartment. Even though the apartment was fabulous, I found it just too much to bear and made him move elsewhere. To this day, the smell of new carpet takes me back to that time. Somewhere there is a photograph of me standing in the lounge next to some flowers that the production company had sent me. I'm wearing a tracksuit with satin stripes up the side. 'Attractive,' I hear you say, but remember, this was the early nineties! It's one of those photos that I look at and think, 'Oh my God, I know exactly how I was feeling then.' Anyone else seeing it would think, 'Look at that lucky cow, just arrived in Australia, on a trip paid for by the BBC!' But I look at it and see a desperately poorly person.

I've blanked a lot of the trip from my mind because it was so awful. Every minute of the day, I was acutely aware of how far I was from home. I don't know why it affected me so much, but it did. Then Matthew had an accident: he picked up a hot cup of coffee and spilt it on himself. It was awful; it took all the skin off his chest. He's not scarred now, but we thought he would be. Oh my God! That set off another major attack of panic and paranoia.

I became so bad that when it was time to go home, I just couldn't make it to the airport. The blackness was so dark the day before that I couldn't cope with the idea of a twenty-four-hour journey with Matthew. I was terrified of leaving Tim too. So he had to phone the BBC and say I wasn't well enough to do the journey. 'She can't come back for another few days,' he told them.

They were very understanding. 'That's fine. We'll work around it,' they said.

Tim was devastated when we left. He was horribly homesick without us and I hated saying goodbye. When I finally got back to Heathrow, there was a nurse waiting for me, courtesy of the BBC. It was like being met by Nurse Ratched from *One Flew Over the Cuckoo's Nest*. She was in full uniform and everything about her screamed 'nurse present to pick up loony'. I remember finding humour in it, even though I was so poorly.

I was glad of her presence, however unsubtle it was. It was caring of the programme-makers to send her and it made me feel that they were genuinely concerned about me. They clearly had their series to do, but they were also very worried about me and wanted someone to accompany me on my way back to the northeast, to make sure I was all right. These days, they would be a lot less bothered about you and much more concerned about getting you back to work.

Two months later, I discovered that I had another fortnight off, so on a well day I decided to go back to Australia to visit Tim again because he was so homesick. Poor thing, he'd had to leave his wife at home rocking in a corner, with a child that he hardly knew, to go to the other side of the world. He hated Australia. He was the biggest whingeing Pom of them all, just like the character he was playing. He says now that, under different circumstances, he would probably love it, like everyone else does, but unfortunately he filmed two series in the Melbourne winter, which wasn't ideal. In between series, he came back to the UK for the English winter, so he went through four winters in a row. He suffered from serious light deprivation. Luckily, the series was marvellous and he was fantastic in it, so that made up for it to a degree.

I decided that I was going to surprise him. This was partly because I love surprising people, but mainly so that he wouldn't be disappointed if, at the eleventh hour, I found I couldn't go. He had no idea we were coming. I liaised with Melanie and arranged for her to meet me at the airport, although she knew there was a possibility that I might pull out the night before. Just before I left, she told me that her sister-in-law, Mark's sister Lisa, would be on the same flight. Lisa laughs about it now. 'The last person I wanted to fly with was somebody who was terrified of flying and suffering from depression,' she says. 'What a nightmare!'

It was quite an undertaking to do a third twenty-four-hour flight with a small child within three months, let alone do it with post-natal depression. Still, I managed it and arrived a second time, feeling just about OK. We went to Mark and Melanie's house, near to where Tim's apartment was, and waited in the lounge. Mark had invited Tim to play golf with him that day and they arranged to meet beforehand at the house. When Tim arrived at the front door, Mark said, 'Just come in for a minute and have a piece of toast before we go.' He led him into the lounge.

When Tim saw us, his eyes flew open in utter amazement and he put his head in his hands in shock. Then, Matthew, looking just adorable in a little denim suit, put one hand in mine and reached out to his daddy with the other. We all became very emotional. That moment is on video somewhere and it never fails to bring tears to my eyes when I see it. I was much better on that trip. I'm sure I had my off days, but I remember it as a very happy time. As a result of our time with Melanie and Mark, and the support they gave me, we are now the closest of friends and I'm godmother to their daughter Poppy.

Once I got back, I finished off *Spender* and began a really good play at the Theatre Royal in Newcastle. It was called *A Beautiful Game* and it centred around football and the origins of Newcastle United FC. All was going well until, one night at about six o'clock, I started feeling really bad. I was supposed to be at the theatre within fifty minutes, but I couldn't even motivate myself to get dressed. Luckily, Mum and Dad were looking after Matthew; they were brilliant about babysitting when I was working, as was Debbie.

Just as I was thinking, 'I can't go on stage tonight,' a car drew up outside the house and Jimmy Nail got out. He had been somewhere for the day and was just dropping in on the off-chance. Although I fell out with Jimmy all the time on *Spender*, on a one-to-one basis he and I have always got on really well.

It was clear that I was in a state, so he sat me down in the conservatory to talk to me. 'I can't go! I can't go!' I said.

He was fantastic with me. 'What is the worst thing that could happen?' he asked gently.

'I don't know,' I said.

'The worst thing that could happen is that you can't carry on, so you run off stage. The next day, the *Evening Chronicle* runs an article saying, "Play ends because Denise Welch runs off stage." That's it. Nobody will die. People will be disappointed, and they might not get their money back, but that's the worst thing that could happen.'

It was just what I needed to hear. He was giving me a get-out clause if I couldn't cope. 'You're right,' I said. 'It wouldn't be the end of the world.' I went upstairs to start getting dressed.

I managed to get through the play that night. I felt terrible throughout, but what kept me going was the thought that I could just run off stage at any point and no one in the audience would die. It would be OK.

When I told Tim about how Jimmy had come round and helped me, I think he felt jealous because he was a million miles away and wished it had been him who had talked me through the crisis. 'It could have been anybody,' I told him, trying to make him feel better. 'I just needed someone to tell me that the world wouldn't end if I couldn't finish the play.' It didn't make things any easier for him when he was commissioned to do a second series of *Boys from the Bush* in Australia and I still couldn't go with him because I was contracted to do another series of *Spender*.

Of course, Tim was a huge help to me when he was around. When he came back after the first series of *Boys from the Bush*, we made plans to go abroad on holiday with our friends Linda and Paul. Travel never usually fazes me in the least – I'm the kind of person who packs her bag on the morning I leave – but when I'm ill, the whole idea of going somewhere becomes a huge thing in my mind. I spend weeks mentally preparing for the techniques I will use to get on the plane without panicking and how to cope with being in a strange place. This particular time, I got so worked up about the trip in the days leading up to it that I went on a massive downward spiral, to the point where I was as poorly as I had been originally.

Tim was off working somewhere that day, so somehow I drove over to see my parents and they called a doctor out. The depression was so thick that I began to seize up; I couldn't move my hands and I developed a temporary facial paralysis similar to Bell's palsy. The doctor immediately got on the phone to the hospital to arrange for me to be taken in for electroconvulsive therapy, which can help to ease these kinds of symptoms.

When Tim arrived a little later, he took one look at me and said, 'There's no way I'm going to take you abroad.' He could tell that the fear of being ill while I was away and spoiling things for Linda and Paul was making me worse. So he rang them and told them that we couldn't go. It was a huge relief for me. The moment he put the phone down, I started to get the feeling back in my hands and my mouth because the pressure had been taken off me. I slowly recovered again.

In October, we received some terrible news, out of the blue. Mum was diagnosed with cancer, aged fifty-five. She had paid a visit to the dentist with toothache and he identified a suspect patch in her palette area. Not long afterwards, it was identified as cancer of the soft palette and she was prescribed an intensive six-week course of radiotherapy. The whole family was thrown into a state of shock and worry.

Mum was incredibly brave and endured six weeks of agonising radiotherapy, which is unimaginable, especially as she is not exactly a robust woman. It burned her like you wouldn't believe.

Her mouth was constantly full of ulcers. It was just horrendous for her, poor soul. Still, she got through it, bless her, and all was well.

Meanwhile, Debbie had met a lovely Greek man named Peter on the cruise ships. She had always joked that there were three kinds of men she'd never marry: a Greek, a younger man, and a man with no money. Peter was all of those things – and she did marry him, and found the most wonderful husband. Now they were expecting their first child, William. I was terrified that Debbie was going to get post-natal depression. This caused me a huge amount of anxiety. I couldn't bear the idea of someone I loved going through the agony I'd been through and, for some reason, I didn't think Debbie would be able to deal with it, even though she's stronger than me in lots of ways. Fortunately, she sailed through the pregnancy and birth.

The following spring, I went to visit Tim again, during the second series of *Spender*. Now that Matthew was a toddler, he spent the whole time running up and down the bloody plane. The year before, I'd gone to see a GP who'd said, 'Look, I travel to Europe twice a year with my children, who are hyperactive, and I give them a spoonful of medicine that is used as a pre-med on children.'

'One spoonful?' I said.

'Just one,' he said, writing out a prescription.

On the way back, I gave Matthew a spoonful of this stuff at Melbourne Airport. When we arrived at Singapore, he woke up for a moment and yawned, before going back to sleep. When he eventually woke up at Newcastle, everyone said, 'What a marvellous sleeper!'

'I know,' I said proudly, not letting on that I had drugged my child!

Although I've been to Australia three times, I haven't really experienced it as I should have. The third time I went, the weather in Melbourne was terrible again, so we decided to take a trip up to the Gold Coast. We wanted to take Matthew to Movie World, which is Australia's equivalent of Disneyland.

It was a five-hour drive from where we were staying and, as a surprise, Tim chartered a helicopter to take us there because then it would only take half an hour. Unlike me, he loves flying, whereas it scares me to death. So when this bloody helicopter arrived, I got in it feeling absolutely terrified. It was meant to be a pleasure flight, but I was gripped with fear. As far as I'm concerned, there is no such thing as a pleasure flight in a helicopter. To me, that is a paradox. To make things worse, I had to pretend that it was wonderful for Matthew's sake because you cannot express fear in front of your child.

Graham, the pilot, was an ex-paratrooper who obviously loved his job. He seemed bizarrely familiar. I kept looking at him and thinking, 'How could I possibly know the pilot who is flying us perilously over the Gold Coast and may well kill us into the bargain?'

One of the most annoying things about the flight was that I knew I wouldn't ever see a more wonderful strip of coastline in my life, but I was too petrified to look out of the window. All I could think about was how on earth I knew the pilot. 'There's no way that I could know you from anywhere, is there?' I said eventually.

'Well, yes,' he said, 'because I used to be Anneka Rice's pilot on *Treasure Hunt*.' Of course!

Eventually we landed at Movie World. How cool were we, arriving there in a helicopter? Not that cool, considering that I got out with a face as white as milk, trembling with fear. Still,

Matthew and Tim loved it, not to mention Graham, of course, who was in his element.

Movie World was fantastic, except that all I could think about as we went on the rides was our upcoming journey back in the helicopter. At the end of the day, as we made our way back to Graham, we passed a long queue for the coaches. 'How lucky are we?' Tim chuckled as we walked past the line of people.

'Can I go back on the coach with them?' I asked. 'Please!' I wouldn't have cared if it was a ten-mile queue for a coach that would take twenty-five days to get back to Melbourne! Anything would have been better than getting in that helicopter again. Oh my God, the journey back! We flew over a series of bush fires, so it was far worse than the journey there because I kept imagining we'd be burned up in the sky!

From that day, I've always said that the next time I go on a helicopter will be when I'm being rescued from a plane crash – and not a day sooner. Years later, when Matthew had a skiing accident and the air ambulance came for him, I fainted at the side of the slope simply at the thought of getting in it with him. So Tim had to go instead of me because I was too scared to accompany my poor, stricken child. Forget the saying 'Feel the fear and do it anyway.' My version is 'Feel the fear and pass out unconscious!'

Chapter Twelve

When I was twenty-seven, I went to see a play called *In Blackberry Time* by C. P. Taylor, a wonderful writer for Live Theatre. It starred a new nineteen-year-old actor called Robson Green, who lit up the stage. He also happened to strip down to his underpants! 'God, that boy was fantastic,' I gushed to Max Roberts, the director, afterwards. 'He's really attractive in a quirky sort of way too.'

Max introduced me to Robson that night and we got on really well. He was a massive fan of Tim and went on to do his first TV with him. As time went on, it felt like the age gap was closing and we all became great friends, performing in plays together and mixing in the same social group.

I was dead jealous when Robson got the *Soldier, Soldier* gig, filming on location in Hong Kong and New Zealand. 'Can't you invent a Geordie sister for your character?' I begged him. I was only joking though; it would have been impossible to travel so far for work because Matthew was only three at the time. Then, ironically, I got the part of Marsha Stubbs in the third series two years later in 1993, and she had nothing to do with Robson's character.

My friend Rose came with me to the audition, hoping to get

an audition herself. I went in to do the reading as a Geordie, but they told me they didn't want another Geordie character because of Robson and Rosie Rowell being Geordie. 'I'm not really from Newcastle,' I said, quick as a flash. 'I'm from Parbold, near Wigan.' Rose had grown up in Parbold and I parroted a few facts that she had told me about her background. As she always says, there was no way she could go in and audition after that because I'd stolen her identity!

Soldier, Soldier was a hugely successful series about a group of soldiers in a fictional British Army infantry regiment called the King's Fusiliers. It felt like a big career breakthrough for me and definitely goes down as one of my favourite jobs ever. We had a great time filming in Germany and Cyprus. At its conception, it was going to be called *Army Wives*, so the women's roles were very well written, which made it a delight. My character, Marsha, was a squaddie's wife, so it was quite a meaty role. Rob Spendlove played my husband, Michael. Even better, the schedule wasn't too frantic. We weren't trying to complete 500 episodes a week, as is sometimes the case with television today. The girls would often work for three days and then have two days off, which was perfect.

Luck, rather than management, always seems to ensure that Tim doesn't have to go away when I do, and vice versa. Somehow it always works out. Fortunately, he was at home during the filming of *Soldier, Soldier* and by now Matthew was at school. In Germany, if you had four days off, you could go home, so I used to nip back to England quite a lot. The longest that I ever went without seeing Matthew was a fortnight, when we were filming in Cyprus. The third series was filmed in Windsor, which wasn't so much of a problem.

Matthew tells me now that he can't remember me being away

during his childhood. I find this very reassuring when nine-year-old Louis is pulling a fast one on me by saying, 'I don't want you to go to work!'

'Mum, don't let Louis do that!' Matthew says, but it's hard not to feel guilty sometimes. I know that a lot of mums with busy careers feel the same way. Yet I have to remind myself that my children have always been left in the care of people who love them, usually family members. They have never just been left with any old carer. They also understand that Tim and I have to work hard to pay for the lifestyle we all enjoy.

Knowing that Tim was with Matthew, I could really have a good time doing *Soldier, Soldier*, even though I experienced bouts of depression throughout. There are scenes in *Soldier, Soldier* that I've since seen but barely remember doing. I had an especially terrible time in Germany. I was really poorly there. It was particularly difficult being ill away from home and Tim, who is always so amazing with me when I'm bad. I really struggled to cope without him, although I was lucky to have a couple of friends in the cast who were really fabulous with me: Lesley Vickerage, who played Captain Kate Butler, and Annabelle Apsion, who played Joy, Tony's wife. The German weather didn't help. It was often so dull, grey and overcast that the only way I could cheer myself up was to go and stand under the huge studio halogen lights in between takes, shut my eyes and pretend it was sunlight.

When my first series of *Soldier, Soldier* ended, I had some very bad news. Mum's doctors had discovered a secondary oral cancer. Mum was faced with a very difficult choice. Either she opted to undergo incredibly invasive surgery or she had six months left to live. The operation involved pulling tissue down from the soft temple, which matches the tissue in the soft palette. It would leave a big indentation in the side of Mum's head. 'If we do the surgery,' her doctor told her, 'you might never talk properly again. You won't look the same again. We don't know what your swallowing will be like.' Apparently, this operation was quite rare in this country, but more common abroad.

Mum, being Mum, said, 'Sod that. Not having that.' We pleaded and pleaded with her, but she said, 'I know I'm only fifty-five, but I think I've had a good run. I've seen my grandson born.'

It was unbearable for all of us, but we had to accept her wishes, which meant that she had an estimated six months to live. Then the hospital rang up. They wanted her to meet a man in his seventies who had been through the operation and come out the other side. Mum went to meet this man and he persuaded her to have the operation. We were so relieved.

On the day of the operation Mum and Dad's beloved dog Howard died. He was fifteen, which is a good age, but it was still devastating. And then Mum was in surgery for thirteen hours, which was a terrible time. Debbie and I waited tensely outside the operating theatre, desperate for news. Then, when we were finally allowed to see Mum, we were too scared to go in because we were so worried about how she would be. We had no idea if she was going to be able to talk again, or how long the recovery period would be.

Eventually, we steeled ourselves and went in to see her. Mum looked like a car crash. It was very painful to see, so God knows what it must have been like for her. Thankfully, after a couple of days, she started to look better. We began to communicate with sign language. Then Mum began to write everything down. One afternoon, she wrote on a piece of paper that she wanted her lipstick. 'That's a good sign!' said the doctor.

A couple of days later, I was sitting by her bed while she was trying to write another request. She shook her pen, but it wouldn't work. 'Argh!' she gurgled in frustration. I looked up, amazed, and her eyes widened in surprise. She had made a noise! We both began to cry because it was the turning point in her recovery. It meant that she would be able to speak again.

Knowing that she could actually make a noise spurred her on and the speed with which she improved astonished everybody. Within a few months she was looking like Joan Collins again, but with a dent in her temple, which she was very conscious of. Eventually, about five years ago, I took her to the girl who does my fillers, and said, 'What do you think about filling this in?'

She sized the dent up and said, 'I think I can make a difference.' She filled it in with Restylane and now it's hardly noticeable. It worked wonders for restoring Mum's confidence.

The surgeons were astounded by Mum's recovery. They took away two-thirds of her soft palette, which is what enables you to talk, so she speaks slightly differently, using the left side of her palette, but everyone's used to it after eighteen years. The key thing is that they got rid of all the cancer. Her surgeon used to show her off to all the student doctors at the hospital as an example of someone who had gone through hell and beaten a very serious disease.

It was a huge relief for the whole family. And it meant that I could go back to film the next series of *Soldier, Soldier* without feeling anxious about Mum. My character Marsha's husband had now been promoted to officer, and my status rose along with his, which was great. But after two series, I started to get a bit bored. 'Now that I'm an officer's wife, all I seem to do is make tuna sandwiches in the kitchen,' I complained to the producers. 'Can Marsha please have something more exciting to do?'

Soon after that, a script appeared in which Marsha entered a talent competition. It definitely livened up the role, and I recorded and performed the Dusty Springfield song 'You Don't Have to Say You Love Me'. When it was aired, they were going to show just a clip of me singing, but in the end they showed the whole song because it was relevant to the plot (one of the characters had an obsession with Marsha and watched her with mad, staring eyes as she did her performance).

The singing storyline continued, with Marsha then becoming a bit of a 'club turn' – it was quite a leap from making tuna sandwiches! Suddenly, characters would say, 'Marsha's at the local club tonight. Let's go along and see her!' But Marsha also had a drink problem. When *Soldier, Soldier* was repeated recently, I had to laugh when I caught an episode in which I'm singing 'Walk on By' and there's a little alcoholic stumble in my step.

Although I can hold a tune, I'm not a great singer, so I told the producers that I wanted to sing mainly Burt Bacharach songs because they're not too complex. Every week I popped off to the recording studio to record a different number, which was really enjoyable. Then, before I knew it, my agent had a call from Simon Cowell, who worked for BMG at the time. He had heard about the episode and wanted to discuss releasing 'You Don't Have to Say You Love Me' as a single around the time the talent contest was aired on TV.

By then, he had signed Robson Green and Jerome Flynn, who both starred in *Soldier, Soldier*, and they had brought out a version of 'Unchained Melody', which sold nearly two million copies. They had followed it up with another single and a best-selling album called *Robson & Jerome*.

'Oh don't be so ridiculous!' my agent said, guffawing. 'You, bring out a single? How naff is that?'

I bristled slightly at that. 'Well, you can look at it two ways,'

I said. 'It is naff in a way, but in another way, I'm thirty-seven and I'll never get a chance like this again. So I'm not saying that I'm going to try to be Aretha Franklin, but I do like the idea of being able to tick that box and tell my grandchildren that I made a single.'

My agent didn't agree and wouldn't go with me to the meeting. Edward, who worked for her, reluctantly came in her place, and my mum came too. Simon Cowell was adorable, absolutely gorgeous. It's funny thinking of him as he is now, a global superstar, when he was just a record company executive then. 'OK,' he said enthusiastically, 'we're going to sign you up for this and we're going to get you an appearance on this and that show and it's all going to be great . . .' He had it all mapped out.

Edward sat beside me with his tongue in his cheek. 'Get lost!' I thought. 'I'm doing this as an experience and I'll regret it if I don't.' In the end, my agent and I parted company over it, which is just one of those things.

There were lots of promotional plans for the single and then suddenly it all went very quiet, for no apparent reason. Then I heard that BMG weren't going ahead with it. I was disappointed, but it wasn't the end of the world; my universe didn't crumble as a result. I did wonder why it had all petered out after so much enthusiasm had been expressed, but I didn't dwell on it.

A couple of weeks later, I was doing a play in Newcastle with my friend Charlie Hardwick (who now plays Val Lambert in *Emmerdale*) when I received a phone call from Virgin Records. 'We'd like to offer you a one-single contract for 'You Don't Have to Say You Love Me,' they said.

'Whoopee!' Off I went to Abbey Road Studios for the day

with my friend Rose. We had to move quite fast because the talent contest episode was going to be aired in November and obviously the single had to tie in with that.

I had a great producer in Mike Batt, whose varied career includes writing 'Bright Eyes', discovering Katie Melua and helping to create the Wombles! Mike decided that I should have a seventy-piece orchestra to accompany me. I remember phoning my dad and saying, 'Dad, I'm recording my own single with the Royal Philharmonic Orchestra in the studio where the Beatles recorded their songs!'

It was the most surreal experience. 'I would never have given up the opportunity to do this!' I thought as I made my way towards the microphone. It was just amazing. When the orchestra started playing, my spine started tingling. I sang two songs: 'You Don't Have to Say You Love Me' and 'Cry Me a River'.

I can't have been very nervous because in the afternoon, after I'd recorded the songs a couple of times, Rose and I went to see *The Bridges of Madison County*, which remains one of my favourite movies to this day. Later on, Jimmy Nail popped in to see how I was doing and Mike Batt played the tracks to him. 'What do you think?' I asked Jimmy.

'Well, at least you're in tune,' he said. That was his entire critique of my songs.

As it turned out, November was an unfortunate time to release a single because it had to compete with all the pre-Christmas novelty songs. Still, I didn't take it seriously; I was just thrilled to have a record out, although I had no idea how gruelling the promotion tour would be. Let me tell you, if you think that pop stars don't work hard, you're wrong. I was absolutely exhausted after just one month's promotion.

I lost loads of weight rushing all over the country doing interviews and personal appearances. The itineraries were mad: on a typical day I woke up, was picked up from my hotel, flew to Aberdeen, flew to Edinburgh, did two shows, flew back down to Heathrow, did a late chat show and answered the same questions over and over again during phone interviews in the car. Virgin had to take on Rose as my PA because I literally didn't have time to wipe my bottom, let alone answer my phone! Having my best friend with me at that time was a joy. It was a real case of 'If it's Tuesday, it must be Belgium!' I never knew where I was.

I was constantly being asked, 'Are you jumping on the Robson and Jerome bandwagon?'

'Well, of course I am!' I would reply, laughing. 'There's no other reason a thirty-seven-year-old bird off the TV would be asked to go to Abbey Road and make a single!'

The worst moment of that month came as we were flying to Glasgow through a terrific storm. There was loads of lightning and even the air stewards were looking perturbed. 'That's it!' I thought. 'First Buddy Holly and the Big Bopper, next Denise Welch. I'm bound to die in a plane crash because I'm a pop star! I'll be for ever sharing headlines with Buddy Holly!' Drama queen? Me?

We were sitting in a London hotel a couple of days after the single had been released when Tony Barker, the publicist, turned up with the midweek charts news. 'You Don't Have to Say You Love Me,' had gone into the top thirty, which was a really good sign, apparently.

At the end of the week, I went home for Matthew's sixth birthday, which we held at a local community play centre on the Sunday. As we were driving home with Matthew and his pals Kit, Jamie and Boothy, who are still his pals to this day, we switched on the radio to hear the Top 40. 'And at number twenty-four is

Jimmy Nail with "Big River",' the announcer said. 'But straight in at number twenty-three is Denise Welch with "You Don't Have to Say You Love Me".'

'Yaarghhh!' screamed the kids.

It was just so random; I was a number ahead of Jimmy! To my delight, the single spent three weeks in the charts. The consensus was that it may have gone higher if it had been released at another time of year, on the back of the huge popularity of *Soldier, Soldier*. But with all the pre-Christmas releases, it may have underperformed. However, I don't think I could have promoted it for a moment longer because I was exhausted by it, and I wasn't in it to become a major recording star. It was just an experience, and a fantastic one.

I had a real giggle a few months later, when I went into a shop and a compilation album caught my eye. It was called something like *The Gold Collection* and both my songs were on it, listed alongside the likes of Lionel Ritchie! It was a mini Aretha Franklin moment.

I never found out why Simon Cowell had been so enthusiastic about promoting me and then went off the boil. Yet I did wonder about it. After all, it's not as if I'd approached him and said, 'Hey, Simon Cowell, can I make a single?' Someone later told me that Robson had been against the idea of him signing two acts from *Soldier, Soldier*, but I don't know if it's true. Something must have changed Simon's mind, though. Otherwise why would he have booked all those shows and then cancelled them? I'm sure Simon's lived to regret it!

I can't say I would have blamed Robson if he were against it. What I do know is that Robson struggled with the notion of his artistic integrity. He had originally talked about naming the *Robson & Jerome* album *Integrity in Tatters*, although I knew that the record company wouldn't allow it! He didn't want to release a single in the first place, but Simon Cowell offered him and Jerome so much money that they couldn't refuse. 'I'm not doing it,' Robson kept saying. 'I'm not going to sing a song in a Santa hat on *TOTP* with fake snow coming down!' Of course, that is pretty much exactly what happened. But if he was struggling to garner some integrity from the situation, it makes sense that he wouldn't like the idea of his mate from *Soldier, Soldier* coming along and releasing her own single. It just made the whole thing even more naff. Remember how gradually all the cast of *EastEnders* seemed to be trying their luck as pop stars at one point! Either way, I got to make a single, so I was happy.

Some people do a job and that job catapults them into the stratosphere, but my career hasn't been like that. When I came out of *Soldier, Soldier*, which was a massively popular show in which I was very well reviewed, I didn't get called for a TV casting for nine months. Nine months! It was weird and worrying. I felt like ringing up all the casting agents and asking, 'What do I have to do to get your attention then?'

It goes without saying that I enjoyed being at home with Matthew and having more time with Tim, although it can be hard to appreciate having time off when you're an actor and you don't know where your next job is coming from. I did a couple of plays, but I was longing for another juicy TV role. Meanwhile, Tim and I started getting involved with Simon Weston's charity, Weston Spirit, which had been set up to help and encourage kids who were going off the rails to get back on the right path.

Simon had been a bit of a Welsh teenage nightmare when he was young, which is why this cause was so dear to his heart. He joined the Welsh Guards at sixteen and served in Berlin, Northern Ireland and Kenya before he went to fight in the

Falklands in 1982, when he was twenty-one. When his ship was bombed and set on fire, he suffered 49 per cent burns and his face was horribly disfigured. He then had to go through more than seventy major operations and procedures. Obviously, this changed his life. After a period of despair and heavy drinking, he picked himself up and started working for charity. Then, in 1988, he set up Weston Spirit for kids aged between sixteen and eighteen.

When the third Weston Spirit youth centre opened in Newcastle a few years later, Tim and I were invited along to the launch. There we met a group of young people who talked about how a year on the Weston Spirit programme had helped them. It was incredibly inspiring. Many of them had never heard the words 'trust' or 'respect' used at home, but now those words were very much part of their everyday vocabulary.

I have always loved working with teenagers and young people. It was already an area that I had decided to focus on when it came to my charity work, although I hadn't done much more than bits and bobs for the local hospital and the occasional appearance at a charity opening in the northeast up until then. So when Simon and his wife Lucy asked us to come on board as patrons, we were very happy to say yes. Weston Spirit was the first major charity we took on and we began to get to know Simon and Lucy. My friend Pam also became involved.

I'm now a patron of twenty-one charities, but I work hands-on for only three or four of them.

The charity that is probably closest to my heart is the GEM Appeal, which was set up by a friend of mine after she discovered that her two sons had the genetic disease Hunter's Syndrome. The GEM Appeal funds research into genetic and metabolic disorders, and Tim and I are the charity's main patrons.

Every year we invite lots of celebrities to a themed ball to try to raise as much money as possible, in the hope that one day cures will be found for at least some of the many genetic and metabolic illnesses that affect the lives of so many children.

For the other charities I support, I will try to attend at least one event a year, but I don't participate actively in the charity. My dad deals with the administrative side of these things for me and when people approach him now about getting me on board, he says, 'If it will help to have Denise on your list of patrons, then of course she would be delighted to, but she can't be actively involved because she's already got her hands full with other charities.'

With Weston Spirit, I would go and see the kids at drop-in centres, and Tim and I also had them over to the house for a meal from time to time. Some of them had never been a guest in someone else's house before. I had a really nice long chat with one young lad and, as he left, he said, 'That's the first time that anybody's ever talked to us without reprimanding us.' I felt so sad for him. When you ask about their families, you wonder how on earth some of these kids stand a chance.

A few years ago, I went to a centre to give out some initiative certificates. Ten kids had earned them, but five of them had reoffended and couldn't be there. Only one set of parents was there. 'Do you have a relationship with your parents?' I asked one boy.

'Well, I don't see my dad, but I talk to my mum sometimes on Facebook,' he said. My heart just bled for him.

It was always quite hard to raise money for kids like these. Teenage charities don't produce the same emotive response in people as, say, a children's charity does, because we've all got a story of some little bastard who's nicked our car radio. But Simon refused to give up on these kids and the charity grew in status and funding. At one point, we had a 100 per cent success rate of non-reoffending. But, sadly, Weston Spirit had to fold in 2008 after financial difficulties beyond Simon's control. I don't know the full details, but it was just such a shame. Still, working with under-privileged teenagers has remained a passion of mine to this day.

Prince Andrew was the president of Weston Spirit, so we met him on several occasions. I vividly remember the first time we met him, when he invited us to his house, Sunninghill Park, in Berkshire, along with thirty of the young people who had come through the programme and were doing really well.

The night before, we stayed in a hotel in the south for one of Tim's golf events. Tim went to bed early and I ended up having a snog with the girlfriend of a comedian who was also at the do. I thought it was the funniest thing. I had never had any kind of feeling whatsoever for girls and it was the first time I'd ever tried kissing one properly. I was drunk, but not really, really drunk, and it just happened. It really surprised me because when Rose and I were cast in a play at drama school where we were supposed to kiss, we had both been appalled at the thought. We kept trying to make ourselves do it, but then we'd back away in dis-gust. When we did finally force ourselves to do it, Rose said, 'Your lips are so much softer than a man's!' and we both fell about laughing.

This time, unfortunately, I was spotted by a mate of Tim, who decided to tell him what he'd seen. Tim was horrified and immediately said that he wasn't coming to Sunninghill with us.

I felt terrible. The last thing I had wanted to do was hurt him. It made me realise that kissing a woman is just as bad as kissing a man, even though most of my girlfriends didn't agree when I told them about it afterwards. They were all amazed that I'd left it until I was in my mid-thirties! But I think men find it threat-ening because they can't compete.

'Look, I was drunk and it was a silly thing to do,' I said. 'I'm so sorry, it meant nothing. Please, please, please, you have to come to Prince Andrew's with us.' I desperately wanted him to be there because Weston Spirit was very important to us and I didn't want him to miss out on this special occasion because of my bad behaviour. After all, we'd seen these kids grow so much and now they were going to Prince Andrew's house, where they'd be making speeches. So I couldn't bear the thought of explaining his absence. What would I say? I felt very guilty.

In the end, he relented and came along. Pam was with us as well. The house was freezing when we arrived. I couldn't believe it! It was so draughty. Prince Andrew came in and found me hugging a radiator and kindly went off to get me a woolly. Just after that, we filed into a room to be formally introduced to him. When it came to Tim's turn, he said, 'Good afternoon, sir. Thank you so much for inviting us. I have to leave now. My wife's a lesbian.' And he left!

Not a muscle on Prince Andrew's face moved. You'd have thought by his expression that Tim had said, 'Isn't it clement for the time of year?' Not, 'I have to leave; my wife is a lesbian.'

So I was left stranded at Prince Andrew's house, feeling very shamefaced. Still, Pam and I went on to have a real giggle with Andrew. I remember being very taken with the fact that there were photos of Sarah Ferguson everywhere, including the toilet. There was Andrew-and-Sarah embossed toilet paper; everything was 'Andrew and Sarah', even though they were divorced. And the toilet impressed me in more ways than one. 'Oh my God,' I thought. 'The Queen has sat on this toilet!' So, in a way, I always feel as if I've sat on the royal throne!

Denise Welch

When I came out of the bathroom, I noticed a really interesting-looking room on my right. Just as I was peeking in, I heard a creaking sound behind me. 'Do you want me to give you a little tour?' said a voice. I turned round to find that I'd been caught snooping by none other than Prince Andrew! He very sweetly showed Pammy and me around the whole house, which was fascinating.

When we left, Pammy said, 'Right then, bye!' Then she added, in her Yorkshire way, 'Now we know where you are, we'll not be strangers!' I laughed all the way home.

The next time I met Prince Andrew, at a lunch in aid of Weston Spirit, we didn't get on quite so well. It was just after Diana had died and we had a bit of an altercation about how the Royal Family had treated her. I was quite vocal in my defence of her. As he walked past Tim on his way out, Prince Andrew said, looking over at me, 'Rather you than me.'

However, he got into my good books again the next time we met, at Buckingham Palace. This time I was there in my role as vice-president of Weston Spirit. There were about fifteen of us and we had lunch in the room with the famous Buckingham Palace balcony, the one where the Royal Family always wave at the crowds.

After lunch, one of the staff came over to have a chat because apparently I'd been skiing with a friend of his. 'Is there anywhere I can have a fag?' I whispered to him. The next thing I knew, someone arrived with one of those old-fashioned silver cigarette boxes, and I took one.

Andrew was going on about what a filthy habit it was, and I was like, 'Bothered!' But then he waved his arm in the direction of the balcony and said, 'Oh for God's sake, you can go out there and have it, if you want.'

A minute later, there I was, on the balcony at Buckingham Palace, where Charles and Diana had that famous kiss, smoking a tab! And Andrew said that I was the first person to have a fag on that balcony! It was brilliant. We even had a bit of a giggle about it. I desperately wanted someone who knew me to walk past the gates of Buckingham Palace at that moment and look up. I just loved the thought of someone pointing and saying, 'Oh my God, is that Denise Welch off *Loose Women* smoking a cigarette on that balcony?'

Chapter Thirteen

For a lot of people, it's a badge of honour to have been in *Coronation Street*, even if only for one scene. Stars who aren't actors, like George Michael and Cliff Richard, have bent over backwards to do a scene, and big actors like Michael Crawford and Sir Ian McKellen have appeared in cameo roles.

Like so many others, I always wanted to do a couple of episodes of *Corrie*. When I left drama school, I wrote to Judi Hayfield, the casting director, saying how much I loved it. I never really got a sniff at it though, except once when I went up for a tiny part. I remember it vividly: I was sitting in the foyer waiting to go in when self-professed womaniser Chris Quinten, who played Brian Tilsley, strutted in.

'Hi,' he said, grinning toothily. 'Chris Quinten.'

'Oh hi, I'm Denise Welch and I'm up for a part in *Corrie*.'

As he swaggered away, he called out, 'Dressing room 236!' Needless to say, I didn't take him up on the offer. I didn't get the part, either.

Years later, I was doing a sitcom called *See You Friday* with Mark Benton and Neil Pearson when my agent called to say that Judi Hayfield was auditioning for a character called Natalie. It was only ever going to be a three-month part because Natalie was to break up Kevin and Sally Webster's marriage and, of course, the Websters were never going to break up permanently.

I remember going into the foyer at Granada and being amazed to see that actresses like Paula Wilcox, Susan Penhaligon and Maggie O'Neill were also trying for the part. 'There's no way I'm going to get this!' I thought. 'These are big names!' Although I'd done *Soldier, Soldier*, I didn't feel I was in their league.

Taking a deep breath, I went in and read for Judi Hayfield and Brian Park, the producer. Judi told Brian that I'd written to her over the years sporadically and made it clear that she was gunning for me, which helped to settle my nerves. She was so friendly and nice that it was like having an auntie in the room. I found that I really gelled with Brian, which also helped, especially when it turned out that he was good friends with Simon Massey, the director I was working with on *See You Friday*. Sandy-haired and Scottish, Brian had a great sense of humour, as I went on to discover, and we've stayed friends to this day.

'But I need to warn you that this part has got a shelf life,' he said.

'Fine!' I thought. 'I'd just love to have a bit part in *Corrie*!'

I was driving past the MetroCentre in Gateshead when I got the call saying that I'd got the part. Oh my God! I raced home to phone my parents. Nothing beats telling your family that you're going into *Coronation Street*.

That night, when I was asked what I was up to, it was amazing to be able to say that I'd just heard that I was going into *Coronation Street*. People were nearly popping champagne corks with glee. It didn't matter that it was only for seventeen episodes, which was only going to take a few weeks to film; it was *Corrie*!

There was a sudden flurry of publicity because it was the first time that *Coronation Street* had cast somebody who was already slightly well known. Before this, the new cast members tended not to have much career prominence, so the press went absolutely bananas and I was invited to appear in character on the front cover of a whole series of magazines.

It was very daunting to walk into the studio for the first time. I was terrified. I had watched *Coronation Street* since I was a child of about five or six, and so many cast members were institutions: Bill Roache (Ken Barlow), Liz Dawn (Vera Duckworth) and Barbara Knox (Rita Fairclough). All legends! I found it really hard to call them by their real names, not their character names, which some people got really iffy about. For instance, Michael Le Vell really doesn't like being called Kevin. I couldn't help thinking, 'Oh come on, Michael, you've played the part for ten years! It's bound to happen!'

In one of my very first scenes, I had to open the door to Rita Fairclough and say, 'Why don't you leave me alone, you ridiculous old cow!' Imagine saying that to the scariest woman in *Coronation Street*! I couldn't sleep the night before, I was so nervous. I was very honoured when Barbara told me later that she loved doing that scene with me. She was also aware of my work, so I was very flattered.

My first few days were really tough. It wasn't an unfriendly environment, but nobody took me on board and showed me around, or directed me to the chart that shows you what to do and when. Suddenly I felt as if I had gone back to school. All my years in the business just meant nothing.

'You're on PSC on Sunday,' someone would say, just like that, with no explanation, and because I'd been in the business for such a long time, I was too embarrassed to ask what PSC was. I had no idea that it stood for 'portable single camera', which meant that the location day was on the street, as opposed to the multi-camera setting in the studio sets. I didn't know what anything meant, so after I'd bedded myself in there, I made a point of explaining everything to the new people who came in. That's something that's very important to Tim as well: to make new people welcome, whether they are young or old.

I used to tell 'them upstairs' that we needed to offer some kind of starter pack for new people, especially the young actors. I never felt that they gave the young actors enough information, or protected them. In my opinion, there should have been a counsellor there to look after them because some of these actors are children when they come into the show and their lives change as soon as their faces hit the screen.

I was in my late thirties when I went into it, having had an element of recognition through other shows, but even I wasn't prepared for how immediately your life changes when you're in something like *Coronation Street*. Suddenly, everybody knows who you are, everywhere you go. Later on, my wedding to Des was watched by 19.5 million people! You rarely get those ratings anymore, with all the five million other channels on air at the same time. So it was quite a shock to the system.

At the start, working on *Corrie* was a lonely experience. It's changed now, but nearly everybody on the programme lived in the Manchester area back then, so they all disappeared in the evenings. Since Tim and I were still living at the Hemmel in Northumberland, I didn't have a home to go to. Instead, I was going back to a little rented flat in Castlefield on my own. Normally, I quite enjoy my own company, especially when I know that I can pick and choose how often to spend time alone (which is almost never!), but during my first three months in *Corrie* I really felt lonely. It was very strange because I'm blessed with many friends and acquaintances and I'm used to being sur-rounded by people.

I was also used to being on location in shows like *Soldier, Soldier*, where everyone was away together, which meant that the cast and crew congregated in the evenings and had dinner and got pissed together. But now the rest of the cast went home at night, leaving me to wander back to my empty flat.

The Victoria & Albert Hotel in Manchester was a meeting point. Occasionally we filmed at the V&A or people held parties there. It was also where actors working at Granada often stayed. So one night I went there and sat in the bar with a drink and a newspaper, pretending that I was waiting for someone. My plan was to say that I'd been let down if someone I knew came in, but no one did. It's so sad to think of it now; I feel quite sorry for myself, as if I were another person. Oh God, I hated those three months, even though I enjoyed playing the part of Natalie. It was a really good role and I had lots of great emotional scenes.

With some characters, you can see a future, but I didn't see one with Natalie. I thought she'd be someone who went in, had an affair and left; someone whose name would be bandied about for years to come during rows between Sally and Kevin. But she turned out to be a character that people loved to hate, which meant that she was good for viewing figures. People just couldn't believe that Kevin Webster was having an affair. All the soap operas tend to ebb and flow, and I think that *Corrie* had been at a low ebb before Natalie came along. Suddenly she was part of an exciting storyline starring Kevin and Sally, and the viewers loved it.

I was thrilled when I was asked if I would extend my contract for another three months. However, I was also incredibly home-sick. At the time, Natalie's house was off the set; it was a real house that we used in Chorlton, and all the scenes of Natalie at home had to be done on a Sunday. So I hardly ever had a chance to get back up to the northeast, where Tim was at home looking after Matthew (thankfully, his work wasn't taking him away for more than a couple of days at a time). Sometimes I went up on a Friday night, but I'd often have to come back on the Saturday night. Matthew was only seven and I really missed him.

Quite soon after I'd agreed to do the extra three months, I was asked to sign for a further six months. Torn between my family and my career, I immediately rang Tim. 'I'm either going to say no, or you and Matthew will have to come down,' I said, 'because I'm just miserable being away from you.' I was adamant that I couldn't bear a whole year of hardly ever seeing them. I missed Matthew terribly.

It was a dilemma. I went to see Judi Hayfield to discuss it with her. 'I know it's difficult for you to say, but if you honestly think that this is going to be a runner, then I will take Matthew out of school and put him in school here,' I told her. 'But I don't want to then be told, "That it's then." I know it's impossible for you to give me a guarantee, but what would you advise me to do, off the record?'

'Off the record, I think it would be advisable for you to do exactly that,' she said.

So Tim was dragged kicking and screaming down to Wilmslow, less than a decade after I'd dragged him from London back to the northeast. He wasn't happy. It wasn't his kind of place at all. 'Wilmslow? I don't want to live in Wilmslow,' he protested. 'It's so posh, they've got their own blooming credit card there! I don't want to drink in a wine bar!' Still, I wanted to be in south Manchester because my auntie Julie lived there, and in the end I managed to persuade him.

I don't know how I would have felt if it had been the other way round because I'm much more selfish than Tim. If he'd said, 'I'm really miserable; I want you to up sticks,' I don't know if I would have agreed to move with our child to a place where I didn't want to live. It was very good of him.

It was a tough decision, but what choice did we have? We were all settled in our lovely home up in the northeast and we really didn't want to sell it. Then Tim had a brainwave. My sister Debbie and her husband Peter were living in a little house in Prudhoe with two kids and another on the way. The house was like a noose round their neck because it was in negative equity and they couldn't sell it. 'Why don't you move into our house until you sell yours?' he suggested. 'You can stay there until Denise finishes *Corrie*. She's only going to be away for a year.' Debbie and Peter thought it was a brilliant idea. We rented a house in Wilmslow and they moved into the Hemmel. They're still there to this day because of course we've never gone back to live there! So it's become our family home, in a way. I love seeing my nieces and nephews growing up there.

Unfortunately, my mental health was very poor during much of my time at *Coronation Street*. I don't blame *Coronation Street* for that; it was just a particularly bad period. Obviously, things weren't helped by the fact that the schedule was really gruelling. Filming four episodes a week (five, by the time I left) is tough going. I was constantly tired and had very little free time, and I wasn't helping myself by having too many at the end of the day at the Old School Granada bar. I had been drinking heavily on and off since the onset of my illness, and my intake had increased dramatically during the third series of *Soldier, Soldier*, which was filmed in Windsor. This wasn't just a case of trying to escape my bouts of depression by drinking; there was a lot of socialising among the cast and crew, as I've said. Either way, by the time I started doing *Coronation Street*, I was knocking it back. I wasn't just drinking a lot either; it was around now that I started to take drugs as well.

Not having touched it or thought about it since I'd been offered it more than ten years before, I tried cocaine again a couple of years before I got the *Corrie* job. It was the night before I went up for a part in a Catherine Cookson drama and I was staying with a girlfriend in London. She and I hadn't seen each other for absolutely ages, so of course we were just 'rabbit-rabbit-rabbit' from the moment we got together. I had to be up early for the casting, but we were still chatting and drinking wine at about one in the morning and neither of us wanted it to stop.

'It's frustrating because I'm not going to see you again for so long, but I'm so tired!' I said.

'Do you know what I've got under the settee?' she said. 'I've got some of that cocaine. I've had it for about a month.'

My eyes widened. 'Do you do it then?' I asked.

'No, not really. It's just that someone asked me to put it in my wallet and never asked for it back.'

'Oh go on then,' I said. We had a little bit and stayed up all night. Then I went skipping off to my audition the next day and got the part.

This ignited my interest in cocaine. Suddenly, I could see its potential for propping me up. After that, I started doing it every now and then, when I was offered it. At first, I only accepted it when I was tired and needed a little 'livener'. Then I occasionally did it just for the fun of it. Very occasionally I used to take some home on my weekends off during the third series of *Soldier, Soldier* and Tim and I would do a little bit recreationally. Later down the line, I started buying it regularly. There were plenty of people in my life doing cocaine who could link me up with a dealer.

I find this difficult to write about because it will be the first time my family finds out how bad things were. As time went on, I became convinced that cocaine alleviated my symptoms when I was ill. The truth is that when the depression is that thick, nothing can make it go away, but I began to use it as a crutch to help me get through. It was so stupid of me to fall into that way of thinking because there is nothing more painful and depressing than a big cocaine comedown. I always felt worse the next day, but I'd do anything for temporary respite.

One line of cocaine gave me a feeling of normality; it did what antidepressants took five weeks to do. Of course, the effect would only last for forty minutes, so it was very short-term relief, but then I'd think, 'Just one more line, just one more . . .' The next morning I felt terrible again, so it was a vicious circle. What made things worse was that when you're doing cocaine, you want to drink all the time as well. I have a very addictive personality and one thing leads to another.

I suppose I can blame much of my drink and drug intake on my depression; I was often self-medicating, for all the good it did. There were times when my mental health was terrible and it had nothing to do with the cocaine, although that was obviously making it worse. But when my illness was really bad, it felt like the only way to get through it was to take cocaine. Sometimes I did it in the day as well as the evening, either because I'd been out all night and I had a whole day of work stretching ahead of me, or because I was so depressed.

In my warped mind, I was certain that cocaine was enabling me to feel better and to function. And I did function – obviously I did, or I wouldn't have been a successful actress. Still, I'm not going to claim that my times with drugs were purely about self-medicating. Taking cocaine was sometimes recreational. I felt that I was doing a lot, but when I talk to some people, I realise that I was quite a lightweight. I discussed it with Tara Palmer-Tomkinson once, when we both appeared on a game show called *Russian Roulette*, which was presented by Rhona Cameron. Bizarrely, if you got a question wrong, the ground opened up and you plunged screaming down into the bowels of ITV, where you landed on a mattress. Amazingly, I won, which meant a nice bit of money for my charity!

Before we started filming, I asked Tara, whom I like very much, how much cocaine she was doing at the height of her addiction. She told me that she used to take eight grams a night, pop two or three Rohypnol to get herself to sleep, wake up at 2 p.m., have a cup of tea and a piece of toast, and then start taking cocaine again. That's proper addiction! Thank God she's through it now and looks amazing.

It's one thing experimenting with cocaine when you're very young, but I was really quite old to be getting into that lifestyle. After a night caning it, you have very poor sleep, if any at all, which takes its toll when you're nearly forty. There were times when I would go straight to work after being up all night. Trying to function on no sleep was hell and would make me ten times more depressed. So then the only way I could see to feel better was to get some more cocaine to help me through the day.

I started lying about how much I was taking it. Tim knew that I dabbled at parties, but he had absolutely no idea that I was doing it to the extent that I was. I would be very sneaky about when I'd do it and I'd conceal that I'd been out all night by saying I'd fallen asleep on the settee or something like that. I became very, very clever at lying.

My growing dependence on cocaine meant that I put myself in some incredibly dangerous situations. Sometimes my safety was less important to me than having a wrap of cocaine in my hand-bag. My desire to top up my supply would outweigh everything else. I was always scared of running out. It didn't matter to me if someone saw me waiting on the corner of the street for a strange car to pull up with a delivery. On the pretext of going out to get cigarettes, I would leave the house at midnight to drive eight or nine miles to some dark street to meet a drug dealer.

One night I was so terrified of experiencing a comedown that I found myself sitting alone in my car in a dark backstreet in Moss Side at three o'clock in the morning, waiting for a dealer to show up, because that was the only place he would agree to meet me. I shudder to think about it now. People are murdered in Moss Side at three o'clock in the morning! It was absolute madness. What the hell was I doing? I often found myself with the wrong people in the wrong place at the wrong time.

My plan was to go home, do some more cocaine and be back on the *Coronation Street* set in four hours' time, at 7 a.m. When I got back, I sat alone in my lounge, with Tim and Matthew asleep upstairs, and laid out a line of coke on the coffee table. I knew I had to keep going; I had to stay awake, because I'd feel so much worse if I went to bed and had even an hour's sleep. I felt so empty and alone in the stillness of the night. I fought the urge to cry as I rolled up a banknote and inhaled a line of coke, which instantly began to numb the pain. Feeling better, I began to potter around, doing little household chores until it was time to shower and change for work at around 5.30 a.m.

I got myself into some terrible situations. One particular disaster started with a few drinks at the Television and Radio

Industries Club (TRIC) Awards in London. I was at a table with Brian Park and various other people. We'd all had a few to drink, as you do at these awards, and especially that night because they weren't being televised.

Adam Rickitt had recently joined the show, taking over the role of Nick Tilsley. He had hit the screen a month before and he was totally unused to the attention. A youngster from an upper-middle-class family in Cheshire, he had never been subjected to anything like it before; he had certainly never been papped before. So I thought it was unfair when I heard that he'd been hauled over the coals for giving the finger to some paparazzi in Manchester, after someone with a camera had jumped out at him and said something unpleasant to him. 'How dare you give him a hard time?' I said to the producers at my table. 'It's absolutely outrageous! He's just a kid!'

Enraged, I got so drunk that I only have flashes of memory after that. We all went back on the train, I know that, because I can remember being at a railway station at one point. The next thing I knew, it was three o'clock in the morning and I woke up on the settee in the sitting room of a house I didn't recognise, with someone's coat over me. 'Oh my God, where am I?' I thought in a panic. It was a terrible moment because it was 3 a.m., I hadn't gone home and I had no idea where I was.

After I'd crept across the room and inspected the photos on the mantelpiece, I realised that I was in the home of one of the *Corrie* scriptwriters. Ironic, really, because I was thinking at the time, 'You couldn't write this!' It seemed a good moment to leave, but when I tried to open the front door, it was locked. I tried the back door, but that was also locked. 'What the hell am I going to do?' I thought. 'I don't know even know which part of the country

I'm in!' I ended up having to tiptoe upstairs, past the teenager's bedroom and into the writer's bedroom, where he was in bed with his wife. I gently shook him awake and said, 'Can you let me out? Please get me a taxi!' How embarrassing! Needless to say, it didn't take long before everyone at work found out about it.

I was working so hard and Tim and I were spending so much time apart that it started causing real problems in our marriage. It didn't help that my depression drove me to drink more and do drugs and cause arguments. We began having terrible, destructive, alcohol-fuelled fights, real humdingers, although they never took place when Matthew was in the house. Alcohol was a major factor. We very rarely had massive rows when we were sober; all our arguments in those days were fuelled by alcohol and we fought about ridiculous things.

'Why did you do such-and-such four years ago at so-and-so's party?'

'Well, I saw you do such-and-such!'

'No, I didn't!'

'Yes, you did!'

We have the same old disputes today after a drink and they are never resolved.

The arguments never became violent, but I was impossible to argue with because I would never shut up, so it was very frustrating for Tim. After a really bad row, he would get so annoyed that he'd wait until I was asleep and then throw buckets of cold water all over me to get me back. When I woke up shrieking and moved to another bed, he'd wait until I was asleep again before throwing another bucket of water on me. It was surreal, like living through *The Poseidon Adventure*!

I would never say I was the perfect wife, not in a million

years. There's no doubt that I've been hard to live with! One night, I'd been out judging Mr Gay UK in Leeds with Sir Ian McKellen, or 'Serena' as everyone calls him. Funnily enough, the compère that night was Jane McDonald, whom I didn't really know then, but I'm now on the *Loose Women* panel with. That was also the night I met Chris Biggins, Neil, Nick and Paul, who all remain my dearest friends to this day. I was with my gay friends and we all got absolutely ratted. We partied into the night and it was such fun that I didn't want it to end, so I said to everyone, 'Come on, let's all go back to Wilmslow!'

When I say everyone, I mean *everyone*! All kinds of people came with me, from members of the cast and crew of *Changing Rooms* to a load of Mr Gay UK contestants. We descended on the King's Arms pub in Wilmslow, two doors down from our house, where Tim was having a quiet drink. Poor Tim! Since Matthew was staying with a friend, I took everyone back to the house, despite Tim's protestations. He was in a foul mood by now because he had been drinking whisky, which brings out the worst in him. A tussle began: he wanted everybody out and I wanted them to stay. We began to argue and the next thing I remember is trying to smash a lampshade over his head.

He'd had enough. 'Everybody get out of this house, NOW!' he shouted. It was awful.

I remember standing there and shouting, 'But you can't throw people from *Changing Rooms* out of our house!' These poor people found themselves in a garden in Wilmslow, with nowhere to stay.

After they'd gone, he started throwing water over me and just wouldn't stop. Eventually, I had to get in the car, drive to the V&A hotel in Manchester and pretend that I'd just come from a swimming pool party!

Another night, in the northeast, we started arguing at dinner and Tim was so angry with me by the time we got home that he punched out every square of glass in the French windows in the front room. He cut his hand very badly and I was still so angry with him that I remember thinking, 'I'd like you to die now; I would actually like it if you died!' But, of course, I couldn't let him die, so I had to tie a tourniquet around his hand and drive him to the hospital. He still hasn't got full movement back in that hand.

We just don't have fights like that anymore. We're too old now; we just can't be bothered. There's something quite nice about getting older in that sense. Our relationship is much calmer and more harmonious, although there's life in the old dogs yet, as we always chuckle to one another.

After two years on *Corrie*, I was very honoured to become a barmaid at the Rovers Return. Of course, the reality of working behind a bar in a fictitious pub is that you spend an awful lot of time trying to find different ways of emptying an ashtray in the back of the shot. The problem is that you have to be there while everybody else's story is going on, so it was just like being a well-paid extra a lot of the time. It was incredibly tedious if you weren't in the storyline, so to relieve the boredom, Roy Barraclough, Jane Danson and I used to invent crazy subplots and lesbian love stories behind the bar. We had to do something, or we would have gone mad, just standing around for hour upon hour, pretending to look busy.

The end of August 1997 was a strange time for me. First, Princess Diana died. I was devastated because I just adored her and felt an empathy with her because of her mental illness, even though hers didn't manifest itself in the same way that mine did. It didn't matter whether the origins of our illness were different or not, the reality of the illness was the same, and I really felt for her. I never met her, but I recognised her dead-eyed look when I saw her at functions.

When her illness came to light, people used to say she was weak. I couldn't have disagreed more. 'You have no idea what it's like to have a mental illness and stand up and do what she does as a public figure,' I'd say to them. 'She's not weak, she's strong.'

Diana died at a time that should have been really exciting for me because my first scenes as a barmaid at the Rovers Return were being screened, there was lots of interest in my new role in the papers and my family was very proud. But the day she died, I completely went to pieces. It was a Sunday and on Sundays we did location scenes. This particular Sunday, my scenes were in Firman's Freezers with Michael Le Vell. It was one of those dark days with grey skies and it was chucking it down. I felt really upset all day.

Everything seemed so surreal. In the green room at *Corrie*, everyone was going about their normal business; some people were even laughing. I just couldn't get to grips with it. 'Princess Diana has died,' I thought. 'Why aren't they crying? How can everything just be the same?' Amanda Barrie and I were the only people who seemed visibly upset. Then I had to go and do a scene with Michael, who was not the best person to be upset around. It was a horrible day.

The following evening, Sally Whittaker and I were due to be presenting an award at the TV Quick awards ceremony. I phoned our producer and said, 'Obviously the awards will be cancelled, won't they?'

'No, they're not being cancelled and you have to go,' he said.

My heart sank. It may sound ridiculous, but it was almost as if somebody in my family had died and people were making me go on as normal. I felt very weird when I arrived at the ceremony. The only way I could deal with it was to get some wine down me. I know: excuses, excuses . . . Anybody who hasn't experienced depression would find it hard to understand, but I'm not looking for sympathy. I just needed something to anaesthetise the pain and help me get through the evening.

Brian gripped my hand through the minute's silence for Diana. I had to force myself not to dwell on her death because a few minutes later, Sally and I had to go on stage and present an award. It all felt very strange. To make things even weirder, David Easter suddenly arrived at our table, looking like something out of *Thunderbirds* – Troy Tempest, as Tim calls him.

'Who's this?' Brian asked.

'It's my ex-husband,' I slurred, hardly able to believe my eyes. It was a shock to see him after so long. Why the hell was he coming up to say hello? Still, I was polite and introduced him to everyone. Soon he moved on to another table, much to my relief.

By the time we reached the after-show party at the Embassy Club, I had sobered up. Since I hadn't seen David for a while, I'd assumed he'd gone home. But then he took my arm as I was coming out of the toilets. 'Can I have a word?' he said.

Seeing this, my friend Matthew Marsden, who was in *Corrie* at the time, came up and asked if I was all right.

'Of course she's all right!' David snapped. 'That's my fucking wife, you c***!'

'I think you will find that it's your *ex*-wife,' Matthew said, 'and I'm talking to *her*, not to *you*.' At this point, David lunged at Matthew.

Brian dashed over to us. 'I don't want to interfere, but there's a line of press at the bar,' he warned.

'David, can we just stop this, please?' I said angrily. It was as if we had spun back ten years, within seconds. 'I will happily talk to you, but will you please come and sit over here?'

So we sat down together and David began to go over the past. As he talked, I thought, 'Oh my God! You have a completely different view of our relationship to me.'

I was already aware that he did not remember our relationship the way I did. About six years earlier, I had picked up the *Sun* to find an article that quoted David talking about the termination that he had urged me to have. But I didn't recognise this account of what had happened. According to the article, I'd said, 'I'm pregnant,' and he'd reacted by saying, 'Oh my God, that's brilliant!' Then I'd apparently said, 'I don't want it. I'm having an abortion.' It was unbelievable stuff, just a load of rubbish.

In order to make the point about me being some kind of wayward lass, the photo the paper used to illustrate the article was a publicity shot from the daft farce that I'd done called *A Bedfull of Foreigners*, in which I'd played 'Ooh, la la!' Simone, the French stripper. At the end of the play, Simone wore a nun's habit that was split up the back to show her stockings and suspenders, and David was quoted leading the public to believe that this was how I appeared when he walked through the door at night. 'I'd go home and she'd be all dressed up, waiting for me,' it said. It was bonkers!

Sitting in the Embassy Club, listening to him blather on about what had gone wrong in our marriage, I realised that I would never get used to David's way of thinking and seeing. Maybe I would have doubted my version of events if my friends and family hadn't witnessed everything; perhaps David's problem was that, having few friends, there was nobody to remind him of the truth.

I was taken aback when he started to cry over how much he missed Auntie Cynthia. He accused me of not being concerned about how he felt about her. 'Wow,' I thought. 'It's ten years since we split up, so what the hell are you talking about?' I'm not disputing that he adored Cynthia, my dad's sister, who died when she was fifty-seven. She was a wonderful person and Debbie and I adored her too. She and David had got on well because she had only ever seen his good side, but to cry about her now? It seemed very odd.

David told me that I had driven him to drink, which also surprised me, since he didn't drink when I was with him. Or maybe he did, but just not in front of me. I reminded him that I used to beg him to have a drink to relax, or to stay out longer, because I didn't want to go home, but he had always refused. 'No, you made me drink,' he insisted. 'And you were unfaithful to me!'

Things were getting quite heated and Brian said, 'Can we please take this outside? You're attracting too much attention.'

Mal Young, the producer who had given David the job in *Brookside*, said, 'Let's take this back to the hotel.' So Mal, David, my friend Pam and I went back to Mal's hotel, where David and I spent the next few hours talking things through in Mal's bathroom while Mal and Pam died of boredom in the bedroom. When we eventually emerged, they were both asleep. The next day, a rumour swept around Granada that Mal had enjoyed a three-up with Denise Welch and her friend Pam!

I left feeling sorry for David. He was just so wrong about our relationship. I haven't seen him since that night, more than ten years ago, but honestly I hope that he has conquered his demons and found happiness.

Over the years, people have asked me whether I regret my relationship with David. The answer is that, despite everything,

I don't regret it. I wouldn't be the person I am today without having had the experiences I've had, and I suspect that I wouldn't be with Tim if I hadn't been through what I went through with David. Anyway, I try to only regret the things I haven't done, not the things I have done.

Chapter Fourteen

I can't eat when I'm clinically depressed. The idea of food makes me feel physically sick. Of course, you don't eat on cocaine either, so I went through major weight swings in my addicted years. At times, I was completely undernourished. I was always vomiting and saying that I had a stomach bug. My appetite disappeared. My depression, combined with drink, drugs and a relentless schedule, became worse and worse.

God knows what my colleagues thought. I had talked about post-natal depression publicly and been quite open about it, but I didn't discuss it with anyone at work. Over the years, I've hopefully helped to remove some of the stigma and the taboo surrounding depression, but I didn't feel that people would understand back then.

The way I saw it, if I'd said that I had a heart problem, everyone would fuss round me and say, 'Oh you poor thing, you can't come into work!'

However, if I'd said that I was depressed or having a nervous breakdown, then people would say, 'Hey, we're all depressed by the workload. You're not the only one!'

We were working incredibly long hours, we were all very stressed and none of us was seeing enough of our families so I felt I couldn't say anything. I hated the thought of people dismissing my illness as an excuse and thinking, 'Oh yes, she's off with "exhaustion".'

It's difficult to assess the difference between an extreme period of depression and a nervous breakdown, but finally I did have a breakdown, in early 1999. It was more than depression. I experienced incredible anxiety and had all-night panic attacks. It was awful because there was panic raging inside me for no logical reason. I didn't know what I was afraid of; it was a continual fear of something inexplicable.

After a night of terror and cold sweats, I'd drag myself up in the morning, fraught with anxiety, weighed down by a thick, black depression, and I'd be sick. Vomiting took away the blackness and nervousness, if only for three seconds, so it was actually a relief when it was happening. Sometimes I would make myself sick in the hope that the physical impulse of vomiting would give me a few seconds away from the pain in my head. That's why, although I've never cut myself or self-harmed, I can understand the reasoning behind it, the idea of moving the pain on to something else.

Then I would drag myself into work. What compounded the illness and kept it going was the fact that I felt I had to go to work, no matter what. It was stupid of me to think I was indispensable because *Coronation Street* wouldn't have fallen to pieces without me, but unfortunately those of us who have been in the business since the year dot are driven by this strong sense of the show having to go on.

In the past, I'd been incredibly poorly physically, but still gone on stage. One night when I was doing *There's a Girl in My Soup*, I had a temperature of 104°F. I was vomiting, shaking and I had diarrhoea. They had to put buckets on both sides of the stage and I filled them up between scenes. In fact, only recently, I did *Loose Women* with a sick bucket under the desk – the day Robbie Williams came on the show. Well, there was no way I was going to miss Robbie, was there?

Of course, it doesn't have to be that way. There are some people who will phone up and say they're poorly after losing an eyelash, and amazingly the show continues without them. But being an integral part of the *Coronation Street* machine, it didn't occur to me not to go in.

I was very good at hiding my illness. I see things I've done on TV or look at myself in magazines, knowing that on those particular days I was in a black pit, and yet you would never know it. However, Tim and my mum can always look at me across a crowded room and tell how I'm feeling. There were many times when I'd seem normal to other people, but Mum would come up afterwards and say, 'You're not well, are you?'

Nadia, who was my make-up artist on *Waterloo Road*, noticed it last summer, when I had a couple of bad days, as I still occasionally do. 'Your eyes are usually very vibrant, but for the last two days there's been a kind of deadness about them,' she said. That was the first thing my mum always noticed too.

So it was really hard, just getting through and trying to pretend I was OK. Even some of my close family didn't realise quite how bad it was.

There was a time when I was so poorly and struggling so hard to stay afloat that I arranged to meet my dealer outside the studio in the middle of a scene. It sounds ridiculous really, but I felt so desperately ill that I couldn't bear the idea of not having some cocaine on me, just in case. It wasn't just any old scene either – it was Betty Turpin's eightieth birthday party! I cringe when I think back to it.

I needed an excuse to leave the set. 'What can I say to get myself out of here for enough time to meet my dealer?' I thought. Since it was a male director, I decided that something girly would do the trick, so I said that I had cystitis and needed twenty minutes to get myself together. I was counting on the fact that most men hate any reference to that sort of thing, and I was right: he immediately let me go.

I rang my dealer, walked off set, sneaked out of the *Coronation Street* building and slipped down a nearby side street to meet him. It was a huge risk because I was a major personality at the time and there were often paps outside the building, as well as members of the public, not to mention the police. But I went anyway because I was terrified of not being able to lift the dark, heavy feeling I was experiencing. It was so stupid! When you're pissed and on coke, you simply forget how famous you are, so you put yourself in crazy situations without thinking it through. If you've run out of what you need, there's a compulsion to score, even though you could easily be found out.

Back in the studio, I nipped into the loo to have a line and went back on set feeling ten times better, almost normal. I knew it was wrong and I was constantly wracked with worry, but I couldn't stop it. One of the most awful things was waking up in random houses with a bunch of people that I would never normally mix with. Sometimes I couldn't really remember who they were because the night before was just a hungover blur in my mind. It was scary. I'd feel totally disgusted with myself: 'Argh! I'm in my late thirties and I'm in an apartment in Notting Hill with people that I don't know!' Like most people who do coke, I spent a lot of time berating myself. It was just horrendous; it makes me feel ill to think of it now. All the while, I was this adored public person. I was lucky that nothing really bad happened to me.

I would hasten to add that at no point in my addicted years did I ever put my child in jeopardy. My sister would probably disagree and argue that although I was physically there, I was mentally absent, but the point is that Matthew was always safe. Whenever I was away or unwell, I always made sure that he was with Tim.

Cocaine didn't make me a bad person. I didn't become horrible to people. OK, I hated it when my family told me I was drinking too much; that would make me very defensive. It's the same with all addicts. You know what you're doing and you know it's wrong, but you don't want anybody to tell you off about it. There was a lot of denial and subterfuge. So it was a pretty grim time, in lots of ways. The mad thing was that if I was feeling good, I'd want to feel even better, so I'd have some more cocaine, even though it made me feel terrible in the morning. Finally, it came to a point where I couldn't go on anymore. I was jeopardising my health and happiness. Something had to give.

By now, Brian and I were good friends. So when he started planning to leave *Coronation Street*, I told him that I was ready to leave as well. Brian was a very successful producer and was setting up Shed Productions with a couple of other people. He'd gone to ITV with an idea about a women's prison series and they'd snatched his hand off, even though the concept was pretty much sketched out on a napkin.

Brian and I met in Soho House in London and he told me that the series would be called *Jail Birds*. It went on to become *Bad Girls*. Would I like to play a bisexual character in the series? I loved the idea. 'That sounds fantastic, just perfect!' I said, swept away by the moment. But it wasn't perfect at all because filming would be in London and Tim said that he didn't feel we could move Matthew again. I began to fret. I wanted the part, but it meant being away from home again. What should I do? I started to get really worried about it.

Then fate intervened. Eight episodes of *Bad Girls* had already been commissioned and the timing meant that I would be able to fulfil my existing *Coronation Street* contract and move straight on to filming it in London. But ITV suddenly decided that they wanted to make twelve episodes instead of eight because they had a lot of faith in the *Bad Girls* project. Unfortunately, this would mean me coming out of my *Corrie* contract early in order to film all twelve episodes. What's more, Brian, as the existing *Corrie* producer, couldn't be seen to be procuring me out of a contract. 'Well, I can't do it then,' I said, when he told me about this latest development.

A couple of hours later, I was told that Caroline Reynolds wanted to see me the following day. Caroline was the producer who was taking over from Brian on *Corrie*, and I'd already spoken to her about how I wanted to leave the show because I was finding it too restricting being a barmaid. I wondered what she was going to say to me.

She was smiling when I went in to see her. 'Look, I know you said you wanted to leave, but we really don't want you to,' she said. 'In fact, we would like you to become the landlady of the Rovers Return.'

'Oh my God,' I thought. 'The LANDLADY?!'

'It'll be a very different experience. We'll endeavour to get you out of the pub as much as possible,' she went on. 'But we need you to sign for eighteen months.'

I went home to talk it over with Tim and we decided that I would do it. It was quite an amazing prospect. I'd only gone into

Corrie for three months and now I was following in the footsteps of Annie Walker and Bet Lynch! How could I turn it down? It was a huge honour.

The phenomenon that is *Coronation Street* sometimes amazed me. I remember Michael Crawford coming into the green room after he'd done a cameo. He was really, really big at the time and yet he was so excited to meet us. 'This is bizarre,' I thought.

It struck me again when I went to a recording of an *Audience With . . .* type of show at some TV centre with my great friend Steven. I was walking through a big crowd, saying hello to the people I knew as I went, when suddenly, in my peripheral vision, I saw someone hurtling towards me like a streak of lightning, stretching out his arms and screeching, 'Oh my God!'

My heart began to race. 'Walk quickly, walk quickly!' I told myself, because I thought it was going to be what's known as a 'window-licker' type of fan. But it was only Sir Cliff Richard! He's absolutely besotted with the show – he never misses an episode – so he was behaving like an everyday member of the public. It was just bizarre to have Cliff reacting like I was the big star and he was just a fan.

I had some very good storylines and great fun as landlady, especially my days with Phil Middlemiss and Lee Warburton. I also made a good friend in Kevin Kennedy, aka Curly Watts, and we're still close to this day. But it was extremely hard work. I was nearly always in four episodes a week, which meant getting into work at 7 a.m. and staying until 7 p.m., plus there were often pre-shoots – preparation for shoots – when I had to arrive on set even earlier. It was just ridiculous. It was very good financially, much better than it is these days, but I had very little time off. I often felt crushed by tiredness.

When I got my script for each episode, I'd go through it to see how many scenes I was in and who I'd be working with. If there was a colon by your name – a double dot, as we called them – it would mean that you weren't speaking in the scene. Sometimes I'd look through a script and see scene after scene in which I wouldn't be speaking; in other words, hours and hours of washing up ashtrays stretching out in front of me. You cannot imagine the absolute boredom of it. A scene in the cornershop felt like going on location. Oh my God, what joy! Every time I did a scene at the Barnes' home or went to Sally Webster's house for a chat, I was in heaven. Anything, anything to avoid being behind the bar.

So it was a nice diversion to be asked to appear as a guest on a lunchtime chat show called *Loose Women*. It was in the days when Kaye Adams, Nadia Sawalha and Carol McGiffin were on the panel. *Corrie* also allowed me to co-present the show with them one day, which made a change from washing up glasses.

In the following weeks, I started to wake up with an impending sense of doom, a terrible sick feeling in my stomach at the thought of the day to come. 'I just can't do this,' I'd be thinking. 'I don't want to go to work.' After about a year, I thought, 'I'm going to have to leave.'

My sensible side said, 'What do you think you're doing? You're the landlady of the Rovers Return, people would kill for this role!' But I had to follow my gut instincts.

The production team was very supportive; they didn't beg me to stay. They were disappointed, but they understood. Then, just after I'd handed in my notice, I discovered, at the age of forty-two, that I was pregnant with Louis. I thought, 'Oh my God, have I done the right thing financially? Should I go back cap in hand and ask if I can reverse my decision?' I battled with it, but eventually I decided that leaving *Coronation Street* really was the right thing to do.

I had never wanted to have just one child, an only child, but my illness and my fear of feeling even worse after another bout of post-natal depression made me think twice about having more children. I was terrified of a repeat of what had happened when Matthew was first born. Tim and I never sat down and made a conscious decision not to have another child, but it was kind of accepted between us. Anyway, Matthew was a very happy only child. Tim and I always made sure that he was 'only, not lonely' by filling the house with his pals and cousins whenever possible. Funnily enough, he had no hankering for a sibling. I think he was put off by seeing his friends having horrible battles with their brothers and sisters.

Although the pregnancy wasn't planned and it wasn't discussed, when I got to about forty-one, my biological clock started saying, 'It's now or never!' I seemed to have no control over it. I tried to suppress my broody feelings. 'It's not practical,' I thought, 'and Tim doesn't want another child because he doesn't want to lose me to depression again.' Yet I became slightly lax when it came to contraception, although that was partly because I thought I probably wouldn't get pregnant anyway, what with being in my early forties and having been a bit of a boozer and a caner.

It happened one weekend when Tim and I were in Amsterdam. Since Tim had never been there before, whereas I'd been and loved it, I arranged to take him there for the weekend. When I was doing *Soldier, Soldier* in Germany, we were so near Holland that we used to pop over to Amsterdam quite a bit, so I knew it well and was looking forward to showing him the red-light area and the sex shops and all those daft things.

Although I don't like marijuana, Tim used to enjoy a smoke

in his younger days, so we went into a cafe to have a joint while we were there. Of course, I made the typical English tourist's mistake of forgetting that we don't put as much in a joint in England as they do in Holland. Those ready-rolled joints in the Amsterdam cafes are like bloody rocket fuel! Tim got stuck in and smoked it like a cigarette and although I only had a couple of puffs, I was so unsteady on my feet a few minutes later that I could hardly walk out of the cafe.

We'd bought some tickets for a live sex show in the evening, but when we went back to the hotel, I started vomiting really badly. I was just stoned out of my head. Tim couldn't believe the state I was in after just two puffs; I was definitely too poorly to go out. He was gutted because he had never been to a live sex show before and was looking forward to it. But he didn't want to go on his own. It's a completely different thing to go on your own to a sex show; whereas going as a couple is something you have to do if you're a tourist in Amsterdam!

I woke up at God knows what time the next morning to find him flicking through the naughty channels on our hotel TV. I felt guilty, so I said to Tim, 'Go on then; pull my nightie down when you've finished!'

That was Louis. Tim always said, 'Don't you ever tell that story on *Richard & Judy*!' So I didn't tell it on *Richard & Judy*, but I did tell it on *Loose Women*!

If I remember correctly, Tim went away to work when we got back, so Amsterdam was literally the one time in that month that Louis could have been conceived. It was obviously meant to be. Louis was born in March 2001, and I was forty-three in May.

It was really weird because a fortnight after the weekend in Amsterdam, I just knew. Without saying anything to Tim, I went out and bought a pregnancy test. It was that whole thing all over again: in two minutes your life could change! I didn't dare to look at the stick for at least ten minutes. When I saw the positive line, I was totally shocked. I went through a complete range of emotions, from joy to fear and back again.

Tim was watching Wimbledon on television in the lounge. I walked in and said, 'I'm pregnant.' He didn't say anything because it sent him into a state of total shock, not least because he was nearly fifty. We just sat and watched a whole tennis match in silence.

For a while, he wasn't happy at all. He thought that I'd tricked him into getting me pregnant by taking him to Amsterdam. 'Darling,' I said. 'Not being funny, but you would have shagged me in wellies in the kitchen here. I didn't have to take you to Amsterdam for you to shag me, let's be honest!'

He didn't say, 'I don't want you to have it.' He never said, 'Have an abortion,' even though he was understandably worried on so many counts. He was worried about the baby because I was in my forties, and he was desperately worried that I was going to be ill again. He was very worried about being nearly sixty when his child was ten, and he was worried about starting again and going back to square one, especially now that Matthew was eleven and gaining a little independence. I don't think he properly became excited until I actually had Louis. That's not saying that he was so against it that we had a miserable pregnancy. We didn't at all. But I know that he would admit to having reservations all the way through.

On the other hand, I was very excited. After my initial wobble, I was really glad that I was pregnant. I instantly stopped drinking and taking drugs and I just seemed to bloom all over again. For the second time I was struck by the wonder of it all and the miracle of birth. All the same, I was obviously very concerned about having a child in my forties. I spoke to our very good friend Gordon Falconer, who is an amazing gynaecologist, and he suggested that I have an amniocentesis, the test for congenital problems such as Down's syndrome.

I decided to take his advice. I needed to find out if there was anything wrong with this baby because it's best to be prepared. So I went ahead and waited anxiously for the results. I don't know what I would have done if the test had uncovered a genetic abnormality, but as it happened, it was all fine, and it was another boy. Fortunately, I was never bothered about having a girl, perhaps because Debbie has two girls. I was just so thrilled that there was nothing wrong, or so we thought.

Gordon and I also discussed the birth and he was very happy to agree to an elective c-section. I wanted a caesarean because I wanted everything about the birth to be different to how it had been with Matthew. It was nothing to do with being 'too posh to push'; I simply didn't want any memories of the past to set something off in me. 'That's not a problem at all,' Gordon said, because he's such a wonderful person.

Mothers usually get excited about telling existing children that a new baby is coming, but I was worried about telling Matthew because I didn't know what his reaction would be. He was eleven at the time. 'If there was anything in the world that you could have, what would it be?' I asked him.

'A scooter, an orangutan or a baby,' he said.

'Well, it's not the orangutan or the scooter,' Tim said.

Matthew burst into tears with happiness, and then we burst into tears. It was brilliant that he was so excited, and we got him a scooter anyway. Sadly, we had to draw the line at the orangutan.

I was also worried about telling Mum and Dad. I couldn't be excited until they were excited as well because I've always had this childlike desire for parental approval, even though they've made so many mistakes themselves. It's a funny thing: I just want everybody to approve of what I'm doing. But I was terrified that they would say, 'What the bloody hell have you gone and done that for?' It would have been an understandable reaction because my depression had caused them a lot of anxiety and it had been very painful for them to see me suffering so badly. But during this time, there were more periods of wellness, which is why I didn't consider not having the baby, so of course they were pleased when I called them with the news. They were worried, but really pleased. 'Now I can be pleased too,' I thought, which was ridiculous really.

The other person I was anxious about telling was my best friend Rose, who had been through four failed IVF treatments. A year younger than me, Rose had discovered that her fallopian tubes were completely shot to pieces, so I was absolutely dreading telling her that I was pregnant. It made it worse that my pregnancy had been totally unintentional, while she'd gone through all this agony with no baby at the end of it. Still, I had no choice but to tell her.

It was just horrendous and I spent ages trying to find my moment. Being my best friend, she was of course wonderful about it when I finally came out with it, but inside it must have been killing her. However, much to my joy, four months later she became pregnant. I was in the green room at *Coronation Street* when she phoned and said she was pregnant. It was just so amazing! I was thrilled that we were both pregnant at the same time.

I had only told close family, Rose and Brian about my pregnancy, warning them not to tell a soul because I wanted to get the timing of the announcement right. Then one of the newspapers left some flowers on my doorstep and a note saying,

'Congratulations!' I don't know how they found out. I doubt it was anyone from my family, though! In fact, I often tease Brian that it's a big coincidence this came out the day after he was at the *TV Quick* Awards. I suspect he got drunk and let it slip to some journalist. 'I did not!' is always his indignant response. But I'm not convinced; I know what *I'm* like after a few sherries! There's a reason Tim calls me the Gob on the Tyne.

There didn't seem much point in denying it. So I spoke to the producers about it and they said, 'Would you mind if we wrote it into the script?'

'I would love it, of course,' I said. 'I'd like to work as much as possible through my pregnancy.' And so the pregnancy flew past because I was working hard and barely had a moment of free time.

There was one last hurdle to overcome before I left *Corrie*. For the fortieth anniversary episode that December, the producers decided that it would be great to do a live one-hour special. I shivered when I heard about it. I said, 'Listen, I don't want to be in that!'

I love live television when I'm presenting; I much prefer the live show of *Loose Women* than the pre-recorded show because I enjoy the dynamic when it's live. But when you're a character in a drama, you can't suddenly say, 'Whoops, I said the wrong thing! What I meant was . . .'

In its early days, *Coronation Street* was always filmed live, back when Ena Sharples was one of the star characters. God knows how they did it. They had a lot more rehearsal time, but it must have been tough. Luckily, I didn't have a huge amount to do in the one-hour special. Bill Roache had the lion's share; all power to him. Still, I was terrified. Just before it came to my bit, I went into the green room, where all the bigwigs were watching it on the monitor. At the end of part one, David Liddiment, the director of programmes at ITV, said, 'Twenty-three million people are watching this.'

I thought, 'Get out!' Imagine forgetting your lines and drying in front of twenty-three million people! It would be like missing a World Cup penalty or something. So my heart was racing when it came time for me to go on. I had to walk from the Rovers Return bar into the living room, where my scene took place. Jack Duckworth had gone before me to do his bit and knocked down the coat rail as he went, which immediately made me tense up and want to start laughing. Nobody had made a mistake up until that point and I was petrified. I was so nervous that I thought I was going to give birth on set! But I got through it, and that was my last day working on the longest-running soap opera of all time. To make it even more special and memorable, little Matthew came in as an extra. Which meant that, after all the darkness and misery I had been through during my years on *Corrie*, I left on a high.

Despite the many dark periods I experienced during my time on *Coronation Street*, in lots of ways I had a fantastic time and it has definitely been the highlight of my career so far. When I was having one of my better days I always had a laugh on set, and one particular episode, when Dad appeared as Natalie's father-in-law, will for ever stick in my mind. He went for the part and got it without anyone knowing he was my dad, and being on set with him in the Barnes' house was probably one of the most surreal moments of my life! Without doubt it was *Corrie* that established me as a well-known actress and I'll for ever be thankful for that. But being on the show also gave me the chance to make many life-long friends, such as Beverley Callard, Sally Whittaker and Kevin Kennedy, and for that reason alone I wouldn't change a thing.

Chapter Fifteen

It was incredibly emotional saying goodbye to Matthew as I left for the hospital. I was in racking sobs. Until now, he had been my only baby and we both knew that the next time I came home, he wouldn't be my baby anymore. Just like every other mother, I wondered if I'd be able to love the new baby as much as I loved Matthew. I just couldn't imagine loving another person as much as I loved him.

That night, in my hospital bed, I started to feel fearful. I couldn't help it: I had a fear of the fear. I worried that simply being scared might trigger my depression. But I was OK. Although the c-section was quite an uncomfortable experience, it was a hell of a lot better than thirty-six hours of labour.

'Bloomin' 'eck, it's like a shopping bag!' Tim said, referring to the foetal sac, as he watched Gordon at work at the other end of the bed.

'Shut up!' I shouted.

And suddenly there he was, my little Louis, and he was fine! He was 7lb 3oz of pure sweetness. Tim and I were thrilled.

After he was born, Mum and Dad and Matthew came in to see us. Matthew was very clingy because he was obviously a bit worried, but I soon reassured him with hugs and kisses. Then

Rose arrived and burst into tears at the sight of Louis because in a few months she would also be having a baby. I was over the moon. Everything seemed wonderful.

After being unable to breastfeed Matthew because of my depression, I desperately wanted to breastfeed Louis, for both our sakes. Matthew had been totally fine on formula milk, but I was a mother and naturally wanted to breastfeed if I could. So off we went, Louis and I, but for some reason it just wasn't working. He would latch on to my nipple and then very quickly come off it, which meant he wasn't getting any milk.

The nurses kept testing his blood sugars, which were fine, so there didn't seem to be cause for concern. 'This can happen when the baby hasn't come down the birth canal because he can be a little bit blocked with gunk,' they explained. 'We often see babies who don't feed very much in the first couple of days. As long as their blood sugars are fine, we don't worry about it.'

Since Louis wasn't crying or perturbed in any way, I tried not to fret, even though he still wasn't feeding by the evening or during the night. When the midwife arrived in the morning, we tried some different feeding positions and continued checking his blood sugars, which were still fine. However, he was totally constipated and he wasn't eating.

Tim arrived and burst into tears of joy. He was so delighted that we had this baby; he said that he couldn't believe that he'd ever had reservations about it. He was also thrilled that giving birth hadn't plunged me into post-natal depression.

'Yes, but it's early days,' I cautioned, because I didn't want to build his hopes up. 'I feel fine, but I just wish he was feeding.'

'Well, the nurses aren't worried,' Tim said happily. 'That's the main thing.'

The third day arrived. I was on my own in the ward with the

midwife, trying another feeding position with Louis, when suddenly he vomited up a mass of liquid the colour of greenest bile. It was like a scene from *The Exorcist*.

'OK, I think we'll just pop him down to special care,' the midwife said.

'What's the matter with him?' I asked, distraught.

'Oh, it could be a variety of things,' she said chirpily. 'The best thing is for us to pop him down to special care and they can sort it out. Don't you worry, everything will be fine.' She seemed so calm that I didn't panic, although obviously I was anxious.

And so the nightmare began. They took Louis down to special care and said they'd call me soon. Half an hour later, Gordon arrived. I could see that he was upset, although he was trying to hide it. 'What do you think it could be?' I asked.

'It could be variety of things, Denise,' he said soothingly. 'It's not remotely uncommon for babies to vomit or for them to be taken to special care. When they're newborns, we take extra precautions.' He left me with the assurance that he would stay in touch with developments through the night.

Louis was in special care for a fortnight. They put my tiny, sweet baby in a little incubator, where he had all kinds of wires and tubes coming out of him. It was heartbreaking. Only occasionally was I allowed to take him out and give him a little cuddle, with all his wires attached. Oh how I longed to hold him tightly in my arms and take him home! The doctors did endless tests and eliminated all kinds of possible illnesses, without coming up with the answer as to what was blocking up his system. At one point, they thought it might even be meningitis, so they took him away for a lumbar puncture. They wouldn't let me stay with him while he had it because it's just too horrendous for a new parent to watch.

I was worried sick. Sleep was elusive; I was lucky if I managed to drift off for a couple of hours before waking up in a panic. The distance between the ward and the special care unit seemed to grow longer every time I walked it – 'the green mile' I called it. Every time it came to pressing the buzzer at the door, I was terrified out of my wits; I always hesitated because I was dreading the sound of the nurse's voice when she answered. I knew I would be able to tell by her tone if it was bad news, so every time she casually said, 'Oh hi, Denise!' I would practically collapse with relief. The tension was endless.

I'd go in and they'd say, 'Right, we're going to try him with a little syringe of milk and just see if he'll take it now.'

So we'd give him the syringe of milk. If he kept it down, I would cry with joy and all the nurses started beaming. Then I'd go back to my room on the ward, only for them to phone an hour later and say, 'Sorry, Denise, he's brought it up again. He's still not keeping it down.' This went on for two long, agonising weeks, while they fed him intravenously.

Meanwhile, Tim was holding the fort at home, trying to keep everything as normal as possible for Matthew, who was being very brave despite being very concerned that I wasn't coming home with the baby. I could see that Tim was becoming increasingly upset as well. Every time I phoned and told him that Louis had kept the milk down, he'd say, 'Fantastic! Shall I bring the carrycot in, then?' He desperately wanted me to say that we could bring Louis home now, but I couldn't.

'I just can't stand this anymore!' I told the doctors finally. 'I'm tired of hearing about what he *hasn't* got. When are we going to find out what it is?'

They decided to send him to Alder Hey Children's Hospital in Liverpool for a surgical opinion. The ambulance came, equipped with an incubator, and Tim and I travelled with him. When we arrived, we discovered black poo in his nappy. 'God, it's all fine! It's all over!' we cried joyfully.

'Just calm down,' the staff at Alder Hey kept saying. 'We still have lots of tests to do. We need to do a bowel biopsy.' They suspected that the problem might be something called Hirschsprung's disease, which occurs in one in five thousand babies; it's when the nerve endings in the bowel don't form between the fifth and the twelfth weeks of pregnancy. Otherwise, they said, it could be malrotation, which is a twisted bowel. If it was malrotation, Louis would need immediate surgery; if it was Hirschsprung's, we wouldn't know for three weeks, when the test results came through. I tried hard to concentrate on what they were saying. The thought of my baby going into surgery appalled me.

Thankfully, he didn't have malrotation, so emergency surgery was ruled out. Now we had to wait for the Hirschsprung's diagnosis. If it was Hirschsprung's, there was only a surgical solution. If it wasn't, we had to go back to the drawing board.

I was lucky enough to stay in the Ronald McDonald Children's Charities house at Alder Hey, a wonderful house where people whose children are sick can stay when they are at the hospital. It meant that I could go straight to see Louis when he woke up in the morning. God, it was a lifesaver for me. Even though I only lived forty minutes from the hospital, I would have slept in a chair by his bed every night if not for the Children's Charities house. It's even more of a lifesaver for people who live further away. Even so, the nights were terrible; I kept waking up, convinced that I could hear the phone ringing with bad news.

While we were waiting for the diagnosis, they were washing out Louis's bowel with regular enemas; you could see the relief on his little face every time they emptied him out. After a week, we were shown how to do these rectal washouts ourselves. 'What would be the chance of taking him home?' I asked. 'Do you think we're OK doing this ourselves until we get the diagnosis?'

The doctors went off, had a conflab and decided that it would be OK because we lived relatively close by. It was just so wonderful to take him home and introduce him to everybody, even though he needed a lot of care and we didn't know what was ahead of us.

A fortnight later, the hospital phoned to confirm that Louis had Hirschsprung's disease. I was so relieved that we finally had a diagnosis. I knew there was going to be surgery, but my fear had been that it wasn't going to be Hirschsprung's disease but something they couldn't operate on or couldn't even diagnose. It was also incredibly fortunate that Graham Lamont worked at Alder Hey; he's a brilliant consultant paediatric surgeon and a Hirschsprung's specialist. What's more, there were two Hirschsprung's research projects being conducted there at the time. So Alder Hey was far and away the best place for Louis.

The next worry was that the doctors couldn't tell how much of Louis's bowel was affected until they actually went in and saw it. The results of their investigation would determine what level of aftercare he would need; in other words, if a very long piece of the bowel was affected and needed to be removed, he might have to have a colostomy bag, or worse. So off he went to surgery. Oh God, to watch your child heading for the operating theatre is just horrendous!

I was told that I should go home and wait until they called me. It was important to be with Matthew and my family, they said. I drove home, but I couldn't cope with trying to be normal for Matthew; I couldn't cope with not being near Louis. So I got back in the car and drove to the hospital. I just had to get back there.

Louis had seven inches of large intestine chopped out, which is not too long when you think of how long the intestines are. I was so relieved when I was told that the operation had been successful and the doctors were convinced he wouldn't need the colostomy bag. Of course, suddenly we went from no nappies to going through about twenty a day. It was literally one after another! It was pouring out of him because there was so much and it was so loose. Hirschsprung's children will always be quite loose, but what made it worse was that Louis hadn't had any practice with working his bowel. Oh my God, it was constant, but obviously I couldn't have cared less. It was just so amazing that he was better. At last we could take him home for good.

A week later, I took him abroad, after I'd checked with the doctors that it was safe to do so. We went to Cyprus with Mum and Dad and Debbie and Peter and their kids, and it was just fantastic. At last I could enjoy being a mother without post-natal depression; I was simply tired and stressed. It just goes to show that it's not psychological, but physical, doesn't it? I suffered terribly with depression the first time I had a baby, when I had money in the bank, a much-wanted, perfectly healthy child and a husband who adored me. Yet when Louis nearly died, I didn't get it! Of course, I had days when I was clinically depressed, but that was to be expected because I was a person who suffered from clinical depression. However, it wasn't connected to having Louis.

We often got together with the Greek side of the family in Cyprus, an island we all love. This time we were staying in the

Amathus Beach Hotel, where we had been several times before. It's a five-star hotel by their standards, although maybe it's only a four-star by ours. Either way, it's a fantastic place.

On our second night, Mum rang our room and said, 'What time are we meeting downstairs?'

'I don't know. I've got to get Louis sorted first,' I said. 'Why?'

'Well, Litza is in here doing your dad's make-up.'

'You are joking, aren't you? He's not dressing up! This is not funny, Mum,' I said. 'I've laughed about it before, but we have only been here one night. This is a five-star hotel and we don't know people here. I really will be angry if he dresses up.'

'Well, you tell him!' she said, putting the phone down.

I got on the phone to Debbie, who said, 'No way! I'm just not having it. Not here!'

So I got on the phone to Dad and said, 'Now listen, Dad. It's all very well when it's just you and Mum at the end of a trip and you've dressed up after you've made friends with all your Brit pack, but we have just arrived at this hotel and we don't know anybody here. Tim and I are on the television, so could you please just not do it, for once?'

Typically, Dad just started laughing hysterically. Litza came on the phone. 'Oh, let him do it. I love to see him do it!' she pleaded.

'No, Litza, it's just not the right time,' I harrumphed.

We all presumed that Dad wouldn't go through with it because we were all so cross, and he doesn't like us to be cross with him. But when we went downstairs, there was Raquel Welch wearing high heels, a lime-green mini-skirt and an off-the-shoulder white shirt, with massive blonde hair and hoop earrings, drinking at the bar. Now, as Dad grew older, Raquel had begun to look slightly seedier. Where once he had been a pretty guy dressed up, now he was a man in his sixties, with a pot belly, which wasn't quite so attractive.

We were absolutely furious. We kept a safe distance from him but, true to form, Raquel had them wrapped round her little finger in no time. The Cypriots got him singing at the piano; they loved him. Later, he did a double act with Tim at the piano, by which time I was over my anger. Debbie was still furious though. She didn't speak to him for two days. 'I'm not going to be dictated to by my boring children,' he declared, making us sound like Saffy from *Ab Fab*. But is it so very boring not to want your sixty-three-year-old dad to dress in a lime-green mini-skirt and high heels? 'Yes,' my mates would chorus! They love Dad.

Two months later, in September 2001, the Twin Towers were attacked in New York. Like everyone else, I remember exactly where I was on that awful day. It plunged me into depression. I was filming *The Vice* with Ken Stott and we wanted to stop shooting when we saw what was happening, but the production schedule meant that we had to carry on, even though everything suddenly seemed pointless.

The next night, I went up to London, feeling very shaky and unwell, and some friends persuaded me to go for a drink in a bar in Knightsbridge. Everything seemed so awful that I decided to get drunk, which was unusual for me then because I had given up partying when I got pregnant with Louis. It hadn't been easy to give everything up and sometimes I had felt tempted to be excessive, but I had never succumbed. However, tonight I needed a drink.

Halfway through the evening, while I was visiting the loo,

a beautiful Asian girl started chatting to me about her life. She introduced herself as Myra and it was clear from what she said that she came from a very wealthy background. She talked about having an apartment in a smart area of London, a boat on the Thames and a complicated family life, which fascinated me.

'Can I buy you a drink?' she asked as we left the bathroom.

'That would be lovely,' I said. We went on chatting for a while and exchanged numbers before I went back to join my friends.

For the next month, I was at home almost non-stop, being a full-time mum to Louis and Matthew. Myra called constantly, inviting me to parties and events in London, but I had to keep turning them down. 'I'd love to come, but I've got a parents' meeting that night,' I would tell her. Or 'Sorry, but I'm taking Louis to baby swimming that day.' After a while, I'd see her number come up on my phone and not want to pick up. She was very persistent and it felt a bit like she was stalking me.

One weekend, I flew to Spain to do a photo shoot with Gabrielle Glaister, who played my sister in *Corrie*. Gabrielle left on the Saturday and I was on my own in the hotel when Myra called to ask me to a party she was throwing the following week. It turned out that I was actually free, for once, so I said that I would try to go.

Ten minutes after I'd put the phone down, she called again. 'If you come to my party, some of my friends might be doing coke. Do you have a problem with that?' she asked.

I laughed. 'Well, it's not exactly uncommon in the industry I work in,' I said. 'So don't worry, I won't be shocked or offended.'

'Do you do it?' she asked.

'I used to, but not really anymore,' I replied. 'Only on high days and holidays; very, very occasionally.'

'You don't know anyone who could get me some, do you?'

I paused. 'I don't know any dealers, no,' I said. It was such a long time since I had bought cocaine that I had no direct contact with that world anymore. 'But I might be able to put in a couple of calls and get a number for you. I'll see what I can do,' I added.

'Great!' she said. I put the phone down and thought nothing more of it.

The following weekend, my parents, Tim, Matthew, Louis and I drove down to Somerset for our friend Mark's fortieth birthday party. We had remained close friends with Mark and Melanie since we'd all met in Australia, and everyone was looking forward to a great night. It was a 1970s-themed bash at the lovely hotel they now owned in Ilchester.

We arrived at the hotel with our wigs and 1970s clothes at about teatime. Suddenly, my phone rang. I picked up to hear someone saying something about being from the *Sunday Mirror*. 'I can't hear you, mate,' I said. 'Let me just go outside.'

'Denise, I'm really sorry,' he said, once I could hear him. 'Don't shoot the messenger, but we're running a story about your cocaine use tomorrow in the *Sunday Mirror*.'

I went cold. 'I beg your pardon?' I said quietly.

'I'm really sorry, but we have it on tape.'

I was totally taken aback. What on earth was this about? 'What do you mean?' I asked. 'I don't know what you're talking about. Who did this? Who taped me?'

'I can't say,' he said.

For the next three hours, I racked my brain trying to work out who would have sold a story about me, accusing all kinds of people in my head. Stupidly, I didn't phone a lawyer or my agent. At ten thirty that night, my friend Steven called me. He'd been to Kings Cross station to get the papers. 'Denise, it's terrible,' he said. 'It's on the front of the *Sunday Mirror* and it says, "MY COCAINE EXCLUSIVE".'

There were pictures of me on the night after 9/11. Someone had followed me to the hotel when I left the bar in Knightsbridge with my friends. In one of the pictures, a man had his arm round me and the article said I was having an affair with him, which was rubbish. It also said that I'd done drugs all night, which was totally untrue. By now, I very rarely touched cocaine at all.

At one o'clock in the morning in Somerset, I suddenly clicked. I know who it was! Myra! I phoned her. 'Myra?' I said.

'Denise, hi!' she replied brightly.

'Hi, Myra, I just hope that your parents are very proud of you,' I said, and I put the phone down. That was the last time I spoke to her.

It turned out that she was the cousin of Mazher Mahmood, the undercover reporter known as 'the fake sheikh'. Nice family. It was very galling to think that she had been taping me for a month, hoping to get me to admit that I took drugs, and yet every single conversation we'd had, apart from the final one, had been about me taking Matthew to school and doing baby things with Louis. That final conversation was the only one she could have nailed me with.

Of course, I then had to tell my parents and Matthew. Everybody was fantastically supportive because they felt really sorry for me. It was a horrible setup. I've never seen Myra around, but if I ever do, I would love to pour a pint over her head! It seems so mean that she would be tempted to do what she did, knowing what a devoted mum I am.

*

Despite having Hirschsprung's, Louis thrived, thank God. I had to be cautious with him, however. The doctors had told me to watch out for sickness and diarrhoea and always get it checked out, even if it didn't seem serious, even when he grew up and became a teenager who threw up after drinking too much vodka that he'd nicked out of the cupboard. It was important to be vigilant.

I wasn't a neurotic mother; if he was sick, I didn't panic, but I did watch him closely. So when he stopped wanting his juice and began to be sick when he was around twenty months, I tried not to overreact. I let it go for a little while, but when my doctor friend David happened to pop round, I asked him to take a look at him. David felt his tummy and said, 'Hmm, it's quite soft, which is a good sign. I'd be worried if it were hard. So I'd wait until the morning and then pop him down to the doctor's and get him checked out if he isn't any better.'

During the night, Louis's poo turned black and his tummy became rock hard, so I took him straight to my GP in the morning. Since Tim had just got over a nasty bout of gastroenteritis, the doctor assumed that Louis had caught it from him. 'You need to get him up to Macclesfield General Hospital to rehydrate him because he's very dehydrated,' he said.

At first, I was relieved that it was only gastroenteritis. But when Louis didn't improve after attempts to rehydrate him at Macclesfield, I started to get quite concerned. He just didn't want any fluids.

The hours ticked by and I began to feel really anxious. The doctors told me not to worry, but how could I not worry? 'Just give it another hour,' they said.

Other medics began to pop in and gather in corners to

discuss Louis, without telling Tim or me anything. At around 10 p.m., when we'd been at the hospital for twelve hours, I said, 'He doesn't look right to me. If you can't tell me absolutely that this is gastroenteritis, then I want him to go to Alder Hey.'

I felt that he would be in better hands at Alder Hey, where the doctors knew Louis's case history. Much to their credit, the doctors at Macclesfield listened to me and called an ambulance. My poor little boy was taken out on a stretcher, with a drip in his arm. Tim and I went with him.

In an emergency like this, I had always imagined myself to be the kind of person who yelled at the ambulance driver, urging them to 'Drive faster, drive faster! I don't know what's the matter with my son – we have to get there quickly!'

But in actual fact, a sense of calm came over me in the ambulance, some strange and wonderful coping mechanism took over. I vividly remember talking to the paramedics about the scandalously low salaries they earned and how many hours they worked. I was just having a totally normal conversation with these two great girls.

We arrived at Alder Hey in Liverpool and Louis was wheeled in. We were met by a doctor and a nurse, who immediately said, 'Let's check him out.' They examined him, went away and came back again. 'Right, Mr and Mrs Healy,' the doctor said. 'He's gone straight to the top of the emergency surgery list and we're taking him down to the operating theatre now.'

My heart began to pound. 'What do you think it is?' I asked. 'How long will he be in surgery?'

He frowned. 'Well, we think it's probably acute appendicitis and if that's the case, he should be away between an hour and an hour and a half.'

Shuddering with fear, I reached for Tim's hand. It was clear that Louis's condition was very, very serious. A burst appendix could lead to peritonitis, which was potentially fatal.

Four and a half hours later, Louis still hadn't come out of surgery. There was no word about how he was doing, either. Tim fell asleep; it was the only way he could deal with the stress of waiting, I think. It was more catatonia than sleep. Meanwhile, I kept looking at my watch and going to and from the nurses' station, where a very kind male nurse kept saying, 'No news is good news. We would hear if it was bad news.'

'But it's been four and a half hours!' I whimpered.

'I know, I know,' he replied, 'but we're not allowed to phone the theatre.'

All kinds of things went through my mind as I waited for news. I thought about Mum and Dad. Mum had lost four babies, which was just terrible for her. She had two very late miscarriages and had to give birth to a dead baby at around seven months. I only remember one of her pregnancies, when I was nine and Debbie was six. One of my clearest childhood memories is of feeling hugely excited about the new baby. Dad was going to take us to the skating rink and Debbie and I were wearing our little skating outfits. Then Dad called us downstairs and I saw that he was crying. It was the first time I'd seen him cry and it was a real shock. He told us that Mum had lost the baby. He didn't say it then, but it had been a little boy and he'd had encephalitis, so he was severely disabled. He was going to be called Christopher Lorne.

This was my first experience of loss. It was horrendous seeing my dad so upset. At nine, I had a real sense of the sadness of the situation, but it was different for six-year-old Debbie. After Dad had broken the news, she said, 'Can I have my cornflakes now?' At the time, I felt she was being really insensitive, but obviously now I realise that she was too young to understand.

I don't remember Mum coming out of hospital or witnessing her heartbreak. I don't remember the aftermath of it all; I just remember Dad breaking down in tears. Now that I was waiting to see if my own child was going to survive, I experienced a deep sense of sorrow for Mum and Dad and what they had been through. Surely there is nothing worse in life than losing a child.

Five hours after Louis was wheeled away, a doctor came to find us. 'How is he?' I asked desperately.

'OK, he's out of surgery and he's in intensive care,' he said.

I gasped with relief. 'Oh my God!' I said.

I woke Tim up and told him the news. He was mortified that he'd been asleep; it really upset him and I felt really sorry for him. 'Everybody has different ways of coping with things,' I consoled, 'and sleep is one way.' I knew this because it was one of the ways I coped with my illness. Still, he felt devastatingly guilty.

We immediately made our way to intensive care, where Louis was on a ventilator, with tubes coming out all over. There were two nurses watching over him. 'Well, that was really touch and go!' a doctor told me.

Apparently, Louis had adhesions caused by the stomach surgery he'd had at six weeks old, which meant that his bowel hadn't knitted together properly. It can happen to anybody who has had stomach surgery, we were told. They removed about fifteen inches of gangrenous small intestine, which had twisted and cut off the blood supply. Much later, when he was completely out of the woods, they said that if we had left it another hour at Macclesfield, they might not have been able to help him. So if I

Left Playing the temptress: as Natalie Horrocks in a steamy scene with Kevin Webster, played by Mike Le Vell.

Right Me and Jules Hesmondhalgh on Nat's wedding day.

Below Hiding a dark secret at Betty Turpin's eightieth birthday.

Above Leaving the *Corrie* set for the last time after the live episode, December 2000.

Opposite On a promotional photo shoot, Texas, 1998. Working on *Coronation Street* enabled me to go to so many amazing places I would have never otherwise visited.

Above As a sober birthday girl in Malta. Tough when you're mates with this lot! From left to right: Dee C. Lee, Trisha Penrose, me, Angie Lonsdale and Gaynor Faye.

Left Friends for ever.

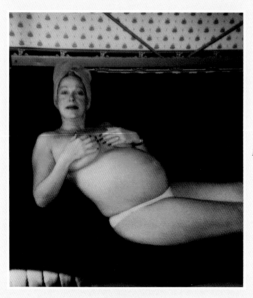

Left Demi Moore I ain't!
The night before Louis
was born.

Below Praying for little Louis.
He was only three weeks
old when he had to have his
operation. Alder Hey, 2001.

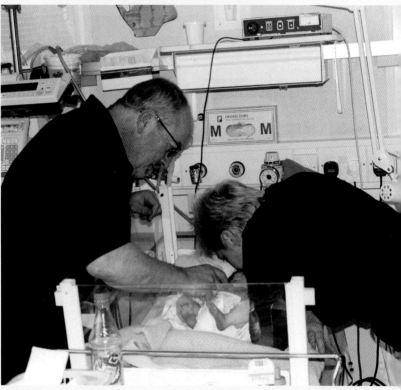

Above Looking more like a mad auntie at a wedding than Louis' mum at his christening! August 2002.

Right Rose, me, Louis and Harrison. Who'd have thought it?

Right Behind the painted smile. Dressed as the Wicked Queen, with Louis, just days before my breakdown. Stockport, 2004.

Below The Golden Girls! With Lynda Bellingham, Coleen Nolan, my Tim and Jane McDonald at our annual ball for the GEM Appeal.

Top Robbie Williams joined us on his favourite show, 2009. We always manage to work hard and still have fun on *Loose Women*.

Above Girls behaving badly. Me and make-up artist Janet having fun with Neil Morrissey.

Right I was so proud when I won Best Actress 2009 for *Waterloo Road* at the TV Quick & TV Choice Awards.

Above The Love Boat. On an Ocean Village cruise to the Caribbean, Christmas 2009.

Below The most important people – and dog! – in my life.

hadn't insisted that he be moved to Alder Hey . . . well, it doesn't even bear thinking about.

After the operation, Louis had to be nil-by-mouth for quite a long time, which was awful for both of us. 'Mummy, water, water!' he'd beg, but I couldn't do anything to help him. It's terrible to have to say no to your child in that situation, when you'd do anything to make him feel better. A lot of the time, I was breaking up inside. I'd have to leave the room to cry, then wipe my tears, put on a smile and return to his bedside, pretending that everything was fine.

Eventually, they said that he could have the occasional ice pop. Ice was better than water, apparently, because it helped to control his liquid intake. They had ice pops in a rainbow of different colours in the freezer, which made things a little bit more fun for the poor mite: 'Which colour do you want now?' I'd ask.

But then I came back from the loo to find the alarm by his bed going off and nurses panicking all around him. The new nurses had come on duty to find that his tongue and lips were completely blue. They thought he'd had a cardiac arrest, when in fact he'd just been sucking on a blue ice pop! It's funny now, but at the time it was just terrible. Those bloody monitors! My heart still races horribly whenever I have to film in a hospital and I hear that beep, beep, beeeeeeeeep noise.

Louis's recovery was slow and difficult. He was very up and down: he'd be really quite well for a few days and then he'd have a day when he was completely floppy, which sent me into a total panic. Every little thing he achieved was like a milestone. 'He wants a piece of toast. Oh my God, it's a miracle!' I used to plead silently with him to keep his food down because he couldn't come home until he stopped vomiting. The day my friends Dawn and Ashley came to see him, even though Dawn absolutely hates hospitals, Louis had just eaten some toast. We started celebrating, at which point he covered everybody in vomit. Not surprisingly, Dawn hated hospitals even more after that.

Once again, I was in the Ronald McDonald house, for what seemed like an eternity. Every morning I'd get up and go over to Louis's ward, so that I would be there when he woke up. Then I'd lie on the bed with him all day until he went to sleep at night. We used to watch *Bear in the Big Blue House*, among other things, and he now says that's one of his earliest memories. He doesn't remember much about the hospital, but he hasn't forgotten lying on the bed watching TV.

The whole experience was very hard for Tim and Matthew. I was also worried for Mum and feared that the stress might bring her cancer back. Tim spent most days at the hospital, while Matthew was at school. He kept saying, 'Look, you're exhausted. Why don't you go home tonight and I'll stay with Louis?' But I couldn't leave. I just couldn't. It was as if there were still an umbilical cord between me and Louis.

I made one exception, though. I was in the middle of making a documentary for *Tonight with Trevor McDonald* when all this happened. Jonathan Maitland and I were testing out the Atkins Diet and a nutritionist was due to come to my house to do a weigh-in. For some crazy reason, I left Tim and my mum at the hospital with Louis to do a totally unimportant bit of filming. And when they weighed me, I couldn't help thinking that it probably wasn't a very accurate gauge of how well the diet worked, even though I had stuck to it, because the pounds drop off you instantly when your child is that poorly!

It's very strange, the actor's work ethic. I think it's interesting that Les Dennis's autobiography is called *Must the Show Go On?* It's the performer's dilemma because in this industry you are trained to think that it must. Tim went on stage the night his mother died and then thought, 'What the hell am I doing? It's only a play and they'll get their money back if it's cancelled.' Even so, he saw it through until curtain down.

It's weird because it's drummed into you and it's very hard to resist that sense of obligation, especially if you're worried about losing the job. As an actress, you can't help but be fearful of taking your foot off the pedal because you can become yesterday's news very quickly. It's only really in the West End – and then only if you're one of the more important members of the cast – that you have an understudy. The rest of the time, you have to be there, or there is no show. So you really don't want to let the rest of the team down, although what better excuse can you have than your child being in intensive care? On the other hand, Louis was in safe hands, I knew the filming had to be done at some point and I wasn't going to feel any happier doing it two days later.

Louis was in hospital for another fortnight before he stopped vomiting and started putting on a little weight. Finally, we were able to take him home. And that was that, touch wood; he's been fine ever since. He farts for England, though, which is a characteristic of someone who's had Hirschsprung's. I know this because after I went public about what had happened to Louis, I was contacted by a man named Gerry, who was only the second child in England to be operated on for Hirschsprung's. Gerry went on to run a Hirschsprung's society for a while and he was thrilled that I had spoken about it because I was the first person off the telly to draw people's attention to it.

Now in his fifties, Gerry has gone on to have four children and his life is good, but the one thing that has remained, and probably will remain for ever, is wind. Still, as he points out, you can develop a sense of humour about it, which is exactly what Louis has done. He loves farting – the longer, the louder and the more public, the better!

Chapter Sixteen

My friend Jane, an old friend from school, was a typical house-wife for a long time. She stayed at home and brought up the kids. Her husband John went to work and came back at five o'clock. That was their life.

Things have changed now and Jane works part-time in a doctor's surgery, but back when she was a housewife, Jane would say to me, 'I would never, ever have an affair. I mean, I just can't imagine it. I couldn't cope with it, not in a million years.'

In those days she was obsessed with Kevin Costner. So one day I said to her, 'OK, it's not completely impossible that I, as an actress, might work with Kevin Costner one day. Now, if I invited you to come on set, would you come?'

'Well, of course I would!' she said.

'OK, so Kevin Costner is sitting having a coffee with you and he says, "It's lovely to meet you. Would you like to have dinner with me tonight?" What would you say?'

'Well, of course I would.'

'OK, so you have dinner with Kevin Costner. John's not around and Kevin Costner wants to sleep with you. Would you?'

'Well, of course I would!'

'And that's my point,' I said. 'You think that you could never have an affair because it seems so far outside the realms of possibility. You can't see beyond John and the kids and getting their tea on the table. But I've been meeting people who I find as attractive as you find Kevin Costner throughout my working life, a long way from home and my husband. I'm not saying I've taken it, but the opportunity to sleep with them has often been there.'

So when it comes to infidelity, isn't it just a case of 'There but for the grace of God, go I'?

In 2004, I started working on a series called *Down to Earth*. Pauline Quirke and Warren Clarke had starred in the first series, as a couple who move down to Devon from London and take over a farm. My dear friend Angela Griffin and I tend to follow each other around different series, and she and Ian Kelsey took over the *Down to Earth* farm in 2003. Then, Ricky Tomlinson and I joined the show in the third series; we played Jackie and Tony Murphy, who owned the local pub.

It was a wonderful job because it involved filming in beautiful places in Devon, like Dartmouth. The downside was that it meant leaving Louis, who was still only three, but it was a very well-paid job and Tim was at home to look after him.

It doesn't excuse anything, but it just so happened that Tim and I had been going through a really bad time in our marriage. We'd been having terrible problems. For a while his drinking had been escalating; he was drinking too much and doing it secretly. Now, I had never known him to have a problem with drinking before. He could give it up whenever he wanted to and never drank while he was working. We were both capable of having a massive drinking session with our pals, but now, rather than getting drunk socially, he would go into the garage to tipple on the quiet.

'Have you been drinking?' I'd say when he teetered back into the house. He always denied it. 'How is it, then, that we've both had two glasses of wine, but you're pissed?' I'd ask.

I hated him drinking spirits, which can often make people aggressive. Whisky is terrible: it either turns Tim into a know-all or he's suddenly really up for an argument – with anybody, about anything. He has never, ever come close to being violent, but drinking can make him very argumentative. He began coming back from the pub so drunk that he'd lurch through the door and step sideways instead of forwards, before losing his balance. He became what we call in Newcastle a 'falling-down drunk'.

I don't know why it happened. Maybe I hadn't been around enough, or it was something within him. It was obvious that he was numbing his pain with alcohol, and he was mainly doing it secretly. Perhaps his secrecy had something to do with the fact that he kept a lot of his anxieties to himself because he felt I couldn't deal with them. Much of our marriage had been about my pain, and it was almost as if he wasn't allowed to be depressed himself. Occasionally he'd say, 'You haven't got the monopoly on being depressed in this house, you know!'

'You don't know what it's like to be really depressed!' I'd retort.

Whatever the underlying reason, his drinking began to get worse. 'I can't handle this,' I told him. 'OK, I drink, and sometimes I drink a lot, but you are turning into the falling-down man who comes back from the pub. It is just horrendous. I dread you walking into the room.' I was starting to become quite unhappy.

Partly because of the deteriorating state of my marriage, I was really looking forward to starting *Down to Earth*. However, as luck would have it, I went on a right downer two days before it was due to begin. Suddenly, I was really, really bad. It wasn't that I was worried about the job, but I always get a bit anxious about going away, so maybe it was subconsciously linked to that. Certainly it was nothing I was conscious of. Fortunately, Darren, who used to drive me, really looked after me on the way down south. Darren died last year. I really miss him.

During the journey, I had to stop and be sick several times, a sure symptom of my depression. It was that panicky feeling all over again. Since the series had been going for some years, a lot of the cast and crew had worked together before, which didn't help. And however much I try to de-stigmatise my illness, I'm still not going to walk in on the first day and say, 'Hi, I'm Denise. I've got clinical depression and I'm in a state.' At least Ange was there, though. I told her to watch out for me.

I started on a Friday and I had to film all day. My ability to act withers away when I feel that bad; it's like a thick blackness. I found I couldn't move my mouth very well and, whenever that happens, I develop a bit of a stutter. My ability to learn lines also suffers. Still, I somehow got through the first day, although it was awful. My character was supposed to be quite jokey and comedic, which made it particularly difficult.

There was a big cast and crew outing planned for that night. I really didn't want to go, but the peer pressure got to me. 'Come on! You've got to come with us!' So I stupidly did something that I've done so many times before and drank in my room before I went out. Then off I went out and got absolutely hammered, not to the point of falling-down drunk, but not far off. I ended up going to a bar with mostly members of the crew, including a guy called Steve, a set carpenter. The bar was full of locals, who immediately surrounded me, at which point Steve said, 'Look, everybody, let's go somewhere a bit quieter for Denise.' This struck me as very thoughtful and gentlemanly of him.

We went somewhere else and then on to a nightclub, where Steve and I spent most of the time talking. Then we went back to the hotel and drank champagne until three in the morning. The crew was mainly staying in another hotel, but Steve and a few others were in our hotel because a block of rooms had just become free.

In my drunken state, I became convinced that one of the make-up girls didn't like me, which turned out to be totally unfounded. Actually, she was just a bit guarded, but I'm pathetic if I have a sense that somebody doesn't like me. I get really paranoid about it. Why don't they like me? What have I done wrong? Eventually, everyone started going to bed and I heard Steve saying to some guy, 'Am I in 201?' Ding!

When I got to my bedroom, I had another drink. Now that I was on my own again, I began to feel down. I started thinking about how nice Steve had been to me, and how interesting I found him. He had made it obvious that he found me attractive, which was very flattering because he was good-looking and younger than me. On a whim, I called him and invited him to my room. I can't excuse it, but that's what happened. Why did I do it? I just don't know. Maybe it was out of general neediness, or I simply thought it would make me feel better. Being away from home was definitely a contributing factor.

The next day, Steve went out to play golf with some of the crew. I wasn't working, so I spent the day hanging around, not doing much, and I agreed to go out for dinner with a couple of cast members later on. I was feeling slightly better, but still not great. I didn't eat all day, which is always a bad sign; as I've said, my appetite is the first thing to go when I'm not well.

When he came back from playing golf, Steve came to my room to pick up his sunglasses, which he had forgotten to take with him earlier. He asked how I was and suddenly I found myself telling him all about how I was feeling. To my surprise, he was incredibly understanding. Here was someone ten years younger, who I thought was fit and had slept with, suddenly turning out to be a friend I could talk to as well. Slowly, a relationship began to develop.

We hid the relationship from everybody, of course. Well, we thought it was a secret, but afterwards people said, 'We knew about it from early on.' Your body language changes when you are with someone, even if you don't notice it yourself. You're just different when you are around that person. Anyway, why would the set carpenter spend so much time in my trailer having lunch?

Over time, Steve and I became very fond of each other. I found that I was able to separate what was happening with him from my life back home with Tim and my children. It felt as if I was living two lives. You know when you hear about these people who have managed to conceal their second family in Sussex from their original family in Northumberland? I can understand how they do it, I think. It's known as compartmentalising your life; you just put things into separate boxes. It didn't help that I was spending very little time at home. Sometimes I would literally get home at midnight on a Saturday night, after filming all day, and be picked up by Darren at teatime on the Sunday, having spent less than twenty-four hours at home with my kids. It was tough on us all.

Still, the job was amazing in so many ways: we filmed in beautiful places; the people were all lovely; it was fun and well paid; and I lived in a gorgeous cottage in Dartmouth, which I loved. By about the fourth month of filming, Steve and I were spending all our free time together. I was very fond of him; I suppose I loved him. I knew that he loved me. The relationship continued quite happily for four or five months.

I can't lie and say that I felt guilty about it. As long as it went undiscovered, it simply felt like my private affair. I didn't want to leave Tim for Steve; I've never wanted to leave Tim for anybody. Having said that, there have been times when I've wanted to leave him and I know there have been times when he has wanted to leave me. We are so thankful that we've stayed together.

Steve wanted me to leave Tim, partly because he knew I was unhappy at home, but mostly because he wanted me to be his partner. But I was very firm on that score. 'If I ever leave Tim, I can't guarantee that there will be anything between us,' I told him. 'I wouldn't be leaving for you.' Perhaps the problems I was having with Tim made me feel closer to Steve than I would have felt otherwise; I don't know. What I do know is that I've experienced more guilt over the way the affair was discovered than over anything I've done wrong in my entire life. It makes me go cold to think about it.

One weekend, my parents came down for a visit with my sister and her kids. Steve came over one night, in a group, for a barbecue and I suspect that my sister realised then what was going on between us. I thought I was being very clever about it all, but obviously I wasn't.

The next day was lovely and sunny and so we decided to go to the beach. Just before we left, Steve texted me to say, 'Can you get away for half an hour and at least come and have a cup of tea with me, or something?'

I called him back and left a message. 'Hi, darling, it's me. What a nightmare that we can't get together, but I will try to nip off if I can. Speak to you later. Thanks. Love you!'

Half an hour later, Dad and I went into Dartmouth to get some sandwiches to eat at the beach. I was driving, so I waited in the car while Dad popped into the bakery. Just then, my phone rang. It was Tim. 'Hi, darling!' I said.

'I want a divorce,' he said flatly.

I gulped. 'What?'

Still he showed no emotion. 'You have left a message for your boyfriend on my answer phone.'

My insides turned over and I wanted to be sick. Instantly I realised my mistake: I had dialled Tim instead of Steve and left a message that ended with 'Love you!' It was clearly for someone other than Tim, and clearly directed at a man. I hadn't registered because they both had the same generic Orange answer-phone message. What a fucking nightmare.

Tim was on the set of the fourth series of *Auf Wiedersehen, Pet* when it happened. Jimmy Nail later told me that the cameras were about to turn over when Tim looked at his phone and noticed that he had a message. 'The way he reacted to it, we thought somebody had died,' Jimmy said. It was the worst thing I could ever have done.

What could I say? I couldn't deny it. 'Listen, all I can say is that I'm sorry,' I told him.

'It's fine,' Tim said calmly. 'I just want a divorce and I want it as quickly as possible. Speak to you later.' He hung up.

Just then, Dad got in the car with a bag of sandwiches. 'Right! Let's go to the beach,' he said heartily.

It was absolutely horrendous. I didn't want to tell anybody, so I went to the beach with my family and went through the motions with a smile on my face. Then Jimmy Nail rang. 'Hang on, everybody!' I said brightly, walking off down the sand. 'Just got to take this call!'

'For God's sake, what's happening?' Jimmy said. He was just trying to help his pal, but his tone put me on the defensive, so we had a bit of an argument, unfortunately.

It was awful because I couldn't tell my family and I couldn't go home to try to sort it out. I was convinced that I could make everything all right if I had the chance, but I had to continue my week of filming *Down to Earth*. I tried ringing Tim. He answered the phone, but remained cold and monosyllabic. I would have much preferred it if he'd shouted at me.

Since he was filming in London, I said, 'I'll come to London at the weekend.'

'Well, please yourself, but nothing is going to change,' he said. 'I've heard how you feel about this person.'

I felt terrible. 'I know what it sounds like, but—'

'I'm not going to shout at you,' he interrupted. 'I'm just saying that nothing will make a difference now.'

Things changed two days later. Tim had obviously begun to put two and two together about the lies I had told and the excuses I had made to cover up the affair. He exploded inside and began sending horrible texts. 'Now I know where you were on such-and-such day,' he'd write, sometimes coming to the wrong conclusion, but often getting it right. 'I can't believe you have done this and ruined everything.'

It was completely understandable and I deserved it. I had no comeback and felt absolutely terrible about the way the affair had come to light. If I had sat him down beforehand and said, 'Look, I've got to tell you . . .' I would still have felt guilty, but I would have done the correct thing by telling him and letting him make a decision. What's so awful is that the message I left went on haunting him. He remembered it for a long time afterwards and probably still does to this day. He quoted it at me word-for-word many, many times.

Of course, Steve was horrified because he thought it was over between us. What happened next is all a bit of a blur, but I do remember that I went up to London to talk things over with Tim. I told him that I would end it with Steve and I begged him to give me another chance. It wasn't going to be as easy as that, though. At one point, it looked as if he couldn't forgive me. However, eventually he said that he didn't know how it would pan out, but he was prepared to give it another go.

Then I made a really big mistake: I slept with Steve again because I still had strong feelings for him. I felt very confused afterwards. I didn't know what I wanted to do. I didn't know if my reaction had been so desperate because I felt so guilty, or because I really was terrified of losing Tim. There was even a time when I thought, 'Actually, I don't know if I want to stay married.' Things had been so bad between Tim and me.

Then again, I wasn't sure whether I wanted a relationship with Steve, either. It was easy for me to go back to him, though. He was a fit, thirty-six-year-old carpenter and the sex was fantastic. End of story. I'm not going to lie about it. He worshipped me and was great in bed; we were incredibly compatible in that department. With my marriage being in the state that it was, obviously that had been something that had gone way off the boil. Sex is often the first thing to go, especially when you're with someone who you are not finding attractive at the time. There have been times when it's been vice versa, and Tim hasn't found me attractive, but right then it was the other way around.

So I carried on with my two lives. Tim was obviously paranoid because I was still working with Steve, but I kept promising that I wasn't seeing him. By now, we were filming in Marlow in

Buckinghamshire, which is where Steve happened to live. I was staying in a hotel and he often came to stay with me, but again I thought that I was getting away with it. Then I slipped up again by saying the wrong thing and Tim found out for a second time. At this point, I was more confused than ever. When Tim confronted me, I said, 'I don't know if I want to be married anymore. I don't know if I want Steve, but I don't know if I want you, either.'

I phoned my mum for advice. 'You've got to do what's right for you,' she said. 'We will support you, whatever you decide.' Mum and Dad adored Tim like a son, but they were also aware that I was unhappy. If he had told them that he was leaving me, they would have been equally supportive of him and said, 'We understand why you are going. She is a nightmare, but we love her.'

While I was on the phone to her, Mum said, 'Nobody can make the decision for you, Denise, but just don't step out of the frying pan into the fire.'

'No, I'm trying to separate the two things,' I assured her.

One night, Tim said he wanted to speak to Steve. So I put Steve on the phone. The call started off with them being quite courteous to one another, but then Tim began saying horrible things.

'OK, old man,' Steve said. 'Calm down.' It was just horrendous!

'How can you be with someone who talks like that?' Tim asked me, referring to Steve's London accent. There were some quite comical moments in amongst all the drama and horror, although I couldn't see them at the time.

That weekend, I went home. 'I'm going to leave you both,' I told Tim. 'I can't handle this anymore.' By now I knew that I didn't love Steve enough for him to be my life partner. I was incredibly fond of him, but I knew that he would probably want children and I couldn't give him children.

So I told Tim that I was going to leave him. 'What I did was wrong,' I said. 'It should never have happened. I should have sorted my marriage out with you before I did anything with anyone else. At the same time, I just don't know how we can go back. There were lots of problems beforehand.'

He started crying. We were both so sad. 'Please, please, I don't want you to go,' he said. 'It was horrible finding out about this affair and discovering that you've had strong feelings for somebody else, but I also accept that you were unhappy with me for a long time, so I have to take some of the blame.'

'Well, in a way you do,' I agreed, 'but don't just say that to keep me.'

'I'm not,' he said. 'This is my responsibility as well and I admit that. I promise that things will be different in the future.'

'It's not just you, it's me,' I said. 'I need to think about it. I just don't know what I want to do.'

The series ended and the night of the wrap party arrived. I decided that this was the end of the story between Steve and me. I thought, 'I'll go to the party, but I won't sleep with him and that will be that.'

However, it's one thing to decide something when you're sober, and quite another to follow it through when you're legless. So, inevitably, Steve and I went back to my hotel together. The next morning, at about eleven, we woke up to a knock at the door. 'No thanks!' I called out. But the knocking persisted. 'It's room service,' came a voice from the other side of the door. 'Can we come in?'

Eventually I opened the door and was greeted by a journalist.

'Hi, Denise, I'm from the *Sun* newspaper. We know that you are in your room with Steve and we know that you are having an affair with him.'

My mouth dropped open. 'Er,' I said.

'I'm sorry, but we've been following you for a fortnight,' she went on. 'We have photographs of you going into the hotel together and leaving together. Is there anything you would like to say?'

Of course, I should simply have said, 'I don't know what you are talking about!' because the photos weren't actually incriminating and I could have easily bluffed my way out of the situation. But instead I burst into tears. What a giveaway!

'I need to get my head together,' I told her. 'I'll come down to talk to you in a few minutes,' I added, knowing that I wouldn't.

I felt as if my life was over. The repercussions of the story appearing in the paper stretched out in front of me, including the ripple effect that would be caused by all my aunties reading about it. I knew I had to act fast, so I rang the owner of the hotel and asked her to come up to my room. Once I'd explained the situation, she arranged for a car to wait for Steve and me at the back entrance. We drove off to Heathrow together. 'Well, what does it matter if we are seen in the same car now?' I thought. 'I might as well be hung for a sheep as a lamb.'

Obviously, it wasn't just awful for me; it was bad for Steve as well because he sensed that we couldn't recover from being exposed in the national media. 'I'll talk to you later,' I said as I got on the plane to Manchester.

At home, I had to face the nightmare of telling my parents and Matthew that I was going to be in the papers. Matthew was about fourteen years old at the time, vulnerable and incredibly sensitive, so I found it very hard to tell him. It was easier telling my parents and sister because they already knew about the affair. 'What about Debbie's kids?' my parents said. 'What about your kids?'

'I'm sorry, but there is nothing I can do about it now,' I said.

Matthew was incredibly grown-up about it, but he has since said it was a defining point in his life. It was the moment he realised that his parents weren't gods, but simply two people who had fallen in love, got together and had a baby. Tim and I had been through many ups and downs before then, but Matthew had not really been aware of any major conflict. We do row and bicker – no matter who is present – but we don't air our terribly dirty linen in front of people, and certainly not in front of the children.

The story about the affair came out a couple of weeks later. The only photo used was of Steve and me leaving the hotel one morning. I must have got up late that day because I had a towel on my head in the picture, having come straight from the shower. I was on my way to the car and Steve was beside me. It was so frustrating because it was an image that could easily have been explained away. Having said that, the article stated baldly that one of the cast or crew had tipped them off, though they weren't named. I was sad about that because I'd thought I was friends with everybody.

The day the story broke, the press gathered at the top of our drive, hoping for a reaction. I didn't have a publicist at the time, so I spoke to my agent and we decided not to do an embarrassing Posh and Becks type of display (remember those piggybacks at the ski resort?). We contemplated hiding our faces, Gwyneth Paltrow style, although it drives me mad that she does that. Who cares about Gwyneth Paltrow?

In the end, Tim and I decided to smile at the photographers

on our way out, but not talk to them. By then, I'd learned to say nothing. So on the day, all they got was pictures of us driving out of the drive. However, the tabloids never give up. They kept sending us flowers. How I hate it when they do that! This went on for a few days until finally we decided to give a single interview. We did a photo in the garden and when it came out, I was just horrified. For some reason, I'd decided to wear a turquoise jumper and luminous cerise-pink lipstick! What on earth made me decide on that combo?!

In the accompanying article, we simply said that every marriage has a blip and we were not going to talk about the affair because I had already admitted to it. We were both taking responsibility, we were working through it and we would like our privacy to be respected at this time. There was no denial of the affair, nor any justification of it. We were slowly getting over it by talking it through and spending quality time together. It wasn't easy. We both hated the publicity, but accepted that it is something you have to live with when you're in the public eye.

'Well, the next thing will be Steve selling his story,' said my dad, knowingly.

'No, he absolutely won't do that,' I insisted. 'He cares too much about me to do that.'

Unfortunately, Steve and I hadn't had time for a proper farewell. We couldn't meet up again and so we didn't meet up again. When the story came out, I rang him and said, 'You realise that we can't really have any contact, don't you?'

In a way, it was better that it happened at the end of the series. It would have been harder on all levels had the story broken while we were in the middle of shooting. It would have been desperately difficult for Tim to know that I was still near Steve and embarrassing for the cast and crew. What's more, Steve and

I would have had to see each other every day, which would have made it so much worse for us both.

It was a horrible time for us as a family. I was really wobbly as a result. But life went on. Another series of *Down to Earth* was commissioned; Angela and Ian left, but Ricky and I stayed. Before we began filming, the producers came up to Manchester and we had lunch. 'Obviously, we are not going to employ Steve again,' they told me.

My heart sank, even though I had known it was inevitable. 'Oh dear, I feel really responsible for that,' I said.

'Well, you know,' one of the producers said, 'it's unfortunate, but we just don't think it's healthy. It's not fair on Tim and we don't want the press attention.'

Steve was furious, so I heard. He had lost a fifty-grand job, but I was still employed. It didn't seem fair. Apparently, he was told, 'But look, Steve, be realistic. They can do the series without you. They can't do it without Denise. So who are they going to choose? It is unfortunate, but if you play with fire, you get burned. That's just how it is.'

It was another reason for me to feel guilty.

Chapter Seventeen

Nine months went by and I got on with the second series of *Down to Earth*. I only saw Steve once during that time, in Marlow. 'There's that Steve,' my driver said as we passed by in the car. I was tempted to stop and say hello, but I didn't know how it would make either of us feel. I certainly wasn't going to go back to him, so what was there to say? Tim and I were back on an even keel and very glad that we had made it through. We were spending as many of our days off together as possible and enjoying time with the kids.

Earlier in 2004, I had finally achieved my dream of doing a play at the Manchester Royal Exchange. It was thrilling to be offered a leading role in *The Rise and Fall of Little Voice* at my favourite theatre, playing Little Voice's 'sloshed, slutty' mother. The director had thought of me because she'd seen me in a play nearly twenty years before, when she was eighteen and I was twenty-eight. 'One day, when I'm a director, I'm going to work with that actress,' she had promised herself. So we were both fulfilling a long-held ambition.

It was my first theatre piece in seven years because I'd been busy with television for some time, including *Where the Heart Is*, *Holby City*, *The Bill*, *Doctors* and *Born and Bred*. *Little Voice* was a sellout and the reviews were just amazing. It was really something to be proud of and I received two awards.

Even better, I was absolutely fine throughout it. I'd had a few grey days when I had felt horribly emotionless, which was hard, but I had survived. Then came the matinée before the last evening show. Suddenly, a thought popped into my head while I was in the dressing room: 'I haven't had my depression throughout the whole run; I bet I'll get it on the last day!'

With this thought – WHOOSH – it came upon me. I was able to bring it on myself that quickly. I dried on stage during the matinée. The audience didn't know, but I just blanked. It was terrifying. I have no idea how I managed to get through to the final curtain.

When I was up for my first best actress award for *Little Voice* in September 2004, Mum and Dad came down to Wilmslow for the award ceremony and stayed over. I felt so proud to collect it in front of them and I thanked them in my speech. The house was quiet when I got up the next morning. Tim was still in bed, as were Mum and Dad, and Louis was being looked after overnight, so he wasn't around either. I decided to go and get the Sunday papers. Although I sometimes read the serious papers and I'm up to date with the news, I particularly love the gossip papers – 'my comics', as I call them.

I drove to the nearest garage, where all the newspapers were in a rack outside the shop. On the front of one newspaper, I saw a headline that screamed, 'MY NIGHTS OF WILD SEX WITH CORRIE STAR'. Gleefully reaching for a copy to see who it was about, suddenly my knees went and I collapsed at the realisation that it was about me.

I nearly died on the spot. Sometimes you can get away with having a story about you in the paper. A lot of people only see the front page of the Sunday tabloids, so if you're featured inside, you can sometimes go unnoticed. But this was on the front page of the *Sunday People*! I couldn't believe it.

'Are you all right?' said the man in the shop, with a knowing look. How embarrassing!

I tried to keep it casual. 'Yes, can I just have this, please?' I said, quickly paying for the paper. I drove home, parked the car, went straight into the cabin by the swimming pool in the garden and called Steve. 'How the hell could you do that to me after you promised not to?' I demanded. I felt so betrayed.

'I was set up,' he said.

'I've just read it, Steve. It's an interview with you!'

'Honestly, I was set up.'

I didn't know at the time that the interview was in the *Mail* as well. It was all very odd. In the *Mail* there was a picture of him, posing under a tree. That's not being set up, is it?

Later, when I thought it all through a bit more logically, it struck me that what probably happened was that he'd got pissed and spilled the beans without really meaning to. He is not a horrible person and I just don't think that he would have done it any other way. I happen to know that the press had been on at him to tell his side of the story more than once. I can imagine they offered him money – that's usually how it works, isn't it? – but I don't know if he took it. I can see how, after being pestered, he might give in and say, 'All right, then.' I'm sure it wasn't a case of him phoning the paper and saying, 'Hello, celeb desk? I want to tell my story!' It doesn't make it right, but I think that's what happened.

If it hadn't been on the front page, I might have tried to bluff my way through the situation. But with it being so prominent, I couldn't ignore it. My mind was full of visions of all the aunties at the post office seeing my picture and the headline 'MY NIGHTS OF WILD SEX WITH CORRIE STAR'.

So I went to find Dad. 'I told you that would happen!' he said.

'Yes, all right, Dad, what can I do?'

Then I had to tell Tim.

I went upstairs just as he was getting up. 'Steve's just sold his story,' I said, handing him the paper.

'OK,' he said, taking it into the loo. He was away half an hour. When he came downstairs, he said, 'Well, you clearly broke the guy's heart. That's the end of it.' That was all he said.

In a way, it was the best thing that could have happened. Since Tim knows that I could never be with anybody who has sold a story about me, in a way it was closure for him. If there had ever been a chance that I would go back to Steve, he could be sure that it wouldn't happen now. So it was actually quite good for him. He never mentioned it again.

I think our marriage became stronger after that. What happened made us both more realistic about what *could* happen. Tim hasn't been an angel; as he later confessed, he's had the odd one-night stand here and there. However, he always justifies his behaviour by saying he hasn't actually had an affair, which isn't really a justification because a one-night stand might easily have led to an affair if the circumstances had been different. I found a girl's telephone number among his things once. Although I don't think anything actually happened, I know that it was something he was pursuing and it might well have developed into more than a one-night stand if the girl had wanted it to.

I wasn't happy to hear that Tim had had one-night stands, but that was more because he'd given me such a hard time about the affair with Steve than anything else. I don't want people to think that I'm condoning infidelity, but sexual infidelity is just not the end of the world for me. I've said this on *Loose Women*. I'm just being honest, whether people like it or not, agree or disagree. As far as I'm concerned, there are worse things that my partner can do than sleep with somebody he doesn't have feelings for, outside the marriage. If he went with a beautiful hooker in somewhere like Australia, where prostitution is legal in some states, I wouldn't be threatened by it. Some people would be, but I wouldn't.

I don't want people to think Tim and I have anything other than a close relationship, or that we have anything like an open marriage. On the other hand, we don't see infidelity on a one-night basis as necessarily spelling the end of our relationship. A one-night blip can be just that: a blip.

I've always said to Tim, 'If you have a one-night stand, don't tell me. I don't want to know.' I think men sometimes think that if they offload their guilt, then they're absolved of their wrong-doings. It's like murderers who think that saying one prayer before they die means that everything is forgiven. Of course, if it goes further than a one-night stand and you want out, for whatever reason, then it needs to be discussed, but I don't see the point of burdening your partner with it otherwise. However, in our case, it was a matter of coming clean and moving on, which we have done.

Matthew reacted really well to the story Steve sold and its aftermath. It was embarrassing for him, but he has an amazing network of friends. We were driving back from the northeast after Christmas, a few months after the story came out, and he said, 'Mum, if you and Dad split up because you're not happy, it's OK with me as long as Dad lives within walking distance.'

It was then that I realised that if Tim and I did stay together, we wouldn't be staying together for the children. Matthew was letting me know that he understood that Tim and I were having problems and he didn't want us to stay married just because of him. Meanwhile, Louis was so young that, to be honest, the physical separation of his mum and dad would not mean all that much. As it is, he thinks we have houses all over the country because of all the places we've stayed in when we've been working on location. So Tim and I were free to split up if we wanted to, in a way – or at least we didn't have to stay together for the children. Instead, we stayed together because we wanted to be together.

It's about realising that we do have a responsibility to the marriage, to listen and take each other seriously when one of us says, 'I'm going to leave if you keep doing that.' It's dangerous to ignore it and think, 'You won't leave. We're married!'

As you get older and the electricity fades, you have to work at these things. Now I find that I don't want to be married to anybody else because we know each other so well. Also, I know that the things that irritate me about Tim would still irritate me about someone else. We're there for each other, even if we hate each other at times.

Tim and I are very different on many levels. For instance, I'm a wine bar girl and he is a pub person, and although that sounds like a petty difference, it's quite fundamental to our natures. He's always losing things; he is incredibly forgetful in the short term. Yet his memory is incredible in the long term, which mine isn't. He loses his glasses, his keys, all of those things, all the time. However, because he's so funny and nice, people always look at me as if I am such a nag when I get frustrated at him losing yet another thing. 'Leave him alone! He's only lost his glasses.' But when it's happening every day, it's very irritating; when every time you have to get on a plane, he can't find his glasses or the car keys or his passport. Fortunately, Matthew understands Tim's annoyance with me, as well as my frustration with him.

My snoring annoys Tim, and I'm not surprised because it is really bad! I've tried nasal strips and everything else, but I don't want to have laser treatment for it because it can cause complications. I do understand how difficult it is for him, though. He is a light sleeper, so he probably lies awake waiting for it to start, which doesn't help. Again, it sounds trivial, but it has developed into something. The fact that I'm not doing anything about it means I don't love him enough to go and do something about it, blah blah blah. However, he talks in his sleep, so when I'm not snoring, he's laughing at his own jokes and whistling for the dog!

Also, I like sleeping in a separate room. No matter how much I love a person and want to have sex with them, that's the way I prefer it. I think it's healthy to have your own bed and dressing area, but Tim feels that the love is lost if you are not sleeping together. However, I don't like spooning. I can't bear all that cuddling. I just want to have the sex and then it's a case of 'Thank you very much. You move over there.' I'm a nightmare, aren't I?!

Another thing that annoys me is that Tim has a tendency to not own up to certain things that he has done. In his mind, he's a good guy, who doesn't drink, doesn't smoke and has never done drugs. Well, he *is* mostly a good guy, but he can be very naughty. He does drink, he does smoke and he has done drugs. 'Just admit it,' I say.

'Yes but the reason I did it is that—'

'No, just admit it!'

'But—'

'No, just say that you did it!' It drives me mad! There always has to be a reason, which is a form of denial. Whereas I hold my hands up and say, 'I did that. It was wrong, I admit, but I did it.'

Some of our problems stem from being separated by work so often. I think that a little bit of absence can make the heart grow fonder, but too much absence definitely doesn't. Too much absence means that you start living your lives separately. On the other hand, although we have spent much of our married life apart, we might not still be together after twenty years if we hadn't because I'm not a 24/7 person. I'm not a Paul McCartney type, the sort of person who would be happy not to spend a night away from my partner in thirty-six years. I'd rather kill myself! I need to be independent within the relationship.

Still, there's a constancy to our relationship that we both find comforting. We are used to each other and we rub along together. I can be completely myself with Tim. With everybody else apart from your partner, even with your parents, you're never completely yourself, are you? There's comfort in being able to be so completely relaxed with someone, though I'm sure that makes you take each other for granted as well – and we do. We have to pull each other up now and again.

I've been feeling guilty recently because I've been away working so much and I feel I should have invested more time in Tim. On the other hand, on our last wedding anniversary, he went shooting with Mark Knopfler and rang saying, 'I've just remembered it's our anniversary and it's the best anniversary I've ever had!' That would horrify some wives, but it just made me laugh. 'Thank you! That's brilliant!' I said. We don't have the most conventional marriage in the world, but it works for us.

Some of my friends say, 'If my partner had sex with someone else, that would be it.' Well, maybe it would be and maybe it wouldn't, because you never know until it happens to you. Still, I tend to counter that kind of statement by saying, 'But surely there are other strands to keep you together?' People share their lives, not just their beds – they have children, common interests and a shared past, among other things.

Interestingly, I have a couple of friends who have convinced themselves that they haven't been unfaithful because they haven't done what I call 'willies and fou-fous'. But they have met secretly and they have done everything else but willies and fou-fous! (I know, I'm fifty-one, but I don't know what else to call them!)

I say, 'No, from the minute you met secretly, you started having an affair, in my opinion.'

To me, snogging is one of the most sexual forms of fore-play. When you snog somebody, don't tell me you aren't totally thinking about sex, whether or not you go on to have it.

People say, 'It was only a snog!'

'That's because you've had to put the brakes on,' I reply. 'But the natural thing for you to do after snogging is have sex.'

Similarly, I disagree when men say that getting a blow job isn't being unfaithful. Yes it is! I think they justify it in their minds because it doesn't involve full penetration. But what difference does that make? None whatsoever.

In late 2004, I signed up to do a pantomime in Stockport. Panto is good fun and you can earn really good money if you're head-lining, but I had always said that I would only do it around Newcastle or Manchester. That way, we could be based either at my home in Wilmslow or at the family home in the northeast.

I was to play the wicked queen. It wasn't a big production and we only had a week's rehearsal before we opened on the Saturday. The Thursday before we opened was the day of the

Manchester Evening News Theatre Awards, which are like the northern Baftas, and I was up for another award for *Little Voice*. So my agent had liaised with production so that I could have the afternoon off. It was a bit scary to miss a rehearsal because we were set to open two days later, but I decided to risk it.

I felt absolutely fine at the morning rehearsal before I rushed off to the Midland Hotel in Manchester. That evening I won the Best Actress in a Leading Role award, which was really prestigious and just amazing. I was over the moon because it was such a grown-up award and I was up against some fabulous actresses. I was also thrilled that Mum and Dad were there to see me get it.

Brian Conley presented me with the award. 'I've heard you've given up drinking,' I said to him afterwards.

'Yeah I have, Denise, and I feel great. It was really, really hard, but I feel seriously great.'

'I think I'm going to give it a try too,' I told him.

However, I was somehow persuaded to go to the after-party, where I definitely didn't give up drinking. Fast-forward to the next morning, when I woke up feeling absolutely dreadful. I was shaking and I could feel my depression coming on. Now, this may have happened if I hadn't had a drink, but I thought, 'I've done it again! I've compounded this illness with my drinking.' I then got this ridiculous idea into my head that because I'd won this award, everybody would have really high expectations of me in the pantomime. I became convinced that I would be rubbish.

That was the start of another breakdown. My depression came rushing back and I opened the show severely depressed. It was just horrendous and I quickly became worse and worse. There were two shows a day at the theatre, which had once been a cinema and still had an organ. Before every show began, the organist played in that kind of Blackpool Tower, seaside style. The music haunted me; I just couldn't get it out of my head. It reminded me of nightmares I'd had as a child.

Every day I wanted to crash the car on my way to the theatre. I just wanted to put an end to my depression in any way I could, but I couldn't tell anyone how I was feeling. I had to appear strong because I was leading the company and it was important for me to engender confidence in everyone else, especially as there were children in the cast. So I had to put on this fixed smile and carry on. It would have been easier if I'd been working with people I knew, but the cast and crew were all new to me. The only person I could confide in was my dresser, Davinia, who was very supportive, thankfully. I don't know what I would have done without her.

As is usual with my depression, I lost my appetite and hardly ate a thing for three weeks. So I rapidly lost weight and my costumes kept having to be taken in. When people tried to encourage me to get something inside me, I'd buy a Greggs pasty and pretend to eat it. I wanted to eat, but everything I put in my mouth felt like sandpaper. If I drank, I retched. I could barely drink a thing, so my fluid levels were down. I was becoming very, very poorly.

One day, everything was so black and horrendous as I moved about the stage that I kept thinking I was going to run off. The idea kept repeating in my head. 'I'm just going to run off and run home!' The whole theatre seemed to be swaying. Halfway through, I dried during a big speech. It was just awful. When I got home, I was shaking. After that, I was a nervous wreck all the time. But I had to go on. I didn't have an understudy. There was no one to take my place.

I came home two or three days before Christmas Eve, feeling very wobbly, and poured myself a glass of wine. Mum and Debbie were there. 'Just stop drinking!' they said.

'I can't,' I said. 'It helps to have a few drinks.' Of course, I hadn't eaten anything, so it wasn't really doing me any good.

Just then, Tim came into the room looking very serious. 'What's up?' I said.

He frowned. 'I need to talk to you. Come into the next room with me.' It was terrible news: our beloved boxer dog, Sadie, had choked on a stick and died. I was devastated. We'd had her for seven years, since she was sixteen weeks old, ever since Tim had picked her out at a kennels when Matthew was ten. Although she was supposed to be Matthew's dog, she was very much Tim's. She was the runt of the litter and had been left at the kennels too long, so she hero-worshipped the man who had saved her.

I felt overloaded with sadness and grief. Again, I wanted to crash the car on my way into work the next day. I was constantly upset. Then, on Boxing Day, I got into work and heard about the Indian Ocean tsunami. I was appalled by the news about the numbers of dead, the stories of horror and the terrible TV footage; I think this was what finally knocked me over the edge. Overwhelmed with paranoia and distress, I began to think that my children were going to die, and that all my family was going to die.

The following day, two and a half weeks into the production, I came off stage for a costume change during the first half and collapsed in my dressing room. Davinia found me on the floor. 'That's it!' she said. 'You can't go on like this anymore.'

But I went back on stage. What else could I do? The show had to go on. However, when I came off for the interval, Tim was in my dressing room. Davinia had called him and he'd come straight to the theatre. 'I'm taking you home,' he said.

'No, I have to do the second half, I have to do the second half!' I insisted. So I limped through the rest of the show and then he took me home.

While I was on stage, Tim went to find the company manager, 'I'm really sorry, but you won't be seeing Denise again,' he told him. 'She's not coming back.'

I didn't have an understudy, but he didn't care about that. He brought me home and I gradually started to get better. But then, of course, I panicked about letting the show down. 'It's only a blooming pantomime, Denise,' my agent said. 'So you disappointed a few kids who came to see you in a pantomime!'

Most of the press was moderately sympathetic about the fact that I'd had a breakdown. But one local paper really got their claws in. The girl playing Snow White had broken her wrist, so she had a plaster cast on, and the paper said something like: 'Denise Welch let down her fans by pulling out of the show, citing "nervous exhaustion", whereas brave Snow White battled on regardless of her broken wrist.'

I tried not to let it upset me, but it did. It was just ignorance, but it brought to mind that old media cliché 'she fell out of a nightclub citing nervous exhaustion'. What they didn't realise was that I would have gone on and done the pantomime if I'd had a plaster cast from head to toe, but my illness meant that I simply could not continue. I had no choice in the matter, not least because my parents and Tim took over and forbade me to carry on.

Amazingly, the show did go on, despite my fears; they found somebody to read the part of the wicked queen. Of course, the audience was disappointed when they were told I was sick, but it didn't ruin their Christmas. Then, two or three days later, they found an ex-*Brookside* actress to replace me; she had played the part the year before. They stopped my wages, of course, but they were actually very understanding.

My recovery was very slow. My illness seemed to come on thicker and faster and the periods of wellness began to get shorter. Some time later, Tim and I went to Turkey with Mum and Dad and the boys, and some friends and their teenage sons. I'd been drinking heavily before we went and the holiday marked the start of one of the most intense periods of depression I'd experienced.

I drank to numb the pain, but it didn't seem to help. Then Tim had to go back to England and I wanted to go home with him. 'Why don't you stay here with us?' Mum and Dad suggested.

'No, I want to go home!' I kept insisting.

About a week later, I flew to Spain on the spur of the moment, to visit my friends Kevin and Clare Kennedy, who had been dry for about four years. While I was there, we talked about my drinking and I told them that I wanted to stop. 'If I don't stop, I won't get well,' I said. I had become convinced that drinking was intensifying and prolonging my bouts of depression. I no longer took cocaine; I had left behind that particular addiction when I became pregnant with Louis. I can't say that I completely stopped after that – I've had a couple of blips since – but obviously I didn't do it when I was pregnant. Now it was my drinking that was out of control, and I was desperate to do something about it.

Kevin and Claire were very sympathetic. They suggested that I ring a friend of theirs when I got home, which I did. As a result of that phone call, I started going to Alcoholics Anonymous in Knutsford. Meeting up with a group of recovering alcoholics immediately made me realise the severity of my problem with alcohol. It was definitely the step I needed to take, even though the AA setup wasn't really for me and I only went to a few meetings. Alcoholics Anonymous is a brilliant organisation, though. It has saved countless lives.

I stopped drinking after that first meeting and I didn't have another drink for two years. I didn't even risk eating a portion of sherry trifle, nothing. However, although I benefited in millions of ways by giving up, it didn't actually stop my depression. That really upset me because I had desperately hoped that it would be the key to getting well. Of course, I didn't expect the illness to vanish completely, but I was certainly hoping that it would stop coming so regularly. But no, it was still happening just as often.

Still, I didn't start drinking again, partly because I knew that my family preferred it that I wasn't drinking. It was a relief for them because they felt they didn't have to worry about me so much. People worry about you when you drink too much, even your friends, even if you sometimes get pissed with them and have a lot of fun. And to this day, Debbie would say, 'Oh, it was just brilliant when Den didn't smoke or drink. She was a different person.'

What's more, I loved the fact that I could suddenly remember everything. Never once in those two years did I think, 'Oh God, I was talking to the head of ITV! What the hell did I say?!'

I rather liked the way being the sober one commands respect. And I loved always having my car with me. I also realised that after eleven o'clock at night, there is no other party. When I'm drinking, I'm always the last to leave in case I miss something. But when I was sober, it struck me that all you miss is pissed people talking over each other, who will not remember what they've said in the morning. The good part of the evening – the

interesting conversations, the great food and the happy tipsiness –
tends to last until about eleven o'clock. After that, it's just
drunken people. Of course, when you're one of them, it's great.

The downside of not drinking was finding that when I went
out with my friends, even my friends who aren't big drinkers, I'd
be on the same level with them only until their second glass of
wine. Then things would change. I often found myself saying,
'Yes, I know, you told me that. I know, you told me that! I know,
I know. Yeah, you said that, but tell me again.' After a very short
drinking period, the interesting conversation that you've just been
having will simply turn into babble. I became very adept at going
to the toilet and not coming back.

I found that if I hung around after those two glasses, people
would start saying, 'Oh, you're so boring now you've stopped
drinking!' Or, 'Just have one. Just have one. Just have one.' It was
much easier to slip away quietly. At first, I'd worry that they
would really miss me, but it soon became clear that, after the
initial thought, they don't give a damn that you've gone.

'Where's Den?'

'Yes, where is she? Time for a top-up. Your round?'

I loved getting home and thinking, 'Ooh, half eleven: crumpets, cup of tea, television!' What I didn't like was never getting
excited about going anywhere. You know how it is when you're
going to a party, or out for dinner, or somewhere exciting? One
of the highlights is your first glass of champagne or vodka and
tonic. What's better, when you're on holiday, than that lovely
six o'clock vodka and tonic, as you're getting ready for dinner?
It wasn't getting drunk that I missed; it was that anticipation.

I'm very lucky to be invited to some fabulous events, but I
also have to go to quite a lot of corporate functions. Inevitably,

when I get there, someone will say, 'You're on a fantastic table. You're sitting next to Keith from accounts; he's hilarious!' Even before I've met him, I know that Keith will be wearing a Disney shirt, red braces and a skinny bow tie. 'He's crazy and mad. Crazy, crazy Keith!'

Now, with a full glass of champagne, I might find it fairly amusing to sit next to Keith. But sober, it's like 'Kill me now!' Without the champagne, you find that all you are doing is checking the time, waiting for the night to end. And you can't just slip away in that situation. You've got to sit it out until eleven o'clock at night.

The good mostly outweighed the bad – oh, but poor Tim! He was so proud of me that I'd given up, but as a result he had a dog's life. I became utterly intolerant of his drinking, even though his heavy-drinking days were long behind him. So he would go to the pub and come back after having two pints and I'd give him the inquisition the moment he walked through the door. 'How many have you had?'

'Two pints.'

'Argh! OK, but why are your toes digging into the carpet like that? How many have you really had?'

'Flower, I've driven back. I've just had two pints.'

'Well, you stink of booze!' I'd say accusingly, making a cup of tea and saying an abrupt good night before going to bed.

Even after two pints, people change, and that's very irritating when you're sober. I have a couple of mates, who will remain nameless and I love them dearly, but dear God, I wanted to punch their faces in after two glasses of wine. One of them does this thing where, after two glasses of wine, she'll start telling a story and fussing over tiny details that don't matter at all, like the precise date and time that something happened. Well, when I stopped drinking, my boredom threshold didn't so much drop as plummet to the lowest depths. I started arranging to meet people at lunchtime, when fewer people drink. However, after a while, it got to the point where I became a proper stay-at-home because all the excitement of going out had disappeared.

Then, when I was three days short of two years off the booze, I was on the set of *Waterloo Road* with one of my best friends, Chris Geere, who played Matt Wilding the drama teacher. It was a beautiful, summery Friday and we'd had a really tough week of relentless days and long, long hours of filming. Everybody was saying things like, 'I just can't wait to get home and have a cold beer,' or 'Ooh, I've got a chilled bottle of champagne in the fridge!' Meanwhile, I was thinking, 'I'm going home for another cup of tea! Whoop-de-doo!'

Suddenly, I said to Chris, 'I'm going to have a drink tonight.' But I didn't go out and end up getting oblivious-to-the-world drunk, like a lot of people do when they have their first drink in a long time. So the way I see it, I chose to step off the wagon, not fall off it. Obviously, I was a cheap date that night. I had two glasses of red wine and stopped.

People have asked me if I regret starting again, and I don't think I do because I prefer my life with alcohol in it. Whether or not I was an alcoholic, I don't know. People like to label every-thing. What AA say is that it doesn't matter how much you drink, you're an alcoholic when you become powerless over alcohol. So even if you're only drinking once a month, if on that occasion you become powerless once you take a drink, then you're an alcoholic.

All I know now is that, on occasion, I get absolutely ham-mered. So do all my friends; I don't do it any more than my friends. I still love to party. I know I drink too much; we all drink too much. None of my friends who likes to drink only has eight units a week, or whatever the recommended intake is.

Only the other night, at the wedding of one of my good friends, I was trolleyed! But apparently I was entertaining and fun with it. I never upset anybody when I'm drunk; I never get aggressive with anybody. I have been known to get a bit belligerent with my family, but that's only when they're telling me I shouldn't be drinking, which is a natural reaction when you're being told what to do by your family. You're always going to say, 'It's none of your business! If you had the pressures that I have . . .' Still, as a social drinker, I'm not aggressive at all. I love being around people.

As it happens, I'm nearly always working or looking after my children, so I don't often get the chance to get drunk, but every time I do, I always seem to end up in the papers the next day! Still, I have never been in a position where I can't look after my children, as they will tell you. It certainly hasn't led to Matthew having a problem with drink; he barely drinks at all.

Once I asked him how he felt about my drinking. 'Obviously, all kids hate their parents being pissed because it's so boring,' he said, 'but I wouldn't change you for the world. I like the fact that my life has been a bit rock and roll because it's made me who I am.'

Chapter Eighteen

I can't imagine how my life would have turned out if I hadn't gone into acting. It feels like the only thing I could ever have done. My career has had many twists, turns, ups and downs, and I'm amazed by all the different things I've done.

There have been some very funny moments along the way. Just one example: about six years ago, I was invited to have dinner with Donny Osmond in London, along with a random bunch of women, including Linda Robson, Anthea Turner and my friend Angie Lonsdale. None of us quite knew how the guest list had been compiled, but who were we to ask questions? It was Donny Osmond, our childhood heartthrob! I sat next to Donny for the main course and then Linda Robson sat next to him for dessert. He was so lovely and we got on like a house on fire. We talked about our nervous breakdowns and the various antidepressants we'd tried, which was really interesting!

It so happens that my friend Rosie Lewis, who still lives in the northeast, is possibly an even bigger fan of Donny Osmond than I am, which is virtually impossible. Some years before, a group of us had gone to see the Osmonds in concert and she had managed to make her way right down to the front, where she became convinced that Donny was getting a hard-on every time he looked at her.

Around the time of the dinner, Rosie had just been diagnosed with breast cancer. At least, she had been told that it was 99 per cent likely that she had it. Now, because Donny and I were getting on so well, I did something that I've never done before. 'I'm cringing doing this,' I said to him, 'but if I get my friend on the phone, would you talk to her? She's a huge fan.'

'Of course I would!' he said.

According to Rosie, she was sitting at home in Northumberland having beans and cheese on toast when suddenly Donny Osmond came on the line. Apparently, this had a momentous effect on her bowels. She says that she literally had to go to the loo while she was on the phone to him!

Just before I handed her over to him, she said, 'You didn't say anything about the hard-on, did you?' Well, I had to admit that I had!

'I sure did, Rosie!' Donny said, when he took the phone from me. 'I can remember exactly which one you were.'

They were chatting for ages and I couldn't get them off the phone. After about ten minutes I said, 'Excuse me! I only said to say hello!'

It is lovely to be in an industry that gives you the chance to do things like that for your friends. Even better, although Rosie had nearly worried herself to death and told all her friends and family about the cancer, it turned out that she didn't have it!

Along with the funny times, there have been some very bizarre moments. One particularly weird day that springs to mind was when I was filming *Down to Earth* in Henley, on one of those awful grey days. I was really feeling bad between takes. I definitely suffer from Seasonal Affective Disorder (SAD). For years I couldn't cope with greyness. It was a side effect of my depression. I'd get a tingling feeling in my hands whenever I saw black clouds in the sky, and I'd be overwhelmed with fear about the effect such a dark day would have on me.

Some people have SAD so badly that they just can't operate in the winter, but mine was a daily thing. There was a certain type of greyness that would change my chemical make-up. I have be in the sun as much as possible in the winter. I don't like the cold, but I can cope with a cold, bright wintry day, whereas greyness really gets me down.

This particular day on *Down To Earth*, the series took a slightly odd turn: my character Jackie's fortieth birthday was approaching and, out of the blue, it was revealed that she was a big Chris de Burgh fan. This hadn't been mentioned in the previous three series, but apparently she was just mad about Chris de Burgh. All of a sudden, 'Lady in Red' was playing in the background while she was doing her housework.

Ricky Tomlinson played my husband Tony in the series, and he hired a local lookalike called Chris de Bird to sing at my fortieth. A fairly random storyline unfolded after that: Tony thought he had prostate cancer and went to a holistic healer, played by Paul Kaye. Tony then found out that he wasn't going to die, he saved the healer from something, and it turned out that the healer had been to college with the real Chris de Burgh. So they flew Chris de Burgh in from Norway for one afternoon to be my surprise birthday present.

Now, I think I'm a pretty good actress, but the next scene was challenging. I had to run down the stairs and be amazed to see Chris de Burgh singing 'Lady in Red', while at the same time someone was whispering in my ear, 'Your husband's got cancer.' I just didn't know how to play it!

It was just the most random day: it was pouring with rain, I was suffering from SAD and Chris de Burgh was singing 'Lady in Red'. Then, between shots, I started telling Chris about my SAD. How boring for him! I was saying that the bad weather does more than just piss me off; it actually really affects me. He was very interested in this and asked me whether I had a SAD lamp.

'No,' I said, 'but when I was filming *Soldier, Soldier* in Germany, whenever I had the chance, I used to stand under the big halogen lamps that the crew used to create false sunlight.'

Chris de Burgh then told me that his friend just happened to have a halogen lamp factory just down the road in Maidenhead. Coincidence! He asked for my number and very kindly organised for me to have a lamp from his friend's shop, which came the very next day! We've kept in touch to this day.

My illness has obviously cast a shadow over much of my working life. This was never more apparent than on the day I was on *This is Your Life*. Of course, I had no idea that it had been planned, so it took me completely unawares. As far as I knew, my schedule that day was to open a motor-trade show in London and then come back on the train to open a garden centre in Bolton. This was back when I was in *Coronation Street* and I was being offered a lot of personal appearances.

I remember my agent asked Tim to accompany me, and I thought, 'Why is he coming with me?' Well, it was to stop me drinking, apparently, because they knew I wasn't very well.

I went down to London, opened the show and got back on the train. I really wasn't well at all and I just wanted to get the next event over with and go home. Then, to my surprise, I bumped into my agent, Barry, on the train! He said he was going to Manchester to see somebody.

'Are you all right?' Tim asked.

'No, I'm not well,' I told him. I wasn't sure if I felt up to opening the garden centre. Everything felt a bit weird and sur-real.

'Well, why don't you put some make-up on?' Tim said.

'Oh God, I just can't be bothered.'

'Go on, put some make-up on!' he insisted.

'But why? I'm only going to a blooming garden centre in Bolton!'

When I got off the train, I spotted a man with a video camera. 'What's going on here?' I wondered. I didn't suspect anything, but there was something weird about it. Then Barry and Tim said that the car meeting us was at another exit to the one we usually used. So I followed them there and then bloody Michael Aspel got out of a white limousine! Aargh! It was just a bit too much; I was so poorly. What should have been one of the best nights of my life was an ordeal.

Worst of all, I then had four hours to wait before I went on and I spent them on my own with the make-up girl, which made me feel very panicky. So it wasn't the experience it could have been because of my illness, which was a shame.

There's a nice ending to the story, though, because some time after that, the production company for *This is Your Life* had a massive party for 1,000 people who had been on the programme. I was number 1,000, so that was really cool, and it was a great party. I felt really quite proud looking around at all the other people who were there.

I began appearing regularly on *Loose Women* in 2002, when it was filmed in Norwich. Back then, it was a bit of an also-ran programme, not the major show that it is now. It was bolted together for nine weeks and then would be off air for four or five months.

If *60 Minute Makeover* was on, we'd be nudged to one side or reduced to half an hour.

I was given the Friday slot, with Jaci Stephen, Alison Hammond and Fiona Phillips anchoring, so I'd fly from Manchester to Norfolk every Thursday night on a little hopper plane. The show always seemed to go really well and I loved appearing on it. Jaci, Alison, Fiona and I were a good combination and we had some great debates. So I didn't have an inkling that there could be anything wrong with my contribution until I came back to Manchester one Friday afternoon and my agent called me and said, 'Don't worry about going this Friday. They want to jiggle things around a bit this week.'

'What do you mean?' I asked.

'They're just trying a few new things,' she said. 'They want to try you out in different positions.'

I thought it was odd, but I just let it go. However, when I turned the television on the following Friday, there were Fiona, Alison and Jaci, with Rebecca Wheatley sitting in my place! I was never told why. From that day to this, I've not had one phone call from anybody in the hierarchy at that time to explain why I was replaced. It was really hurtful that nobody had the guts to call me and let me know exactly what the problem was.

I would much rather someone had said to me, 'Denise, I'm really sorry, but we just don't like what you're bringing to the show.' It still seems strange to me because I was the same person that I am now, with the same opinions.

Fiona and Jaci were so upset. They hadn't been told either. They walked in to find Rebecca Wheatley there and said, 'Where's Denise?'

'Oh, she's not with us today,' they were told.

Fiona phoned me later. 'Are you OK?' she asked.

'I'm fine; it's just that I was told not to come in,' I said. She was absolutely horrified and said she would complain. 'Don't do anything,' I told her. 'Don't risk your job on my account. Just let it go.'

Unfortunately, the whole incident brought on an anxiety attack. I was going through a bad time and it made me really wobbly and paranoid, which was horrible.

Fortunately, the producers change regularly on a programme like *Loose Women* and when it moved back to London in 2004, I started doing it again, intermittently. For the last four years, I've become a main member of the team. I love it. I've been friends with many of the other girls for longer than we've appeared on *Loose Women*. I knew Zoe Tyler, Coleen Nolan, Jane McDonald, Lisa Maxwell and Sherrie Hewson before I became a panellist. It's great knowing them all so well because it means you can sense how far you can go with each of them. The magazines are always keen to say there's trouble between us, or some of us have fallen out, but we haven't.

Loose Women has grown and grown – it's astounding – and it's great to have been part of that growing success. We're getting A-list people on the show as guests now, including Robbie Williams, Whoopi Goldberg, Bette Midler and Josh Groban, to name a few. And it's no longer men's guilty secret. Men are happy to admit that they love it as much as women do.

The icing on the cake was winning the *TV Quick* and *TV Choice* Award for Best Daytime Programme in September 2009 and then the National Television Award for Most Popular Factual Programme in January 2010. That was a slightly odd category for us to be in and we couldn't believe it when we won. It was quite a coup, beating *Top Gear*!

The whole *Loose Women* team, both on the panel and behind

the scenes, is fantastic to work with and we always have a great laugh recording the show. I'm an actress first, but I'm exceptionally lucky to have the chance to be a presenter too, and to be taken seriously in both roles. TV drama today can be really gruelling, so it's a refreshing change to do other things.

When I was cast as Steph Haydock in the BBC drama *Waterloo Road* in 2006, I wasn't expecting the heavy workload that it went on to entail. I got the part about two months after I'd finished *Down to Earth*. I remember I took Brian Park to see Tim play the dad in *Billy Elliot* in the West End (it's my most favourite musical in the world and I saw it fourteen times) and he mentioned that he was working on a drama called *Waterloo Road*. 'But there's nothing in it for you,' he said.

A couple of weeks later, my agent got a call saying that there was a character called Steph that hadn't been cast yet. She wasn't a leading role, but would pop up every now and then. They couldn't find anyone to play her the way they envisaged, which was thin and surly, with pointed features. Obviously, I wouldn't have fitted that spec! But when they changed the spec, Brian suggested me and I went to audition for the part. This was slightly irritating, since I'd just played the lead in another BBC drama, but unfortunately everybody has to audition these days.

Once I'd got the part, I made sure that they weren't going to be able to survive without Steph, so the character grew and grew. I loved Steph from the start, partly because I felt sorry for her. She's actually quite sad in the way she bumbles her way through life, desperately looking for love and finding it in all the wrong places, falling for the wrong men and mistaking sex for love. Comedy is my main love, so I enjoy any role that I can make comedic, without turning it into a one-dimensional character. Everyone seems to be as fond of Steph as I am, and I'm often told how believable she is.

However, as many TV actors find, some people seem to have a problem distinguishing between a believable character and the real-life person playing her. It always amazes me. While I was on a cruise with my family for Christmas 2009–10, a woman came up to me and said, 'I love *Loose Women*.'

'Thank you very much,' I said. It's always nice to receive a compliment, even though every man and his dog wanted to talk about *Loose Women* on that ship and I was beginning to question whether there was any point in having an acting career.

'Now, *Waterloo Road* . . .' she said.

'Yes?' I said eagerly.

'Now, I think you're a really good actress, but a terrible teacher,' she went on.

I laughed.

'So why don't you just stick to the acting then?' she said, in all seriousness.

My mouth fell open. She wasn't joking!

'Um,' I said, at a loss for words.

'My advice to you would be to give up the teaching,' she added. I was astonished.

It reminded me of how, when fictional baby Laura was born off camera to my character Natalie Barnes after I'd left *Coronation Street*, I received as many cards congratulating me on Laura's birth as I did for the actual birth of my son Louis. I've always wondered about those people who knit baby clothes for pregnant characters in *Corrie*. Is there any point – while they're knitting the clothes, wrapping them up or posting them – at which it occurs to them that a baby is not going to be born? It mystifies me.

Returning to *Waterloo Road*, I was thrilled to be busy again, but the schedule was punishing, especially when we went from shooting two episodes at one time in the first series, to shooting four episodes at one time in later series. By the last series of *Waterloo Road*, I was often going into work for 6 a.m. every day of the week, and not getting home until 8 or 9 p.m., which was tough on me and my family because it went on for six months.

What sometimes upset me about my filming schedule was that I had less tolerance, simply because I wasn't having the quality time that I would have liked to have with my children, and I was extremely tired when I did see them. I felt guilty about that a lot of the time and annoyed that I wasn't able to share their free time with them. As a result, both my kids grew used to me squawking. I'll be very placid for a long time and then just kick off. I'm not aggressive, but I do raise my voice. It's never really angry stuff, but a lot of it is born out of frustration, especially if I feel people aren't pulling their weight. When I'm working every hour God sends, and Matthew's getting up at the crack of eleven and then saying he's tired at night, and Louis's generally being a little bugger, I'll go off like a pressure cooker!

With both *Coronation Street* and *Waterloo Road*, I was at the total beck and call of the production team and it was impossible for me to plan anything. Towards the end of the last series of *Waterloo Road*, I was trying to get time off to see Louis play a duck in a play and I thought I was going to spontaneously combust. I was so fed up about having no time, and nobody would tell me when I could take time off. Louis was a duck in *Wind in the Willows* – not a big part, admittedly, because I don't remember there being a duck in *Wind in the Willows*, but nevertheless he was a duck and I wanted to see him. 'I don't think it's going to work,' one of the producers told me.

'Well, you have to make it work!' I said.

'Okay, let me see what I can do,' said Debbie, who was our scheduler and my life-saver on more than one occasion. The news came through that it would be OK and I told Louis I'd be going.

All the next day, I kept reminding the director that I would have to leave at quarter past five. So when it came to five to five and we still hadn't turned the cameras round, I knew there was going to be trouble.

'We're really sorry, but Angela has been put in a scene which has changed the schedule, so you won't be able to go,' I was told, twenty minutes later.

'It's a quarter past five, I'm leaving the building, end of story,' I said.

'But you can't!'

'Watch me!' I said, with a burning anger rising up inside me.

What was so maddening was that I went to see Louis play the duck, but then I went home and exploded with rage and frustration because I had been so tense and on edge all day.

Still, my family has always been very supportive of my working life, much more than other families might be, I think. Tim even made a very touching and unexpected appearance on *Loose Women* on our twentieth wedding anniversary two years ago. I knew he was coming on for Valentine's Day and I'd been told that he was going to surprise me, but I assumed that he'd be bringing on a cake or something. 'Please tell me he's not going to wear a thong!' I said to Coleen beforehand. 'If he comes on in a thong with a rose between his teeth, or between his buttocks, I'll have a nervous breakdown!'

I noticed a piano on the set with rose petals strewn over it, but the producers said it was there because they were doing a pre-record with Myleene Klass immediately afterwards. Obviously I believed them. Why wouldn't I? So when I saw our friend Kevin Earle, who's a musical director, walk on, I thought, 'Oh my God!'

Tim sang 'Have I Told You Lately? (That I Love You)' and it was lovely, although it was difficult having the camera on me for so much of the performance because after a while I ran out of emotional faces to pull! Still, it was really, really nice. It was amazing how many viewers started to fancy him after that. Women all over the country were sending in emails saying, 'Oh, I get it now!'

I know a lot of the viewers think, 'God, she gives Tim a hard life!' Poor Tim – he's the butt of all my jokes on *Loose Women*, but he takes it with such good grace. He always says to people, 'It's when she doesn't talk about me that I really have to worry!' He wouldn't allow me to talk about him on the show if he didn't want me to. Obviously, I annoy him with some of the things I say, just as I annoy my sister. 'Thank you for telling the nation that I slept with your best man on the snooker table!' Debbie once said to me.

The problem is that sometimes I get so animated about a subject on *Loose Women* that I forget I'm on telly. Of course, when it's live, there's no going back on it. Still, I'd often rather get the laugh than be bothered about offending people, although I never mean to offend anyone. I do get a bit personal about Tim and me, I suppose, but that's the way I am. Generally, I'm a very open book, sometimes too open.

I don't ever regret the things I've said, not really, although you get a lot of flak if you talk about things like infidelity. I probably shouldn't have visited any of the online forums discussing the show, but seeing how many people hate you can be addictive!

It's usually a fifty–fifty split. You get people who support you, who adore you and relate to everything you say, and people who genuinely hate you and think that you're a complete slapper! I don't read them anymore, but I have done in the past.

I also get criticised for my lifestyle in the magazines, but I've never read the book that says that when you're over forty-five, you've got to stop going out and having a good time with your friends. I hope I'll still be doing it at seventy-five, health allowing! As long as you're not hurting anybody, what's the problem? I'm never unable to do my job or look after my children.

I've spoken about my illness on *Loose Women* several times. I hope it's helped anyone watching who suffers from depression. It's been a long old journey. After my breakdown in 2004, my depression became progressively worse again; my times of being well were shrinking and the severity of the bouts were intensifying. In June 2005, I was up and about again, but I just wasn't well and not eating. I hated the fact that I was worrying my family all the time. They always know when I'm not well; they can hear it in my voice.

I wasn't sure if I could go on feeling that way for the rest of my life. I longed to take a pill and have it all go away. I was so sick of battling it that I used to tell myself that I could always commit suicide if it got too bad. Of course, I also knew that I would never have done something like that because of my children, but I needed to feel I had another option to being so poorly.

I had been trying to convince doctors for more than twenty years that the origin of my illness must be hormonal. Finally, I heard about a doctor in Baltimore who specialised in treating depression with hormones. Desperate for a cure, I was on the point of going to America to see him when I got talking to a friend of mine, who told me about a London specialist called Professor John Studd, so I rang him. The memory is so vivid: it was 22 June 2007 and I was in the corridor at work at *Waterloo Road*.

'My name is Denise Welch and I'd really like to come down and see Professor Studd,' I said to his lovely secretary, Joan.

'He will make you better,' she said, as we arranged an appointment. I didn't know whether to believe her, but something in her voice gave me hope.

I was very lucid the day I went to see Professor Studd. I was pleased that I felt OK because if I'm depressed, I'm almost catatonic. Fortunately, this day I was my normal, chatty self, but soon he cut me off and said, 'OK, OK! I understand totally what you're saying. You don't need to go on about it anymore because I'm going to sort it out.'

After establishing that I had a Mirena coil, the one with progesterone, he said, 'Lie down over there with your legs up in the air because we're going to take the Mirena coil out. It's a brilliant invention, but a lot of people are progesterone intolerant, and I think you've been progesterone intolerant for twenty years.'

Next he told me that I was almost completely lacking in oestrogen. 'No wonder you've been the way that you have,' he said. 'But don't worry, I can sort it.'

I was amazed. 'Have I finally found someone who can cure me?' I wondered, hardly daring to get my hopes up. I told him about how Katharina Dalton's hormone therapy hadn't helped and he said that this was simply because she had prescribed progesterone instead of oestrogen. She was way ahead of her time and had been on the right lines, but with the wrong hormone. Instead, he prescribed me oestrogen in gel form. I wanted it in tablet form because it felt like I was putting on moisturiser, but he said that the gel was a much quicker way of absorbing it.

Professor Studd was refreshingly straightforward about

everything, so I felt that I could be straightforward with him. When he asked about my sex life, I said, 'To be honest, I have no libido whatsoever. Mind, I have been married nearly twenty years!' So then he prescribed me a small amount of the male hormone testosterone in gel form. I was supposed to use a pea-sized amount every other day, whereas a man with a testosterone deficiency would be told to use a full tube every day. It revived my libido, so I used to worry that I would wake up one day covered from head to toe in the stuff because Tim's so desperate for some jiggy-jigs!

I still always talk about my illness in the present tense. I still live and deal with mental illness, but it hasn't come back like it used to since Professor Studd began to treat me. I have a couple of bad days every now and then, but I can always sense that I'll bounce back quickly. It may sound dramatic, but I feel that he saved my life. I've got my life back.

I'm testing it all the time because there are certain situations, like hangovers, worry or lack of sleep, that always used to trigger it, but amazingly they don't anymore. It feels like a miracle. There was a time when I would have found it difficult to talk freely about my illness because I'd think that I was bringing it on by talking about it. But now, for the first time in twenty years, I'm not frightened of my illness. I feel normal; I feel as if I finally have the freedom to deal with my emotions. When I'm sad, I'm sad – and nothing more.

I still take a very low-dosage antidepressant and, at the moment, the combination is working. I'm a huge advocate of antidepressants, when used correctly. They won't help if you're depressed because your boyfriend has split up with you because no matter how emotionally upset you are, that is a normal reaction. Grief is a normal reaction. Antidepressants help with clinical depression because they redress the chemical imbalance in your brain. They get grouped with happy pills and tranquillisers, but they're nothing like them. They simply enable you to see the light at the end of the tunnel.

Like my mum used to say, 'If you've got bronchitis, you think nothing of taking an antibiotic.' But people with depression feel bad about being on pills. I would get to a period of wellness and say, 'Right, I'm coming off those pills,' and Mum would always try to dissuade me, thankfully.

It was incredible to feel well again after so many years of being ill, on and off. Prior to seeing Professor John Studd, I thought that I would find it tough to die of natural causes. It wasn't a case of life being too short, but more of life being too long, especially when the illness was coming thicker and faster. I wondered how long I could keep carrying on the struggle.

But now, at last, I could live my life without worrying about what the next day would bring, about whether the darkness would descend again and plunge me into depression. Everything seemed to fit into place and I felt contented like never before. My career was great – I was dividing my time between *Waterloo Road* and *Loose Women* – and my home life was wonderful too. Everything felt very settled.

You never know what's around the corner though; you never know what life will throw at you. Sadly, just before Christmas 2007, the doctors diagnosed Mum with another oral cancer. It was such bad luck because it was unrelated to her original cancer, and they had said that there was a two million to one chance that she would get another oral cancer. Since radiotherapy nearly killed her twenty years previously, Mum said she wouldn't have it again, so instead they did laser surgery, and they eradicated the tumour. Again, we thought that everything was fine, but when we came back after our Christmas cruise in early 2008, they found another one. This time, they said, they couldn't do any more surgery in that area. Mum's only chance, and it was only a 30 per cent chance, was to have intensive radiotherapy for six weeks plus chemotherapy.

'Will I lose my swallowing reflex?' Mum asked her doctor.

'It's 99 per cent likely,' he replied. Apparently, Mum would have to go to hospital every week for a false saliva top-up.

'I just can't do it,' Mum said. The laser therapy had taken away her ability to get food down, although she could still just about swallow, a reflex that had been slowed down when she had surgery for the original oral cancer.

It was awful, just awful, for us, but at the same time, Debbie and I knew that we couldn't put pressure on Mum to do it. We couldn't ask her to sacrifice her quality of life. So we had to accept we were going to lose her. We decided not to ask for a prognosis because we all know people who have been given a year, and yet five years later they're still here, and vice versa. It seemed pointless to make the situation even more tense than it was.

Mum was just brilliant; she even made jokes about having cancer again. Dad's been very brave too, although I know that he has shared his distress with his close friends. It's been very, very hard for the whole family. In January 2009, Mum was told that she had stage four cancer, which is almost as bad as it gets, and the doctors told her that they were going to focus on palliative care from then onwards. I was devastated. We all were. I wasn't sure whether to embark on another series of *Waterloo Road*, in case I had to leave halfway through.

I felt helpless. As you will now know, I'm not religious, but I do believe in the power of the universe, so, in desperation, I asked the universe to make her better. I'm a great believer in the power of visualisation, so I envisaged a scenario where the doctor went to Mum's bedside, checked her over and said, 'We can't find the cancer!'

And that's what actually happened the following August! It was completely unexpected, just astonishing. The doctors didn't say that there was no cancer there, but they couldn't actually see anything. Nothing had grown. Mum didn't want any further exploration done because as far as she was concerned, she wasn't going to have any treatment. Anyway, if something is lying dormant, why risk flaring it up? Because of her swallowing difficulty, they fitted her with a peg, which enabled her to feed herself liquid meals and water through her stomach. As a result, she absorbed more nutrition and more calories than she had done for twenty years, since swallowing first became difficult. By the end of the year, she was up to seven stone in weight and looking fabulous, like Joan Collins again. It was mind-blowing.

Late last year, we were at a wedding and Debbie said, 'I'm a bit embarrassed about telling people about Mum's terminal cancer because she looks so well, better than she has done in ages!' I saw her point. You know those awful people who pretend that a family member has cancer so that people will give them money? Well, I think that's what people might be thinking about us when they see Mum! That we'll start this Annie Welch fund and then she'll bugger off to Barbados or something.

So, for the moment, life is rosy. I love my work and I feel very lucky to have such a wonderful family. As I've said, Tim and I are so thankful that we've stayed together, despite the difficulties we've had in the past. We're realistic about our relationship. I think we both accept that there are problems in any marriage.

In September 2009 I was involved in a hat-trick of *TV Quick* and *TV Choice* awards when *Waterloo Road* won Best Drama, *Loose Women* won Best Daytime Show as I've said, and I won Best Actress for *Waterloo Road*. It was brilliant. I was very proud, although there was a bittersweetness to the Best Actress award because I knew then that I was leaving *Waterloo Road*. It was the right decision to make, but that doesn't mean it was easy. I'd been there for five series and had a wonderful time working with such fantastic people. Steph has been a great role to play and I'm lucky that they've asked me to go back for a few episodes in the future, so I don't have to say goodbye to her just yet.

I'm not somebody who has a burning ambition to play a particular role, but I would love to do more one-offs. My dream job would be to do several lovely ninety-minute specials that each take me six weeks to film, rather than being constantly locked into a series. I would also love to work with Dame Judi Dench. I just adore her. I love everything she does. It's wonderful that she can be taken seriously as a classical actress as well as a comedic actress. What's more, she will stand and have a natter before going on to play the most amazing part! I like to think that I'm an instinctive actress in the way that she is. She takes her work seriously, but she doesn't take herself or the industry too seriously.

Either way, I would just love to keep working because at fifty-two, I feel very lucky to be getting work when many of my contemporaries aren't. It's much more difficult to get work these days, partly because of the number of reality shows on television. They're just not making dramas like they used to.

Now that I'm back to living with a mad schedule, instead of a totally insane one on *Waterloo Road*, I'm really enjoying having more time with my lovely boys. They are a delight to be around and I'm so proud of them both. Matthew is a lovely, lovely young man with a wide network of friends. He's also a very talented musician and, at the time of writing, is on the verge of signing a record contract with his band, Drive Like I Do. I'm hoping that he will become a major rock star and MTV will come and feature my crib one day!

Louis is a gorgeous bright spark, full of fun, affection and ingenuity. Hopefully, he will become a professional footballer and bring his hunky friends round to see Nana in her dotage! It's when I'm with my sons that I experience my strongest sense of achievement. I have such an amazingly close and happy relationship with them both that I can't help but feel that my life has been a success.

I'm proud of what I've achieved in my life and career, despite all the mistakes I've made and the setbacks that my illness has caused. I think of myself as a survivor, because although mental illness is seen as a weakness by some people, you have to be strong to survive it. As a result of being ill, I appreciate the good times more. I'm never complacent about being well; I never take it for granted. I'm not saying that I never moan about my lot. Everybody does; that's human nature. But there's usually a point in every single day when I'm aware that I'm well and I'm incredibly grateful for it. I finally feel that I'm pulling myself together.

Chapter Nineteen

Have I been too open? This was the question I asked myself again and again as I read back over the manuscript of *Pulling Myself Together* before it was published. I thought very carefully about it. Was I revealing too much?

When I decided to tell my story, I knew it was very important for me to talk about my depression, but did I really need to divulge the dark chapters that followed? After much deliberation, I decided that the answer was yes, because I couldn't have written honestly about my depression without taking the reader to those places. At the same time, I'd heard a rumour that there was an unauthorised account of my life in the offing. Since some of the episodes I described in the book were already in the public arena, I knew that if I didn't give my own account of them, they would inevitably be dragged out and told in somebody else's words. This made me even more determined that if anyone was going to tell my story, it would be me. It was going to be my story in my words.

I've been in the public eye for quite some time now, and given the huge popularity of *Loose Women* and the fact that I'm known for sometimes being quite 'out there' (probably to my detriment!) I sensed that the book would attract a certain amount of interest.

I had no idea, though, just how huge that interest would be. It seemed that everywhere I looked there was another headline about my 'shocking revelations'.

The worst headline by far was 'MY COCAINE SHAME'. When I saw those words in huge, bold letters, I was appalled. I had agreed to the book being serialised in a newspaper because it was a good way to let people know that it was coming out, but I would never have given it the go-ahead if I'd known how it was going to be presented. I had suspected that the papers would focus on the darkest episodes of my life, taking them all out of context, but this was devastating. I was horrified.

To make matters worse, the same week all the madness began I flew to Los Angeles to do a report for *GMTV*, covering a road trip from LA to San Francisco with Carla Romano, who was *GMTV*'s Hollywood correspondent at the time. The job had been arranged months in advance, but some people thought that I had deliberately flown the nest so that I wouldn't have to deal with the fallout from the serialisation.

This couldn't have been further from the truth. On the contrary, it was very difficult for me to be a million miles from my family during a time of such intense scrutiny, leaving them to pick up the pieces. I was in a completely different time zone, having to get up at 4 a.m. to do publicity interviews for the book back home and then carry on with the work I was supposed to be doing in the US, all the while feeling worried sick about the effect all the attention was having on those closest to me and dreading the next day's headline.

Fortunately, none of the headlines were quite as bad as the first day's – I think the headline writers realised they'd gone too far with that one – but it didn't seem to matter, as by then the spotlight was well and truly on me. Literally overnight it felt as though the real me had been replaced by someone known only for taking drugs and having an affair.

My family were fantastic, of course. I had been very open with them about the book and the stories it contained, so they were as prepared as they could be. But it still took them by surprise when the reporters began turning up day after day on my doorstep, and even at my parents' and my sister's houses. None of us had had any idea how big an impact it would have on our lives.

One day I did something like twenty-five back-to-back radio interviews. 'So, did Tim know about this book?' I kept being asked.

What sort of person did they think I was? 'No,' I told them, with my tongue in my cheek. 'I just said to him after publication, "If you want to pop along to your local Smith's today, you'll see a tell-all autobiography on the second shelf when you walk in . . ." *Of course he knew about it!*' I said. 'I've been working on it for a year and there's no way that I wouldn't have told my family about it.'

I wanted Tim to be completely in the loop, so he read the book as I was writing it and was very supportive. There were some things that he would perhaps have preferred me not to talk about, but I fought my corner and he reluctantly accepted. Now I was ringing him from Los Angeles saying, 'Listen, tomorrow's headline is going to be . . .'

He was brilliant about it. 'Don't worry, I'm not even reading it, flower,' he reassured me, knowing how much I needed his support while I was away. He told me that people kept trying to talk to him about it in the pub, but he dismissed it by saying, 'Oh, it was all years ago.'

The cocaine use at *Coronation Street* had also taken place

many years before – nearly fifteen years ago, in fact. Yet in my interview with the paper, it came across almost as if it was a recent thing. Seeing the story spread over a double page was shocking. When you read about my cocaine use in the context of the whole book, you understand that it was a small part of my life and that I was self-medicating to a great extent, to cope with my illness. Reading it out of context gives a very different impression. My book told the whole story; the newspaper serialisation did anything but.

I'd anticipated it to some extent. Before the book was serialised, I had a word with my sister's children, whom I love more than anything in the world next to my own. Being in their mid-to-late teens, they're quite a vulnerable age, but they're cool kids. Nevertheless, it was a bit tricky. I left two copies of the book in the house and told them to bear in mind that much of what I had written was well in the past. There were some unsavoury areas of my life that they didn't know about, but instead of trying to hide them, I wanted them to read the book and see them in context.

'For a week or two,' I warned, 'there will be some attention focused on Auntie Neece and certain stories will be picked out.' They didn't seem too concerned about the whole thing, but Debbie was worrying that everybody at school would gather round their desks saying, 'Your auntie's terrible, isn't she?' And admittedly, Tim and I were both a bit concerned about what the reaction would be at Louis's school gates. After all, the book definitely threw up some contentious issues! Thankfully, though, the other parents have been really supportive. I get the impression from some of them that, had they come up against the same obstacles I did, they may have ended up following the same dark path. In a way I felt that they were quite reassured that other people have their dark sides – and their marital problems and struggles with addiction and depression – and that someone they knew, even if not very well, was talking openly about them. Whatever they thought, I've been lucky not to have come up against anyone with a very black-and-white view of it all; certainly no one has said, 'Keep your child away from mine!' or any of that kind of thing.

Luckily, I also got the same sort of supportive reaction from radio interviewers, despite them asking me some silly questions! Partly because of the press furore, I was prepared for them to give me a hard time too, but perhaps because I had been so open about everything, I never felt that I was being judged. I got the impression that on the whole they admired me for my honesty.

It did amaze me, though, that they only appeared to be interested in two minor episodes in my life: doing drugs at *Coronation Street* and the affair with Steve Murray, which had already been well documented. In the book I had talked about so many other far more interesting and shocking stories, to me at least. Yet not a single interviewer asked me about my ex-husband, who had played such a big part in my life and the book. My relationship with him has influenced the rest of my life, including my relationship with Tim, but it wasn't alluded to once. Nor was the fact that I had had two pregnancy terminations, which I'd never talked about before. One of the terminations took place in very emotional and traumatic circumstances, but it was not mentioned at all. I sometimes think that if I'd done drugs on the set of any other programme, there wouldn't have been the interest in it. But because it happened on the set of *Coronation Street*, there was a frenzy of attention that eclipsed the rest of the book.

I heard a rumour that there were people at Granada who

became rather twitchy when they found out I was going to be talking about doing drugs at *Coronation Street*. Apparently, they were terrified that I might implicate some current cast members. Apart from the fact that I know absolutely nothing about what the current cast gets up to, I would never reveal anyone else's secrets apart from my own. Still, it did make me chuckle that there were a few sweaty brows!

I went back to the cobbles quite a bit last year, as part of the fiftieth anniversary celebrations. There was a photo shoot with about twenty Rovers Return barmaids, from the year dot up to the current day, which was great fun. I saw lots of people I haven't seen for ages, from Irma Barlow (Sandra Gough) right up to Kym Marsh. We talked about old times and how things have changed. In one way it was quite weird to be back in the Rovers after all this time, but in another it felt like I'd never been away, which I wasn't expecting at all.

I was pleased to have the chance to go back and see the set for the last time before the big tram disaster. It felt a bit like the end of an era. I was also glad to be there because some press reports suggested that I would be *persona non grata* at *Coronation Street* after my book was published. I felt it was one in the eye for those people, as I was actually invited back there more last year than at any other time in the ten years since I left the series.

A couple of weeks after the book came out, I called my nieces. 'Has anyone said anything?' I asked. 'No, not really,' they replied, and that was that. I was so glad they didn't appear to be being pulled into it in the way the rest of the family were.

My own kids are used to seeing stuff about me in papers and magazines. They'll be looking at a magazine article with the heading 'Denise Welch goes missing!' while I'm cooking the sausages for their tea, so it's not surprising that they treat the magazines a bit like comics. It's a by-product of my work and they take it with a pinch of salt. Having said that, the tabloid newspapers are more hard-hitting and go into areas that those magazines don't, but fortunately it all goes over Louis's head and Matthew is mature enough to see it for what it is. Still, I had never experienced this level of press attention before, so it was quite overwhelming for all of us.

There were also many positive consequences of writing the book, though, and I was thrilled that it instantly went to number one for several weeks. Many of the people who bought and read it have come up to me or emailed me to say that they've gained so much from it, and it's a wonderful feeling to know that my story has touched or helped people in some way or another. This has meant so much, because I was really hoping that in describing my depression it would bring about a wider understanding of the illness.

I had a very touching encounter in the summer. I was with some friends in a bar in the Algarve in Portugal when a young woman in her twenties came over. She was shaking from head to toe. 'I can't believe I've met you!' she said. 'My mum bought your book for me, because she knows I'm a fan of yours. I suffer from anxiety and depression and I was just so captivated by your story.' Twice this week I've dreamt that I would meet you one day,' she continued, 'and now I've come to the Algarve from the UK and here you are, sat in a bar. You're one of the first people I've seen!'

She said that her mum had never understood her illness until she read my book, and reading it had prompted her to give the first hug she had given her in years. It was all very well to be given a medical explanation of depression, her mum had told her, but until she read about it in laymen's terms, it was hard for her to really empathise. 'I'd never attempted to understand your illness,' her mum said, 'but after reading Denise's book, I now feel as though I know what you've been going through.'

Lots of people have shared similar stories with me and I'm very glad that I've been able to reach so many fellow sufferers. It really makes me feel that I've done something worthwhile. When I went back to see Professor Studd to get a repeat prescription of my oestrogen treatment, I found out that lots of people had made appointments to see him after reading the book or hearing me in interviews talking about it. 'Come and have a chat when you come in,' he said, so after I had picked up my prescription, he came out of his office and there was a girl with him. He introduced us and she started to cry. 'I came here after reading about you,' she said. I knew then that all the fallout from the book had been worth it to be able to help people like her.

And from my own point of view, I think that sharing my story has really helped the people in my life to understand more of what I've been through. Even my dear, dear friends and relatives, who knew about my depression and illness, were moved to tears by the account of my lowest ebb.

However, a few days after the book came out, I started to feel a bit poorly, as all the stress that had been building up in me began to take its toll. Bearing your soul to the nation in your autobiography is quite traumatic; all my girlfriends who've written books say the same, even though they don't suffer from depression. Plus, I was very busy and my schedule was packed, so although I had great fun and met some great people, I was working very hard – probably too hard.

At first I didn't notice that it was affecting me. In fact, I was feeling so well that when I forgot to take my antidepressants with me to Los Angeles, I decided to stop taking them all together.

I'd been feeling so happy and stable for so long that I thought maybe the time had come that I just didn't need them any more. I had no idea what a huge mistake I was making.

Just after getting back from the trip to Los Angeles, I went to New York to make a DVD with some of the *Loose Women* girls. The night we arrived, I went to bed feeling really happy and excited. It was magical to be in New York with my best friends, making a DVD, and we were staying in a gorgeous hotel in SoHo. 'My God,' I thought, 'I've always wanted to work in the States – and here I am working in America twice in a year. How fantastic!'

But when I woke up the next morning, everything had changed. It was as if something had gone 'bang' in my head. I felt unbelievably bad.

If I'm at home and that happens, I might have the option of not doing the show. But I didn't have that option in New York because the DVD revolved around there being four of us, like the four characters in *Sex and the City*, and I had taken on the anchor role of pulling the film together. Luckily, the depression hit me in waves, so we were able to film around it, but it was still really difficult. That was the beginning of a bad run of being poorly and I was really up and down for at least three months after that.

As soon as I got home I phoned my GP for a prescription of my usual antidepressants, but when I started taking them they made me feel ten times worse and I instantly had to stop. The GP changed the tablets, but the new ones had the same effect. So I had to wait until I was out of the worst of the depression and introduce the new antidepressants when I was well. They made me a bit shaky, but didn't plunge me into the depths, and since I've adjusted to them I've felt normal again, touch wood.

They'll never make me feel ecstatically happy and that's not what I want from them anyway; as I've said before, I hate them being called 'happy pills' because they're just 'normal pills' to me. Thankfully, I feel that I've got the balance right again and I'm back to my normal self.

In a way, I'm glad I had that blip because I know now that I'll always need a small dose antidepressant in combination with the hormone treatment that Professor Studd prescribes me, and there's no way I'll take such a risk with my health again. My depression isn't moderate; it's severe and incapacitating when it happens, so although I hate the idea of popping pills for the rest of my life, it's a small price to pay to save me and my family all the heartache it causes.

Something else happened around this time that I'm sure played a part in pulling me down as low as I got: the newspaper serialisation led to a few people coming out of the woodwork and trying to make a quick buck out of me. I suppose it was inevitable, but you'd think that if people were going to do that, they would have tried it before because my life has been quite public for many years. However, as the book started to sell very well, maybe they saw a currency there that they hadn't seen before.

One person's story in particular put a strain on my relationship with Tim. As a result, Tim and I questioned for a while whether we were going to make it to the final furlong. Were we just in this because we were 'Tim and Denise', who were married and had two children? Or did we actually want to be in it for the long haul? When we'd originally had problems, we agreed that we weren't staying together for the children – and that was still the case. But did we think so differently about things that it wasn't worth battling on? We are two very different people. So was it maybe time, at 52 and 59, to review the future?

We took a couple of weeks out to think it through and between us we've done a lot of soul-searching. We've also done a lot of talking, not in the form of shouty arguments, but proper discussions. It was clear that the whole process of bringing out an autobiography was taking a toll on us, from the year it took to write it, to the months promoting it. Not only did it mean that our relationship and whole family life were in the public eye, but the book was demanding so much of my time that I was constantly busy and Tim was having to hold the fort at home. We had never stuck to stereotypical roles in our marriage, but this was a complete role reversal of your traditional couple.

During this time, Tim made it clear that, however much he had been trying to reassure me that he had been letting everything go over his head, he doesn't take the tabloid magazines with a pinch of salt as easily as the children do. Sometimes the articles really wind him up, especially when they drag him into a story that's based on hearsay or something I've said on *Loose Women* that's been taken out of context. I can understand why it seems unfair because he's not someone who likes to air his dirty laundry in public and he doesn't see why he should have to fight his corner or talk back. At the end of the day, he's an actor, a husband and a father, and he doesn't want his life hung out for all to see and comment on. My argument was always: 'Yes, but doing *Loose Women*, which leads to those types of articles, helps to pay our bills!'

This was very single-minded and selfish of me; it was inconsiderate not to recognise that of course some of the stuff written about me would have an impact on him. I wasn't taking his feelings into account enough. My tendency was to say something like, 'Oh well, I'll just give everything up then. If you don't like the fact that there are repercussions, let's all live on fresh air!'

The press coverage affected all aspects of his life, as it did mine. 'How do you think it makes me feel when I go into the pub and people are saying this, that and the other?' he asked me.

After many discussions, we've both learned to compromise more, and to take each other's feelings into consideration. I now accept that it must be difficult for him, while he accepts that inevitably some of what I say on the show, let alone in interviews, will be taken out of context. It's an unavoidable consequence of the sort of job I do. He doesn't want to muzzle me on *Loose Women* because part of my role on the show is to have a pop at him, without ever meaning to be malicious or nasty. But I realise that I need to be more careful about what I say in interviews.

'Sometimes you just engage your gob before your brain,' Tim says, and he's right. So I've had to think before I speak and be a little bit more respectful of him and the children.

I've found that I also need to be more on my guard when I go out because there's been much more of a pap presence on me since the book came out. In fact, one particular publication even tried to set me up by putting some journalists inside a charity event I was at. They were going out of their way to catch me out, rather than stumbling across me having a giggle. That's not very nice and it's also a lame excuse for journalism, if you ask me.

It seems that the papers have decided that they want to portray me as someone who spends night after night falling out of clubs, so that's what the paps are primed to capture, even when it couldn't be further from the truth. Until recently, my view tended to be that I might as well be hung for a sheep as a lamb! But I've since started to rethink things.

One night that really sticks in my mind is my close friend

Pammy's birthday in London last summer. Her friend Kirsty had arranged for Lotan Carter, Louie Spence's nephew, who is one of the Dreamboys' male strippers, to come along and present Pam with her birthday cake, which was good fun and gave us all a real giggle.

We'd been having a great evening, so we all decided to go on to a nightclub called Mahiki, but I had to leave early because I was working the next day. We'd heard there was a big pap presence outside so Lotan very sweetly offered to take me to my car. We couldn't believe it when we stepped out of the club – there were about 35 or 40 paps, going absolutely mad. It must have been a very quiet night on the A-listers front! The people at Mahiki had very kindly ordered me a car and my driver was in a state, using every swear word under the sun because the paps were swarming around his car.

I quickly gave Lotan a hug and got in the car. End of story. After all, only in my dreams would I be taking a Dreamboy back with me – and certainly not in front of 40 paps!

Yet even though I left in the car alone and the paps saw me go back to my hotel on my own, the next day's online headlines all said things like 'Dirty Den out with Male Stripper'. The photos made me look drunk, even though I was sober, and there were references to me being 'in high spirits'.

The implication always seems to be that I'm out of control, which is so irritating because I feel like I'm constantly having to defend myself to people. At work the next day, I felt compelled to say, 'By the way, I wasn't drunk last night'.

Throughout my career, I'd always had a very gung-ho attitude to the way people perceived me. The way I saw it, I wasn't doing anything wrong, so why shouldn't I go outside with Lotan? It hadn't occurred to me how it might be portrayed if I came out of a nightclub with a twenty-one-year-old stripper. But now I have to remember that it might not be very nice for Tim, and I need to think about how I would feel if the shoe was on the other foot.

Tim understood because he knows that the press will do their best to make something of nothing. But the fact is that his mates in the pub see it in a different way. It's not like he would ever try to shackle me and say, 'Never go out!' But in future, in a situation like that, I just have to think, 'Hang on a minute, I'll get a girlfriend to take me out to the car'.

Luckily, we've survived the impact of it all and come through the other side. I don't like to tempt fate – and we are definitely a work in progress – but mine and Tim's relationship actually feels stronger than it's been in ages. As well as learning to consider each other's feelings more, we've both had to do quite a bit of self-analysis: I've realised that I find it hard to compromise so that's something I've been working on. And Tim tends to be a bit stuck in his ways sometimes, so he's been trying to make sure he's a bit more flexible.

The best thing is that we're now enjoying each other's company again. We'd been coasting along in our relationship, and the only things we ever seemed to talk about were domestic arrangements. When life is really busy, it's so easy to just focus on the children when you get home and forget the enjoyment you get from spending time together. We didn't realise it for quite some time but we'd started living different lives.

There was a moment when I realised all of this and I found I was really missing Tim and the way our lives used to be. It was the middle of August and I was on holiday with Matthew and Louis in a beautiful village in Mallorca called Deia. It was a real treat, especially as Matthew doesn't often come on family holidays any more, but Tim had decided not to come, partly because it was going to be very hot there and he's not a great lover of the intense heat. Deia is very hilly and you have to do quite a bit of walking to and from the village, which is tough when it's forty degrees. Since Tim had been invited to go clay-pigeon shooting with his pals in the North East on the same weekend we were flying to Mallorca, he decided to do that instead.

'Don't come then,' I said. 'I just think you're missing out because the two boys will be there.'

I thought it would be fine, but when we arrived, I kept thinking, 'There's something missing.' I loved being with the boys, but Tim's absence was stopping me from really being able to enjoy myself.

We were staying with our friends Jean and Stuart, their daughter Sadie, who played the head girl in *Waterloo Road*, and their son Simon, who is a big buddy of ours and Matthew's. There's not much to do in Deia except have a drink at the one bar in the village, but there was such an interesting bunch of people there that it was really good fun. No matter how busy we were, though, or how many people we were surrounded by, I still couldn't help wishing Tim were with us. Obviously I can have a good time without him, as he can without me, but on this occasion, I just kept thinking how much I wanted him to be there.

After a couple of days, I picked up the phone and called him. 'Would you not reconsider?' I said.

Coincidentally, he was thinking the same thing. 'I'm just online looking for a flight, because I miss you all so much,' he said. 'I'll come tomorrow.'

I think that was the point at which we both realised just how much we really mean to each other, and since then things have been really good. We'll always be Tim and Denise and we'll always squabble and niggle; we're not going to turn into a Stepford husband and wife. But we are good together and it feels like we're in a much stronger place.

It definitely helped when Tim got a regular part in the ITV sitcom *Benidorm*, because it was the first time in ages that he was working on something that he was really excited about. He originally went in to do a cameo and they loved the character so much that they brought him back as a regular. Now he's got one of the lead parts, playing Les/Lesley, which is just hilarious. Half the time he plays a man and the rest of the time he's a rollerblading waitress who careers into shot wearing full drag and roller boots! My father's gutted. 'I've waited all my life for that bloody part!' he rails every time he sees us!

Tim has loved every minute of doing *Benidorm* because the scripts are just phenomenal and the cast are great to work with, and I'm thrilled that he's doing something he enjoys so much. Still, it's hard for us to be apart. I really miss him when he's in Spain and he definitely struggles with being away from home. He was so homesick while he was filming the series last autumn, what with missing me and the boys and worrying about his vegetable patch (and I really shouldn't have let the tomato plants in the conservatory die, even if they were taking over the whole room!). But it was definitely worthwhile putting up with being homesick as he's loved being involved in the show.

One night before they started filming, he came home and told me that Cilla Black was going to do a cameo in the Christmas episode. This had come about because, very sadly, Geoffrey Hutchings, who played the fabulous character of Mel, married to Madge in the wheelchair, had died in real life, before the new series began. This meant that the whole series had had to be rewritten in a very short time. Part of the new storyline was that Mel was living in Marrakech and Tim, in his role as Les the man, was his gofer, picking people up from the airport and taking them to Mel and Madge's villa, among other things.

In the Christmas episode, which is hilariously funny, but also very sad, Mel dies and his chavvy family from England turn up to the villa, which has now been sold to Cilla Black, who has a maid, Consuela, living there with her.

Since Cilla is a pal of mine, I texted her to say, 'Oh my God, you're going to be in *Benidorm* with Tim. How fantastic!'

But she called me to say that she was gutted because she'd turned it down. 'When it came through, I decided that I didn't want to play myself. I wanted to play a character,' she explained.

'But you could make 'Cilla' a character, like in *Extras*, where the special guests play themselves, but with a fictional twist.'

'I know!' she said. 'I'm regretting it now. I was sat with Cliff and Paul O'Grady the other day and Paul told me I was mad to turn it down. "I would kill to be in that show!" he said.'

I think *Benidorm* has become a bit of a cult show, in the same way that *Coronation Street* did, which always had people like Michael Crawford and Cliff Richard wanting to appear in it, if only just to buy a pint in the Rovers! 'Leave it with me,' I said.

So I phoned Derren Litten, the writer of *Benidorm*, whom I had met on a couple of occasions and spoken to on the phone when he was trying to get Tim. 'Look, this is a ridiculous phone call, but I'm trying to get Cilla her job back,' I said. 'So I just wanted to know if the part has gone elsewhere.'

'Well, we've already got a couple of other people looking at the script . . .' he said.

'But Paul O'Grady and Cliff have told Cilla that she's mad

not to do it and she's now kicking herself,' I told him. 'In fact,' I added, 'I think that Paul and Cliff would also like to be in it!'

'And then Dale Winton could come out of the bathroom!' he joked. 'Right, leave it with me.'

The next thing I got a call from Cilla saying, 'Thanks to you, I've got my job back!' It was great; she was chuffed to bits.

Even better, while I was talking to Derren, he said, 'It's a shame you can't come out and do something little.'

'But you've never asked me,' I said. 'I'd love to.'

'Well, I've written most of it now . . .' he said hesitantly.

Knowing it was very unlikely that he could write me in at this late stage, I forgot all about it. Then suddenly I received a call asking me if I'd like to go to Spain to play a small part. Originally, the part had been written for a man, a sinister English heavy living in Benidorm called Reg, who was to threaten Madge because her husband owed him money. Derren reconstructed this into a 'Scary Mary' part for me, with tattoos, my hair slicked back, awful make-up and big earrings. In my scene, I had a karate fight with Madge, who jumped out of her electronic wheelchair to grapple with me. Eventually, Tim, in full drag, put me in a hold, but I karate kicked him into the swimming pool. It was brilliant!

Funnily enough, I was nervous about appearing in someone else's show after being in 'my' show for so long. The thought of having to make an impact in a very short space of time terrified me. But the cast and crew were great and I had a ball, which made me think, 'Oh please, Derren, if you do another series, can Scary Mary come back?' Normally, if I go in to a show to do a guest appearance, I enjoy my time there and then I'm off to the next thing. But with *Benidorm*, I desperately wanted to return, not only because it felt great being able to act alongside Tim, but because of the quality of the writing too.

After that day of filming, we all had a fantastic night on the front at Benidorm, and even though I was keen to get back to the children, Tim and I were having such a wonderful time together that I really didn't want to leave him. Back home, I found I was missing him more than ever, so Louis and I went over to see him for the weekend as often as we could after that.

Doing that small part in *Benidorm* reminded me how much I love acting, although I haven't regretted giving up *Waterloo Road*. When I left the series, it was a bit like when I left *Coronation Street*: I knew it was the right step for me to take, but everyone else seemed to be warning me against it, saying things like, 'It's cold out there'. It's true that many of my friends aren't working and the thought of not being able to find acting work in the future does scare me. But I knew in my bones that the time was right to leave, especially as it meant that I had the whole summer off for the first time in years – something I think I really needed. I did go back for one episode, which I thoroughly enjoyed, but it also confirmed for me that I had made the right decision.

I would never say never to the idea of going back to *Waterloo Road* – I wouldn't say that about anything – but it's a different show now. Amanda Burton has taken over from Eva Pope, Robson Green and Mark Benton have joined and I don't know any of the new children. Of course I'm sure I would have adapted, but it's good to remember it as it was when I was there, with all the original gang, as I really loved it then.

I'm very proud of the work I did in *Waterloo Road* and I was bowled over to win Best Actress for my role in the show at the *TV Choice* Awards in September. It was the second year in a row that I'd won, and as the initial list includes about 100 actresses and the awards are voted for by the public, to go on and win for a second time was just amazing. I was so overwhelmed, and the rest of the cast were thrilled for me.

Whereas I was completely flabbergasted that I had won Best Actress, I wasn't at all surprised when *Loose Women* won another award that night because the show just seems to go from strength to strength and become more and more popular. We did think that maybe it was going to be somebody else's turn after three years running, though! It was such an amazing night; I felt so proud to think of all those people who had voted for me as Best Actress and to know that I'm part of one of the most popular shows on TV.

So there were plenty of reasons to celebrate that evening! Being chucked out of the Dorchester Hotel at 3 a.m., clutching my award, was just too early for me, so I immediately rang Gerry's Bar, a late-night actors' club in Soho, which is one of my favourite haunts and has been going for years and years. The manager, Michael, said he was about to close, but I slurred down the phone that he had to stay open because I'd just won Best Actress and needed somewhere to celebrate!

He agreed to stay open and I ended up taking a totally random group of people along with me, including the adorable Leigh Francis, who is famous for his sketches as Keith Lemon, and he brought along Rufus Hound, who does *Celebrity Juice* with him. James Martin, the chef, also came, with two of my producers and Marc Elliott, who plays Sayed, the gay Asian lad in *EastEnders*. As I say, it was the most incongruous group of people! At 5.30 a.m., I was still trying to order more champagne, but luckily Michael said, 'No, you've all got to go,' otherwise I think I would have really regretted it the next day!

Several potential projects came up after that, including an exciting new sitcom pilot for the BBC and another project for

Sky. Then, right in the middle of everything, I said yes to appearing on *Dancing On Ice* on ITV. Oh my God. The last time I went ice skating I was eleven – and I can tell you that it isn't like riding a bike!

Why did I say yes? I have absolutely no idea. I'm going to blame the very persuasive people who convinced me! I've been asked to do it before – as well as *Strictly Come Dancing* – but I didn't want to do something like that unless I had a current pro-file. So when they asked me on this occasion it seemed like just the right time.

I thought, 'Well, I won't get asked again, so this is my last chance!' After all, at fifty-two years old, will I be given another opportunity to be taught to skate by Torvill and Dean? No, I won't! So I decided to look on it as an experience, as a ticked box, just like when I released my single all those years ago. What's more, I'd had quite a party summer for the first time in years (my friends called it my 'Judith Chalmers summer' because I had so many holidays!) and I wanted to get fit again. I knew the training for *Dancing on Ice* was definitely going to be a phys-ical challenge, the like of which I hadn't experienced before.

Much older people than me do *Strictly Come Dancing*, but I'm one of the oldest people ever to have done *Dancing on Ice* and something about that appealed to me. As long as I could pull it off beyond week one, and maybe add losing a dress size into the bargain, I knew I would be happy to have done it. It was going to be tricky to weave it in with my other commitments, but I was determined to give it a try.

But when I first went skating, just before I made the final decision, I slipped around the ice like Bambi. 'No way!' I thought, 'I can't do it. Not in a million years.'

'Everyone's like that at first,' my manager said, so, not

wanting to be defeated, I went back to try again. Slowly, little bits started to come back to me; I fell over the whole time, but after a couple of attempts I found I could even remember how to skate backwards, which I had learned when I was eleven. Of course, when you're young, you've got no fear of falling, but when you're my age, you're terrified, because it hurts a lot more and you know that your recovery time will be ten times longer.

Everyone who appears in the show risks, if not life, then definitely limbs, but the physical risks weren't the only thing causing concern. My family were more worried that I might get poorly again because of the pressure of appearing on a show like that, and I couldn't ignore their worries as it would inevitably have a ripple effect on everyone close to me. Tim and Matthew quite rightly said, 'We don't want you committing to something like this and then phoning us at three in the morning, crying and saying, "Why have I agreed to do this?" You have to be sure you can handle it.'

Of course, I would do that anyway because I'm a drama queen! But they were right as it would be very difficult to do a show like *Dancing on Ice* feeling poorly. As usual, though, I didn't listen. 'Well, I'm doing it!' I insisted. Again I was steamrolling because I had already made my decision.

Unsurprisingly, I had ice skating nightmares for weeks after I agreed to do the show. Ice skating nightmares coupled with dreams about my teeth falling out – what could be worse? Sometimes I woke up and thought positively about the challenge and sometimes I thought, 'What on earth am I doing?' For someone who spends her life trying to de-stress, it seemed like a massive project to be taking on and I wondered about my sanity. Whatever happens, though, I will never let my depression hold me back from living the life I want to live.

I was lucky to get the partner I wanted. My main criteria were that he should be fit and funny, and he definitely ticked both boxes. I didn't think I'd get him, so I was thrilled when I did. He made learning to skate again lots of fun, so although it was much harder work than I dreamed it would be, during the weeks leading up to the first programme I kept forgetting that I was preparing to skate on a show in front of eleven million people. It just felt like I had taken up a new hobby! Then I'd remember what I had let myself in for. Oh God!

There is always going to be an element of self-doubt before you put your head above the parapet. It was the same before I signed off the final edit of this book; for a few weeks I was really worried about whether I was doing the right thing. Yet in the long run, the outcome has been incredibly positive, despite all the problems along the way.

I don't regret telling my story, although I would have liked to have more control over how it was portrayed in the media. Still, I did it, I bared my soul and the book is continuing to sell well, which is fantastic. It would have been awful – and cringe-makingly embarrassing – if I'd put my life on the line and nobody was interested!

I've had some funny reactions from friends who didn't know certain things until they read them in the book. 'I've known you for twenty-five years,' Pam said, 'but I didn't know your granddad was a professional footballer!' And 'I didn't know you went to drama school with Bungle and Zippy from *Rainbow*!' other friends have laughed.

When Carla and I went to interview Jackie Collins in Los Angeles for our *GMTV* report, we were talking about her latest book and I mentioned that I'd just written my autobiography. 'Could I have a copy?' she asked, although I'm sure she didn't know me from Adam. Anyway, the publishers sent her one.

Then a few months later, she appeared on *Loose Women*. 'The last time I was with Denise, she came to my home in Beverly Hills,' she said. That made me feel very glam and international! 'I tell you what,' she added, 'I've read her book: what a racy read that is!' I was thrilled – I never thought she'd actually read it. And a few days later I saw Barbara Windsor at the premiere of *Deathtrap* and she said that she'd loved it, so I was chuffed to bits.

People have asked if I would do it again. It's hard to say, because if I were to write another book in a few years' time, I don't think it would be quite as explosive! However, I did find the process a lot more therapeutic than I thought it was going to be, because it made me revisit several areas of my life that I thought I'd locked away for ever in a box. I used to pooh-pooh it when people said, 'I did my book for therapy,' because there are other ways to approach self healing or therapy – and if writing helps, you might as well just write a diary. But it really was quite cathartic and I feel a huge sense of relief now that I've got my skeletons out there.

My life's been full of ups and downs, and all sorts of things have happened that I never would have imagined happening. As far as my career's concerned, I'm very excited about the future because I have all kinds of projects coming up. I love doing *Loose Women* as much as ever. There's another presenting job on the cards too, and then there's *Nana on Ice*, of course. There's also some television acting in the pipeline, and I might do some more theatre, which I love. And I'm more excited about life in general than ever before. It feels as though Tim and I have reached a level of understanding and are just entering an exciting new chapter in our lives. So despite everything I've been through, thanks to Tim and my wonderful boys, I feel very, very lucky.

Acknowledgements

I would like to thank the following special people:

Tim, first and foremost, for supporting me in telling my story. My boys, Matthew and Louis, for making me so proud. Mum and Dad, for always being there.

My sister Debbie, for being my best friend and attempting – vainly – to keep me on the straight and narrow!

Rebecca Cripps, for helping me put my story into words and for becoming a friend in the process.

All at Pan Macmillan, who convinced me that I had a story to tell.

Marjorie, for putting up with the Healys for over ten years, and Lisa who took over the mantle. Thanks for making our day-to-day lives possible.

Robin and Julie Arnold, whose friendship is invaluable to me and Tim.

My friend and now retired agent Lindsay Granger, who looked after me for fifteen years and was there for me through so many hurdles, professionally and personally. My love always.

Neil Howarth at Urban Associates, who believes in me and tells me I'm not too old!

My friends, who know who they are and how much I love them.

Lester Middlehurst. I hope he found the peace in death that eluded him in life.

The groovy gang, my best friends in the entire world.

And finally the memory of my beloved grandparents and Auntie Cynthia. I miss you.

Picture Acknowledgements

Section Two
Page 1, top right – Rex Features.

Section Three
Page 1, top – Scope Features; bottom – Rex Features.
Page 5, top – Scope Features. Page 6, bottom – Scope Features.
Page 7, top – Rex Features; centre left – Scope Features;
bottom right – Rex Features.

All other images courtesy of the author.

Every effort has been made to contact copyright holders of
material reproduced in this book. If any have been inadvertently
overlooked, the publishers will be pleased to make restitution
at the earliest opportunity.

extracts reading groups
competitions books new
discounts extracts extracts
competitions extracts discounts
books new events
events books
extracts discounts
new titles reading groups
interviews
events extracts events
discounts books
new books events interviews
events new events books extracts
discounts extracts discounts
www.panmacmillan.com
extracts events reading groups
competitions books extracts new
reading groups